Active Romanticism

The Radical Impulse in Nineteenth-Century and Contemporary Poetic Practice

EDITED BY JULIE CARR AND JEFFREY C. ROBINSON

for Nuala—
"partial sight" al "dependency" have
in you become gifts for poetry.
In friendship,

Jeffrey

THE UNIVERSITY OF ALABAMA PRESS
Tuscaloosa

The University of Alabama Press
Tuscaloosa, Alabama 35487–0380
uapress.ua.edu

Typeface: Minion and Goudy Sans

Manufactured in the United States of America
Cover design: Gary Gore

∞

The paper on which this book is printed meets the minimum requirements of
American National Standard for Information Sciences—Permanence of Paper for
Printed Library Materials, ANSI Z39.48–1984.

Library of Congress Cataloging-in-Publication Data

Active romanticism : the radical impulse in nineteenth-century and contemporary
poetic practice / edited by Julie Carr and Jeffrey C. Robinson. — First edition.
      pages cm. — (Modern & contemporary poetics)
   Includes bibliographical references and index.
   ISBN 978-0-8173-5784-9 (paperback) — ISBN 978-0-8173-8785-3 (e book) 1. Poetry,
Modern —History and criticism. 2. Romanticism —Influence. 3. Poetics. I. Carr, Julie,
1966– editor. II. Robinson, Jeffrey Cane, 1943– editor.
   PN1161.A28 2015
   809.1 —dc 3

                                                                        2014019863

Active Romanticism

Contents

Active Romanticism

Introduction

Active Romanticism

Julie Carr and Jeffrey C. Robinson

Action, the only activity that goes on directly between men without the intermediary of things or matter, corresponds to the human condition of plurality, to the fact that men, not Man, live on the earth and inhabit the world. While all aspects of the human condition are somehow related to politics, this plurality is specifically the condition—not only the conditio sine qua non, but the conditio per quam—of all political life. In antiquity, speech and action were considered to be coeval and coequal, of the same rank and the same kind; and this originally meant not only that most political action, in so far as it remained outside the sphere of violence, is transacted in words, but more fundamentally that finding the right words at the right moment, quite apart from the information or communication they may convey, is action.

Hannah Arendt, The Human Condition

The critical texts of the English and German Romantics were true revolutionary manifestos, and established a tradition which continues today. . . . But in 1800, as again in 1920, what was new was not so much that poets were speculating in prose about poetry, but that this speculation overflowed the limits of the old poetics, proclaiming that the new poetry was also a way of feeling and living.

Octavio Paz

The writer sees himself in the Revolution. It attracts him because it is the time during which literature becomes history. It is his truth. Any writer who is not induced by the very fact of writing to think, "I am the revolution, only freedom allows me to write," is not really writing.

Maurice Blanchot (on Sade), "The Gaze of Orpheus"

The most sublime act is to set another before you.

William Blake

In *Active Romanticism* fourteen poets and critics bear witness to the effects of Romantic poetry and poetics on modern and contemporary innovative poetry. By "active Romanticism" we refer to a poetic response, either direct or indirect, to a "social antagonism" (Marx, Adorno), an attempt to lift a repression that, at its core, keeps democratic pluralism in check. "Romanticism" begins roughly around the time of the French Revolution and other movements leading toward liberation; however, "active Romanticism" does not limit itself to poetry written historically in that time, the period traditionally thought of as "Romantic" (roughly from 1785 to 1830). Rather, by definition it renews itself at any given moment of perceived social crisis. Indeed, we believe that a radical reconfiguring of what has long been accepted as the body of Romantic poetry and the recovery of the radical dynamic of Romantic poetics, perpetually obscured in traditional accounts of Romanticism, would constitute on the level of culture and language a significant response to the conditions of increasing social and environmental degradation on a global scale. Romanticism, Henri Lefebvre has said, following Stendhal, both follows and precedes revolution (295), which suggests that its transhistoricity is deeply implicated in historical event, word in deed.

There are not only important parallels but genuine continuities between contemporary and Romantic poets seeking to find ways for poetry to intervene in social crisis. Crises of democracy could be said to define a form of Romanticism that can spring up at any moment. Romanticism's perennial genius for renewal led the surrealist André Breton to say: "Romanticism asserts itself as a *continuum*" (Rothenberg and Robinson xxiii). The "assertion" Breton refers to often invites formal and linguistic experiment as an interruption in and defamiliarization of inherited elements of the medium of writing, since poets often interpret those elements as fundamental carriers of oppression. Contrary to repeated and vigorous assertions from the nineteenth century to today, the Romanticism we bring forward in the essays in *Active Romanticism* has never come to an end but has continually reemerged over the past two centuries with poets whose politics drive them toward poetic experiment.

Moreover, the full range of Romantic poetry, whether labeled as such or not, although honoring regional and geographical specificity, has never been solely an English-language phenomenon, nor, as comparatists would have it, a phenomenon claimed by a small cluster of nation-states; Romanticism in fact spread and found its home literally across many locales, a reverberation to Goethe's call for a *Weltliteratur*.[1] Cosmopolitan or global poetry permeates the overall vision of an active Romanticism. Essays in this volume include studies of French, German, North American, and Latin American as well as British Romanticism.

This collection thus seeks to correct what we see as a general flaw in the long literary-historical interpretation of the modern and contemporary re-

ception of Romantic poetry and poetics. Along with this effort comes a necessary redefinition of "Romanticism," or Romantic poetics itself. In most
traditional accounts, Romanticism lasted, as the editors of recent textbook
anthologies of Romantic poetry have insisted, for a short, discrete period in
history, its poets burned out by their excessive visionary zeal and youthful
naïveté with respect to the "real" world of the market, of human tragedy, and
of the power of nation-states. Poets, so goes the narrative, subsequently respond to the Romantic with a more "mature" poetry: later (Victorian, modernist) poets such as Browning, Arnold, Yeats, Eliot, Auden, Frost, Bishop,
Larkin, and others successfully, at times heroically, write wiser, tougher, more
ironic poems, being cautious about Romantic excess. As the latest edition
of the *Norton Anthology of English Literature* says, Victorian poets "cannot
sustain the confidence that the Romantics felt in the power of the imagination. The Victorians often rewrite Romantic poems with a sense of belatedness and distance" (1038).

Twentieth-century modernism, according to traditional literary histories,
picks up where the Victorians left off; again, the *Norton* says, "The years leading up to World War I saw the start of a poetic revolution. The imagist movement, influenced by the philosopher poet T. E. Hulme's insistence on hard,
clear, precise images arose in reaction to what it saw as Romantic fuzziness
and facile emotionalism in poetry" (1897). Without denying the spectacular
innovations in poetry and other arts at the start of the twentieth century, in
English-language poetry and throughout the poetry of the West, this collection argues for a much earlier systemic source for innovation in poetry.
Many of the avant-gardes represented here see modern and contemporary
innovations not as a break with a retrograde nineteenth-century past but as
a development from experimental Romantic poetry and poetics.[2]

This proposed revision of the common view of Romanticism as a period
in literary history has immediate implications for the place of social critique
in poetic practice. If it lasts for merely four or five decades, Romantic poetry
and its accompanying political critique die with the death of the movement;
if, on the other hand, it constantly renews itself in the face of perceived social inequity and has the desire to acknowledge the previously unacknowledged, it presents social critique and response as a fundamental principle of
poetry since (at least) the French Revolution. To put it differently, Romantic poetry and poetics reject the common view in both the nineteenth and
twentieth centuries that poetry is an art of consolation, that it represents, in
Herbert Marcuse's phrase, "the affirmative character of culture" (Marcuse
88–133).

By means of the following essays, we are making a claim for Romanticism as an enactment of an avant-garde and innovative poetry, a claim that links vitally a poetry of the past and a poetry rediscovering itself in a present at any stage of subsequent history. Our book insists, against the grain of established cultural expectations, upon Romantic continuities, recurrences, and proliferation.[3] Asserting that Romanticism is a force in the work of a critical imagination sustained over time, we and the writers included here make our own challenge to a cultural hegemony that has refused to acknowledge that connection as having any systemic reality. However, a previous intervention into the canonized version of Romanticism, *Poems for the Millennium, Volume Three: The University of California Book of Romantic and Postromantic Poetry*, edited by Jerome Rothenberg and Jeffrey Robinson, appeared in 2009 and subsequently inspired the idea for the present volume. This large compendium of mostly nineteenth-century poetry from around the world along with extensive commentaries counteracts the more popular view of Romantic poetry mentioned above, attempts to lift the repression not only on many important poems but also on a radical poetics, and calls its readers to the formally experimental and politically progressive core of Romanticism that holds within itself a potentially never-ending renewal in subsequent poetry. This third volume joined the first two volumes of *Poems for the Millennium*, with their focus on "modern and postmodern" poetry, to embody from the mid-eighteenth century to the end of the twentieth the "continuum" of Romanticism. Romanticism in this characterization spreads somewhat wildly, often unexpectedly, across nations and other geographies as an invitation, during an era of enormous stress on communities and environments, for further pointed innovation.[4]

Active Romanticism subscribes to the following premises: (1) The Romantic poet, coming out of the age of the French Revolution and subsequently in similar conditions of social and cultural upheaval, situates himself or herself as a social being, a self with, in Derrida's term, a "constitutive outside" (Mouffe 12). A person becomes a poet at the moment when awareness of social exclusion, inequity, and repression demands response in the way of critique and challenge. Moreover, this social being identifies with a collectivity, a class, through which agency in human affairs seems possible. (2) The condition of poetry exists for the moment of its construction or occupation but may begin again in a new, equally critical, situation; and as such, Romanticism is a "continuum" of formal beginnings that, no matter how great or small or how seemingly apolitical, strikes at the core of a social situation perceived as unacceptable.[5] (3) The condition of poetry conscious of a changing world of heterogeneous subjectivities immediately poses a challenge to form and/or language. One can of course argue that "all" good poetry chal-

lenges inherited forms. However, in Romanticism, when it is an art of democracy, inherited forms, like forms of social constraint, must be recast by
a roughly democratic point of view, an insistence on breaking down hierarchies, whatever that may turn out to mean at the moment. The poetry of
such a moment expresses a crossing of thresholds, a turbulence and at times
hybridity of language, a commitment to mystery as a condition of investigation into new modes of perception, the power and difference of women's
voice and perspective, an opening to eroticism and the breaking of decorum
as an encounter with a fuller humanity, and a general embrace of an expanding field of material seen relevant to poetry. (4) Active Romanticism, finally,
scatters its sparks among later iterations of itself.

But we need to summarize the old space of what we might call institutional Romanticism, a space that many readers of this volume entered as students and that continues today. We refer primarily to textbook anthologies,
as opposed to the work of Romantic scholars, because it is in the former that
institutional Romanticism—a system of exclusion and distortion—gets disseminated to the public, to the degree that school and university students
constitute "the public."

"The deaths in succession of the second-generation Romantic poets—Keats
in 1821, Shelley in 1822, Byron in 1824—cannot fail to suggest a coming-to-
an-end [of Romanticism]" (*New Penguin Book of Romantic Poetry* xxiv). It
seems very important to anthologists and many literary historians to empha-
size the *end* of Romanticism, as if the visionary outburst that usually characterizes accounts of Romanticism cannot be sustained or renewed. Part of
Romantic burnout, so to speak, according to Stephen Prickett, stems from a
Romantic poet's personal absorption in various social excesses. In his 2010
anthology *European Romanticism: A Reader*, he claims of some poets that
"revolutionary activity" or "sexual and social transgression" impeded what
he sees as a primary task of the Romantic poet, "the creation of 'self'" (271).
That some of these poets were sent into exile for their excesses gave to their
poetry of self a mournful cast. Such figures are beset by failure and by pathos and inactivity, or ineffective activity. This view draws on the Victorian and early modernist view of the Romantics—from Arnold to T. S. Eliot
and Irving Babbitt in *Rousseau and Romanticism*—that the Romantics were
swamped permanently in adolescence. Eliot and Prickett associate this fixation in adolescent enthusiasm with radical thinking, part of the Romantics'
supposed failure as persons and as poets.

Not only is there brevity and idiosyncrasy but also an implied hopelessness
in the Romantic enterprise, registered in the Romantic "self" or poet from
whom the account of Romanticism gets its character as a tragic or pathetic

adventure. Shelley is a paradigm: doomed and neglected, as is Keats, who because of his early death did not have time to mature as a poet.[6] A similar view of Romantic poets, loosely identified with the lyric self in their poems, appears in the *Norton Anthology*: Coleridge and Shelley "intimated darkly that the introspective tendency and emotional sensitivity that made someone a poetic genius could also lead him to melancholy and madness" (14). This gloom is further observed by recent Romantics scholar Mark Storey, who claims that the Romantic poets "were only too conscious of poetry's tendency to undermine and vitiate, to desert them, to leave them alone with their shriveled selves" (186).

Less gloomily but still fundamental to the conservative view of Romanticism, the lyric subject as the central dramatic occasion for Romantic poetry, originally theorized and popularized in the 1960s and 1970s by M. H. Abrams, Harold Bloom ("the Internalization of Quest Romance"), Geoffrey Hartman, and their many followers, still appears in all anthologies and in much criticism. The *Norton Anthology*, for example, characterizes Romantic poetry almost exclusively in terms of mental states: "feeling," "spontaneity," "impulse," and their sequelae in the social world, "individualism and alienation." Inevitably this emphasis creates an imbalance between inner and outer: "This attention to the external world serves only as stimulus to the most characteristic human activity, that of thinking" (13–14). Even when it describes Romanticism's celebration of "Imagination," the *Longman Anthology of British Literature* does not attach the mind in its freedom to poetic event or action in the world but sees it simply as a virtue and a glory in itself, "produc[ing] the 'I' as an individual authority, for whom the mind, in all its creative powers and passionate testimony of deeply registered sensations, became a compelling focus" (9).

A shorthand for the "textbook" account of Romanticism might then look like this: (1) Romanticism is strictly a period of literary history (depending on the nation, lasting from the latter quarter of the eighteenth century until the 1830s or 1840s). (2) It values poems primarily as a principle of subjective coherence, a well-bounded version of the poem of the lyric subject; at the same time their extravagant side is fully acknowledged—the Romantic poetry of dream, reverie, madness, alienation, and so on—but is still kept separate from that other coherent, autonomous self of ego consciousness. The latter is never destabilized by the former except in a fundamentally destructive sense.[7] (3) It honors nationalist identifications of its poets and poems as part of distinct movements within Romanticism. And (4) it inclines to accept traditional forms of poetry as indicative both of the boundedness of oneself and the world and of a world immune to social transformations. No matter how willing the textbook anthologies are to situate Romantic poets and the contents of their writing within a historical framework—and they are—they generally refuse to pay attention to the politics of form as fundamental to poetics, and in turn to make poetics a vital locus of literary study. They acknowledge a variety of forms but not the process by which form changes and not the politics behind the process of innovation. In a medium that is quickly disseminated to the public, these anthologies isolate and disarm the radicalism of Romantic poetry and at the same time promote what is in effect a Romanticism of consolation.

In spite of its concern with the historical dimension of poetry, the institutional account of Romantic poetry ironically supports some of those views that associate Romanticism with an art that seeks to transport us outside of history in order to provide an alternative world or a vision or set of permanent abstractions compensating for the present world. Poets of high modernism as well as some avant-garde poets also mistakenly identify Romanticism with escapism or easy utopianism.[8] On a more obviously sinister level, there is a late-nineteenth- and early-twentieth-century art that emphasizes racial purity and exclusivity located in national settings of consummate rural serenity and absorption in myths of the Golden Age and patriarchal heroism; this, many have argued, contributed to the subsequent rise of fascism and other totalitarian regimes. Romanticism has from time to time been associated with this art of fascism, showing an affinity for salvific abstractions such as myth and institutionalized religion, for transcendence of "the real" by means of versions of spirituality, or art itself as a version of such spirituality.

The poetry of active Romanticism, in contrast, seeks to grapple with and participate in, rather than transcend, the intractable or irreducible real. As an event challenging cultural norms and often promoting progressive or radical change, such a poetry *reenters historical time*. The belief in art as an act, an intervention or interruption, characterizes the conceptualization of innovative poetics from the early Romantic Period to our own era. In his brilliant 1833 essay "The Romantic School,"[9] the German late-Romantic poet Heinrich Heine distinguished the work of Goethe, the god of early-nineteenth-century literature, who had just died in 1832, from that of Friedrich Schiller (1759–1805), who, he says, "wrote for the great ideas of the Revolution; he destroyed the Bastilles of the intellectual and spiritual world; he helped to build the temple of liberty, that very great temple which is to embrace all nations like a single community of brothers; he was a cosmopolitan" (34). Goethe's masterpieces, he continues, "adorn our dear fatherland as beautiful statues adorn a garden, but they are, after all, statues. You can fall in love with them, but they are sterile; Goethe's works do not beget deeds as do Schiller's. A deed is the child of the word, and Goethe's beautiful words are childless" (36). He later referred to his own contempt for the "sterility of [Goethe's] writing, the sphere of art which he fostered in Germany, which had a quietive effect on German youth, and which frustrated the political regeneration of our father-land" (36).

What might a Romantic poetry of "the deed" look like? According to Jacques Rancière, Schiller, at the end of the eighteenth century, proposed that a democratic art coming out of the French Revolution constructed emanci-patory visions out of materials at hand by juxtaposing what Rancière calls "art" and "non-art" (42). To attempt to represent persons and their world previously denied representation, either in social life or in art, required that art absorb into its sphere materials heretofore left out.[10] The point of such hybridities was to insist upon a world of art that includes material indicat-ing a more socially and economically fluid society. To Rancière, an art that includes "non-art" is a signal characteristic of avant-gardes from Schiller to the twenty-first century. For example, a late-nineteenth-century instance of the juxtaposition of "art" and "non-art" as a poetry of the deed is the poetry of Arthur Rimbaud written during the Paris Commune of 1871. Kristin Ross says of Rimbaud that he became a "voice . . . that speaks within and by means of a vast cultural system, a system that should be conceived *not* within the limits of some purely literary history but rather as made up of elements and language that are not distinctly literary" (10).

Rimbaud's mixture of "art" and "non-art" refers on the one hand to the content of his poetry, but on the other it refers to juxtaposition as a formal element. In active Romanticism formal innovation is a direct response to the "history" of repression. Looking back on the time of Romanticism, Theodor Adorno said, in *Minima Moralia*: "Not without reason was the epoch of free rhythms that of the French Revolution, the solemn entrance of human dig-nity and equality" (222). Adorno correctly associates the advent of "free verse" not with the early twentieth century but with the late eighteenth and early nineteenth and thus links it to that moment dedicated to social unfettering. "Poetry fetter'd, fetters the Human Race," said Blake in *Jerusalem* in the most comprehensive aphorism of Romantic poetics, a grim chiastic sequence, the negative image of Schiller's word-into-deed, in which a previously fettered poetry predicts the same outcome in the space of the living, the language of fettering absorbed from the French Revolution with its "Bastilles of the in-tellectual and spiritual world" (Heine, *supra*).

The Romantics themselves register the relationship between poetic in-novation and experiment and their commitment to intervene in the social world following the French Revolution. Friedrich Schlegel remarked that by mixing prose with poetry, or rather, by writing "poetry" in the medium of prose, one could expand the possibilities of a deeper, democratic engagement, a vision of a more heterogeneous world and one that further breaks down the division of art and life. Romantic poetry, he said, "is a progressive universal poetry. Its mission is not merely to reunite all separate genres of poetry and to put poetry in touch with philosophy and rhetorics. It will, and should, now mingle and now amalgamate poetry and prose, genius and criticism, the poetry of art and the poetry of nature, render poetry living and social, and life and society poetic" (Rothenberg and Robinson 900–901). As we can see from this passage, the pressure of the representation and also the enactment of democracy in art around the time of the French Revolution imparted to genres a new lability. In the1820s, for example, William Hazlitt and Stendhal insisted that given the immediate need for an art of the people, writers should switch from verse, associated in Hazlitt's case with "power" and Stendhal's with aristocracy, to prose.[11] Poetry in the medium of prose then became a formal innovation that Charles Baudelaire argued for as the "poetry" of the new, mid-nineteenth-century city of anonymity.

The insight that the poetry of a new democracy ought at the very least to mix prose with verse, if not move all the way to prose, indicated a rethinking of poetic language itself. The French Revolution encouraged the experimental incorporation into poetry of what Wordsworth called "the language of conversation in the middle and lower classes of society" (Wordsworth, *The Oxford Authors* 738). As if he were drawing out the implications of these experiments, Wordsworth's German contemporary Schlegel observed that poetry "is republican speech: a speech which is its own law and end unto itself, and in which all the parts are free citizens and have the right to vote" (Schlegel, *Lucinde and the Fragments* 150). In this telling, a sentence is not a syntax under the control of and fully ordered by an invisible, abstract power and utilizing a homogeneous language sanctioned by it, but is an innovation, defamiliarized, taken over by a democracy full of independent subjectivities.

In these instances innovation went against the grain of what poetic language was meant to be, one that identified art with an aristocratic tradition. The results of these "experiments," in Wordsworth's term, in a poetry that mixed a language of the middle or lower classes with an aristocratic literature, might cause "readers accustomed to the gaudiness and inane phraseology of many modern writers" to "struggle with feelings of strangeness and awkwardness: They will look round for poetry, and will be induced to enquire by what species of courtesy these attempts can be permitted to assume that title" (Wordsworth, *The Oxford Authors* 738). "Strangeness" is the affect of a defamiliarized poetic space.[12] As Shelley said in his "Defence of Poetry," poetry "awakens and enlarges the mind itself by rendering it the receptacle of a thousand unapprehended combinations of thought. Poetry makes familiar objects be as if they were not familiar."

In summary, the following late fragment (as the editors call it) of Friedrich Hölderlin epitomizes also the juxtaposition of "art" with "non-art" as well as the emergence of "free rhythms" (free verse) as the breakdown of monumental forms, another important aspect of "active romanticism." Written in the wake of the French Revolution (around 1803), this poem exhibits a "broken promise"[13] of content and form. All of this supports a quiet conversion of the speaker from a person fantasizing an art of democracy to one living out that art and describing what he lives:

I want to build

and raise new
the temples of Theseus and the stadiums
and where Perikles lived

But there's no money, too much spent
today. I had a guest
over   and we sat together (Hölderlin 245)

The first impulse of this speaker wanting to celebrate democracy misses the point about democratic art by associating it with monuments that are made, at great expense, from "art" alone. At this point, however, the economics of his project brings home to him his mistake: he has "no money" and must turn from "monument" to friendship. Monumentality is replaced, then, by the lived reality of social engagement and personal intimacy. As we said earlier about the poetry of active Romanticism, Hölderlin's poet-citizen now enters historical time. The poem produces a revision of the demands of democracy on art registered in form, as stanzas or consistent line length give way to a poem of unpredictable line breaks and vertical breaks. The poem has broken its promise because amid the speaker's earnest desire to imagine an art of democracy, it has refused to deny the reality of economics. Yet that refusal produces what we could call a genuine poem of democracy; intractability enters the equation and the speaker has a solution to it. The poem's open form registers its welcoming vulnerability to events and realities no matter how unpredictable, to what Rancière, praising Schiller as a founder of an aesthetics for twentieth-century avant-gardes, calls "the distribution of the sensible," a principle of inclusivity.

Behind such a complex experimental poetry as Hölderlin's lies a vital presence of subjectivity, what we will call "the Romantic poet as agent," a crucial
element in the constellation of elements named active Romanticism.[14] Here
the poet is not a figure of fundamental autonomy, as mainstream criticism
and the popular imagination would have it, with a reflective and meditative
independence from events and persons, but is one who powerfully asserts
conscious social agency, who participates in the world and disperses himself
or herself in it, reacts to it, reenvisions it, intervenes in its affairs, and inno-
vates.

No Romantic states this principle of active Romanticism more succinctly
than Shelley: "Poetry, and the principle of Self, of which money is the visible
incarnation, are the God and the Mammon of the world" (Shelley, *Poetry and
Prose* 531). The avant-garde, from Shelley's Romanticism onward, seeks to
break down the identification of poetry and the unitary self in order to develop critiques of the world in which Mammon has control. In the Regency
decade (at the end of which Shelley wrote "The Defence"), Keats, Byron, J. H.
Reynolds, Leigh Hunt, and William Hazlitt supported Shelley's view with attacks on the association of poetry and "fame"; poets like Wordsworth (as seen
critically by these poets and essayists) and the poet laureate Robert Southey,
who had linked their fortunes to the government of the Prince Regent, were
thought to subordinate poetry ("Imagination") to Mammon, and thus the
ego or the "self."

We are not saying that Romantic (or contemporary) avant-gardes always
turn away from the self, but rather that they dramatically complicate it. Indeed, the self might be a site of political resistance and exploration. In contrast to the celebration or fascination of Imagination and self that institutional
Romanticism and some mainstream criticism promotes, Adorno's definition
of lyric in "Lyric Poetry and Society," to which we have previously referred,
applies: "the subjective expression of a social antagonism" (Adorno, *Notes
to Literature* 45). The mind in active Romanticism has meaning only when
it acknowledges, responds to, and attempts to intervene in something outside the self.

The Romantic poets themselves, in their statements about poetry as well
as their practice, had no notion of stable and protected selfhood but instead, early and late in the nineteenth century, understood poetic identity
in terms of subjective mobility and lability. Keats imagined a "chameleon
poet" who "has no identity but is continually infor[ming]" other bodies and
characters. Shelley described the poetic imagination as an instance of love,
the "great secret of morals," a "going out of one's own nature," and a poet as
being one who "participates in the eternal, the infinite and the one." Emily
Dickinson remarked to Thomas Wentworth Higginson, "When I state my-

self, as the Representative of the Verse—it does not mean—me—but a supposed person"; Charles Baudelaire characterized the "I" with its "irresistible
appetite for the non-I"; and of course Rimbaud capped this vision with his
famous declaration "Je est un autre" (I is an other). These formulations of the
preferred notion of the poetic subject as highly destabilized become central
to modern and contemporary innovative poetics. The "vatic" in Whitman
to Robert Duncan where the subject takes on a voice from the collective;
the "diasporic," or, in Pierre Joris's term, the "nomad" imagination of poets;
and total immersion into text itself such as that found in surrealist automatic
writing are all major instances of the mobility of subject consciousness.

In active Romanticism mind sees and participates in the world with an
openness to otherness, to the juxtaposition of unanticipated realities, and to
a defamiliarized account of things, all of which requires of mind an extraordinary elasticity and independence. Through recent interpretations of philosophy and aesthetics from the end of the eighteenth century, for example
those by Robert Kaufman and Jacques Rancière, we can see that arguments
by Immanuel Kant and Friedrich Schiller for the freedom of mind as the
means of achieving both an ideal of citizenship and an ideal of artistic creative success in a democratic society center on a release (to the degree that
this is possible) from ideological prescription. Kant's "purposiveness without purpose" and Schiller's *Spieltrieb* (play drive) do not imply "escape" from
the real world but neither are they beholden to reality or ideology or "culture." Their views correspond to aesthetic/political declarations on the British side from Shelley and Keats, who chafe against a poetry of received tru-
isms. "Didactic poetry is my abhorrence," said Shelley, and his war against
what he considered the utilitarian narrowing of imagination he called "calculation." Keats gave his version of the play drive in his Negative Capability
formulation, when one lives in "uncertainties, mysteries, and doubts without any irritable reaching after fact and reason." He said elsewhere: "We hate
poetry that has a palpable design upon us."

Such a rich confluence of poetic and social intention marks the essays in
this book; they themselves participate in active Romanticism. For some of
the essays here, Romanticism is at once ancient source and current practice.
We must, however, caution against the word "source" when applied to the
Romanticism of these essays because the authors see Romanticism as antifoundational. We might best characterize it, then, as a force field—at once
site and opportunity, a way of thought and constructed response. Romanticism, in the versions collected here, demands its reconfiguration, its retelling;
it is a form of critical poetry as we continually rediscover its most generative
aspect. To create in the wake of Romanticism is to re-create Romanticism.

Most of the authors of these essays are poets themselves, and in many cases they chart the present or recent outcomes, sometimes personal, of Romantic undertakings. In this book scholarship and criticism, with some exceptions, are irradiated by the "writerly" perspective on literary history and poetics. This accounts in part for the variety and idiosyncrasies of these studies, and also for something essential to modern innovative art, its own conceptualization. Behind the essays and the material to which they attend lies a passion or energy of commitment required for the crossing of thresholds of the familiar and the hegemonic in order to release imprisoned or repressed elements to view: the erotic; the oneiric; the voices of minority classes; a language, grammar, and syntax not roped in by convention; form made for the occasion. Romanticism requires extravagance and excess to occupy and transform social space. We hope to convince the reader that the truly vital elements of Romanticism live and have their being in the most exploratory and risk-taking instances of modern and contemporary poetry and that consequently what we call "Romanticism" stands for a critical art dynamic that refuses, and has refused over the past two centuries, to be repressed by what the activist London poet Sean Bonney calls "police reality" (64).

The social situations and tensions to which poets (and citizens) respond never fully stabilize; more specifically, in a capitalist society the drive to suppress or exclude elements of that society never goes away. Thus poetry, as a form of resistance and of illumination of social repressions, must constantly react, both to situations and also to capitalism's unerring drive to co-opt language and vision for its own use. Blake understood this when he said in *Jerusalem* (chapter 1, pl. 10): "I must Create a System, or be enslaved by another Man's."

Above all, poetry, not as a conduit for "context" but as the event itself, remains at the center of our interest.[15] In these essays the questions asked in its presence create a site of mind and language and social being working at highest pitch. It may be that the true innovative and interventionist life of Romanticism lies in its more recent reverberations and manifestations, and that Romanticism is continually ready to commit itself to future poetic experiment.

Notes

1. Our use of "active" in "active Romanticism" bears close resemblance to Ezra Pound's in his gathering of poems by contemporaries, *Active Anthology*, 1933. For Pound poetry must be "experimental" and readers must see in it what is "living." Both words project an ongoing, ever-changing relationship to the present, a conscious vitality that continually renews itself with every poem. By

contrast, poets who do not experiment build a "cenotaph" to past experience. "Experiment," says Pound, "aims at writing that will have a relation to the present analogous to the relation past master work had to the life of its time." That Pound generally chose to dismiss Romanticism and later nineteenth-century poetry as a "rather blurry, messy sort of a period, a rather sentimentalistic mannerish sort of a period," shows that, like many modernist poets, he misread Romanticism as escapist, idealist, and thoughtless (1933). Pound's use of "active," with its focus on poetic experimentation, predicted a poetry of participation, but we argue that Romantic formal innovation often lies in tandem with its leftist politics and imagines its "relation to the present" as poetically an intervention into and disturbance of culture.

2. Jerome McGann has been central among academic scholar/critics in encouraging exploration of Romantic trajectory toward late-nineteenth-, twentieth-, and twenty-first-century innovative poetry, in particular *The Poetics of Sensibility* (1996). McGann frames his book with a summary account of modernism's relationship to Romanticism as promoted by the academy; in that history scholars were "reading romanticism through its most conservative venues, where 'the balance and reconciliation of opposite and discordant qualities' would be emphasized. Roads of excess were roads not taken, and that has made all the difference" (2). In the allegory of this last sentence, the subject, "William Blake" (radical, innovative Romanticism), was negated by the predicate, "Robert Frost" (conservative, formally balanced Romanticism). McGann then describes the Romantic territory as comprising a poetry of depth and sincerity (e.g., Wordsworth) on the one hand and a poetry of surfaces and "sensibility" (e.g., the Della Cruscans, Erasmus Darwin, Shelley, Byron, Felicia Hemans, and Laetitia Landon) on the other. Along the way he makes it clear that this latter group of poets anticipates some innovative poets of the twentieth century, in particular Gertrude Stein.

3. Over the past quarter century the number of poems now identified as Romantic has increased dramatically, and anthologies have reflected this. The increase in the number and heterogeneity of Romantic poems and types of poems, however, has not yielded new definitions of Romanticism based on a fundamental vision of inclusivity and recurrence. The work of Maureen McLane, Jerome McGann, Robert Kaufman, David Duff, Julie Carr, Isobel Armstrong, William Keach, Jeffrey C. Robinson, and the recent *Cambridge Companion to British Romantic Poetry*, among others, has begun to articulate a Romantic and nineteenth-century poetics commensurate with the wide range of writing we call Romantic and the association of adversarial politics and poetic innovation. See, for example, William Keach's study, in his book *Arbitrary Power*, of Keats's "Cockney couplets" in his early poems: heroic couplets that break the strict closure implied in the full rhymes and end-stop after the second line found in neoclassical

poetry; Keats's half rhymes and enjambed second lines signaled to his Tory reviewers that "loose" prosody indicated "loose" (i.e., left-wing) politics.

4. In 2012 the University of California Press published *Poems for the Millennium, Volume Four: The University of California Book of North African Literature*, edited by Pierre Joris and Habib Tengour. Here the global reach of Goethe's *Weltliteratur* combines with an already global presence in the first three volumes of *Poems for the Millennium* in a powerful gesture of locating a major world poetry outside of the Anglo/European/North American orbit of influence.

5. See Leigh Hunt's long poem in ottava rima, *The Book of Beginnings* (1823), from early Romanticism, and Lyn Hejinian's *The Beginner*, from the contemporary avant-garde.

6. See Duncan Wu, ed. *Romanticism: An Anthology*, Second Edition (Oxford: Blackwell Publishers Ltd, 1998), 822, 1012.

7. "Self-reflexiveness" is said to characterize the Romantic lyric, as if the self-consciousness of the poet seeps into the very fabric of the poem. See Stuart Curran, *Poetic Form in British Romanticism* and Michael O'Neill, *Romanticism and the Self-Conscious Poem*. O'Neill's book "seeks . . . to trace the curve of imaginative experience described by particular poems" (xx). Romantic poems "display fascination with the theme of the self" (xvii).

8. The purpose of both *Poems for the Millennium, Volume Three* and *Active Romanticism* is to provide a progressive or radical revisiting of Romanticism that disabuses the above critique by disentangling the association of artistic abstractions from the term "Romanticism" itself. In this regard, Charles Bernstein's radical defamiliarization of "escape" in his verse-essay "Artifice of Absorption" (in *A Poetics*) should be noted:

> But escape can be an image of release from captivity
> in a culture that produces satisfactions as a means
> of exploitation or pacification. The problem with
> "escapist" literature is that it offers no escape,
> narratively reinforcing our captivity.
> To escape, however, if only
> trope-ically, is not a utopian refusal
> to encounter the realpolitic of history: it is a
> crucial dialectical turn that allows imaginal place
> outside history as we "know" it,
> in order to critique it,
> an Archimedean point of imaginative
> construction, in which we can be energized,
> our resources shored. (75)

9. First published as *Zur Geschichte der neueren schönen Literatur in Deutschland*, 1833.

10. See the excellent study of "wrong poetry" in Wordsworth's "The Thorn" in Keston Sutherland, *Stupefaction*. "I measured it from side to side, / 'Tis three feet long and two feet wide," lines that flaunt the idea of "poetry." Non-art from one point of view refuses to be absorbed into the poem as lyric.

11. Germaine de Stael's *Corinne* associates the disruption of inherited forms with women. The novel's heroine, Corinne, is an Italian *improvvisatrice* who sings and declaims upon subjects *extempore*, typically in the *ottava rima* stanza, as did many such performers in eighteenth- and nineteenth-century Italy, France, England, and Germany. At one point she improvises a "history" of tragic European heroes and then pauses to switch to tragic female heroes, but in a new verse form, "she preluded for some time on her lyre, then, no longer dividing her song into stanzas, abandoned herself to the uninterrupted stream of verse" (227).

12. Blake and John Clare, as well as Schlegel, rejected the standard system of punctuation that Clare calls "that awkward squad of pointings called commas colons semicolons etc." Blake's renovated poet Milton in the poem of that name says:

> To cast aside from Poetry all that is not Inspiration,
> That it no longer shall dare to mock with the aspersions of Madness
> Cast on the Inspired, by the tame high finisher of paltry Blots,
> Indefinite, or paltry Rhymes; or paltry Harmonies;
> Who creeps into State Government like a caterpiller to destroy! (304)

13. Vanessa Place and Robert Fitterman use the phrase "broken promise" in *Notes on Conceptualisms* to describe conceptual poetry, in which the incorporation into poetry of unanticipated realities in the nonhierarchical world of social democracy breaks the formal and/or substantive expectations with which the poem began.

14. Much of what follows ought to be old news for twentieth- and twenty-first-century experimental poets, but "Romanticism," as seen by academic critics and, more surprisingly, by many poets, still assumes the identification of "the Romantic poem" with the sovereign "I." On the other hand, the essays in *Active Romanticism* show clearly an awareness of a more liberated view of Romantic subjectivity, more available to innovation and social critique or intervention.

15. Even when it has focused on "the poem," academic criticism and scholarship has tended to think about the text either as a conduit of information relevant to literary history or as a poem considered in its "internal relations." New For-

malism, so-called, has brought formal elements into the domain of history, but not often from the "writerly" perspective of poetry as the site of choices about innovation and social agency. More specifically, the literary history of Romanticism has made little effort to privilege as central to its subject the transformations of poetics over time, particularly in its radical manifestations. We hope that *Active Romanticism* will encourage such an undertaking.

I
Bright Ellipses

The Botanic Garden, Meteoric Flowers, and *Leaves of Grass*

Elizabeth Willis

Erasmus Darwin was introduced to me by William Blake. I was in my twenties, had a handful of poems in print, but had not yet published a book. I was unread in both senses of the word: painfully conscious of the gaps in my education and increasingly aware that the poetry I wrote was unlikely to pull me out of the obscurity into which I was born. Then again, few people I knew were reading Blake either, and fewer still had heard of Erasmus Darwin. Within the domain of Romantic poetry, Blake was less flashy than Shelley or Keats; he seemed at once more domestic and less domesticated, more thoroughly deranged. Darwin's genius was even less visible, relegated to the realm of picturesque intellectual eccentricity and moldering in the long shadow of his grandson Charles. I believe I had the deluded sense that I was rescuing him rather than vice versa. He seemed to be all mine.

At the time, I was interested in the resilience of nonsemantic meaning and visual rhyme in Blake's illuminated books and was trying to sort out how to address it and what it meant to my work. I believed that poetry had a hallucinogenic and holy magic, that it was intellectually rigorous and intensely physical. I had the sense that Blake thought of his compositions as animated in ways that were ahead of his time and that remained difficult to articulate. I wanted to understand how he got there. I wanted to watch the thinking in his poems move like the grand gallop of a zoetrope.

In looking through Blake's uncollected visual works, I noticed a reference to an illustration I had never seen in a book I had never heard of. It came from an early period in his career—after Innocence and before Experience—when he took on piecework as an engraver. I had been writing about Blake's *Book of Thel* and the dialogue of visual and verbal meanings in his other illuminated texts, the ways they spoke to—and often contradicted—each other. While "The Tyger" spoke of formal perfection, it revealed something else.

The world was overflowing with dynamic asymmetries. Innocence and Experience wrestled like Jacob and the Angel, stirring up a cognitive turbulence that could not be reduced to a conflict between good and evil. I wanted to articulate the field of meanings a poem produces without those meanings being wholly attributable to poetic devices or visual effects or to any belief structure outside of the poem.

The image I was looking for had been commissioned for the 1791 edition of Erasmus Darwin's *Botanic Garden*. But when I finally located the engraving—*The Fertilization of Egypt*, based on a drawing by Fuseli—I hardly glanced at it. Instead, I was captivated by the visual energy of the text it accompanied. *The Botanic Garden* was stunning in its distracting superabundance of data, its interdiscursive ease, and its wild formal variation. It seemed to be making the implicit—and sometimes explicit—argument that poetry was an ideal medium for acts of intellectual investigation and that it provided an appropriately flexible form for the presentation of evolving scientific knowledge.

As far as I could tell, Darwin's primary interest—the passion that unified his wide range of intellectual, practical, and industrial pursuits—was composition in its largest sense: the relation between the poetic line and the genetic line, between one code and another, the way a life is composed, the behavior of species. He investigated systems in part to determine which were humane and which not, what could be learned from one system that might be usefully deployed elsewhere. He wanted to understand the formation of weather, the uses of electricity, the cruelty of society. I think he was as conscious of the relation between form and content as were Robert Creeley and Charles Olson—and as concerned with the history of violence and the pressure that history places on literary composition as were Aimé Césaire or Samuel Beckett. For Darwin, the intensity of this engagement meant speculating almost simultaneously on the meanings of the Portland Vase, what makes plants happy, the possible applications of a steam-powered engine, the history of slavery, and how to deliver babies more safely. It meant unfencing one disciplinary field from another.

Consider his book titles: *The Economy of Vegetation* (a poem). *Loves of the Plants* (a poem). *Phytologia: or the philosophy of agriculture and gardening; with the theory of draining morasses and with an improved construction of the drill plough. Zoonomia; or the Laws of Organic Life. The Temple of Nature, or the Origin of Society, a poem, with philosophical notes. Plan for the Conduct of Female Education in Boarding Schools.* Such an ambition for integrated fields of knowledge demanded a formal agility beyond the linear development one might expect of a text that wears its content on its sleeve.

Of Darwin's extrapoetic texts, I became especially interested in his *Plan for the Conduct of Female Education in Boarding Schools* (1797). In an era that produced a vast array of conduct manuals for girls, here was a "plan" that sought to change *not* the behavior of young women but that of the teachers and parents who determined their curriculum.

XII.   DRAWING AND EMBROIDERY.   PERSPECTIVE.

XIII.   HEATHEN MYTHOLOGY.

1.1. Table of contents, *Plan for the Conduct of Female Education in Boarding Schools.*

The American edition of Darwin's plan was published in 1798, with its purview expanded from boarding schools to "private families, and public seminaries." Darwin worked specifically on questions of gender and self-knowledge, language patterns and class, treating them concretely as he explored the effect of social patterning on physiology. The section of the book devoted to writing begins by pointing out that because the writer assumes a relatively fixed posture, the body should be made as comfortable and natural as possible, and he goes on to suggest the optimal size, height, and tilt of children's writing desks. The section on reading begins by acknowledging that "reading is as much a language to the eye, as speaking is to the ear" (13). Grammar is described as "an abstract science teaching the texture of language" (16). Clearly the medium by which knowledge is transmitted is inseparable from its received meaning. He advocated for exercise, physical strength, "vocality," and flowing clothing in which a person might more easily breathe and move and think (70). Implicit in this work is a poetics of relation beyond the human: "even the killing of insects wantonly shews an unreflecting mind" and "a depraved heart" (48).

What characterizes our relation to other creatures, to our sex, to the boundaries of our perceived behavior? Can we see ourselves within a frame beyond our species? What species of science, what category of ethics, might inform our attempt to do so? It is this kind of questioning that characterizes and destabilizes in productive ways Darwin's presentation of botanical research in *The Botanic Garden*, where he records a world of passionate negotiation and variation rather than predictable patterns of sexual and political conquest. The sexual politics of *Loves of the Plants* (the second half of *The Botanic Garden*) are, in fact, the opposite of what has come to be thought of as "Darwinian." Rather than reaffirming patterns of domination as "natural" behavior, Erasmus Darwin explores the fact of sexual variety in ways that still transgress prevailing social mores. His classification of plants in the preface to *Loves of the Plants*, for example, includes One Male; Many Males; Confederate Males; Feminine Males; One House ("Male flowers and female flowers separate, but on the same plant"); Two Houses ("Male flowers and female flowers separate, on different plants"); Polygamy ("Male and female flowers on one or more plants, which have at the same time flowers of both sexes"); and Clandestine Marriage. The first footnote of *Loves of the Plants* is devoted to Linnaeus, who has "demonstrated that all flowers contain families of males or females, or both; and on their marriages has constructed his invaluable system of Botany" (2).

This profuse and asymmetrical classification system plays out vividly in the micronarratives that unfold within the poem itself. For example:

Fair CHUNDA smiles amid the burning waste,
Her brow unturban'd, and her zone unbrac'd;
Ten brother-youths with light umbrella's shade,
Or fan with busy hands the panting maid;
Loose wave her locks, disclosing, as they break,
The rising bosom and averted cheek;
Clasp'd round her ivory neck with studs of gold
Flows her thin vest in many a silky fold;
O'er her light limbs the dim transparence plays,
And the fair form, it seems to hide, betrays. (152–53)

The poem's heated content presses against the regularity of its heroic couplets, with footnotes supplying the scientific backstory: "Chundali Borrum is the name, which the natives give to this plant; it is the Hedysarum movens, or moving plant; its class is two brotherhoods ten males. Its leaves are continually in spontaneous motion, some rising and others falling, and others whirling circularly by twisting their stems; this spontaneous movement of the leaves, when the air is quite still, and very warm, seems to be necessary to the plant, as perpetual respiration is to animal life" (152–53). Animal and vegetable behaviors repeatedly rhyme. Cassia—an American plant producing black seeds that inadvertently traveled the Atlantic on cargo ships, resulting in the plant's appearance in Norway—leads the poet to consider other forms of involuntary travel; suddenly we're looking at the transatlantic slave trade and urging Britain's senators to use their power to "right the injured and reward the brave":

Hear him, ye Senates! hear this truth sublime,
"HE, WHO ALLOWS OPPRESSION, SHARES THE CRIME." (117)

The poem leaps from physical pleasures to global commerce to systematic violence. Lush description builds toward political outcry. One form of address shows the possibilities the other excludes. Each must be recognized for its aversions to—or collusions with—the other. The framing of a pastoral need not make the problems beyond its borders irrelevant; rather, it can heighten our awareness of them.

Darwin's expansive sense of form similarly enlarged the work's borders. The central text of *The Botanic Garden* is, unmistakably, a poem, but the generic certainty of this identification is everywhere encroached on, supplemented, or called into question by explanatory notes, conversational interludes, and refigured indices. Apologies, arguments, commentaries, errata, and notes at the edges of the central text compete for the reader's attention. Even the word set at the page's lower right-hand corner to bridge the page turn has a vocal quality:

The Swallow. l. 322.   There is a wonderful conformity between the vegetation of fome plants, and the arrival of certain birds of paffage.   Linneus obferves that the wood

" Breathe,

1.2. Footnote variant in Canto II, *Botanic Garden, Part 1: The Economy of Vegetation.*

Typeset beneath the footnote, the word "Breathe" is an interruption to the notational commentary on "The Swallow" and is visually severed from what precedes and follows it within the central text. A page turn, like a line break, is literally a space to breathe. But here the turn also creates new grammatical alliances: "Linnaeus observes that the wood breathe." Indeed Darwin's pages *do* breathe in the interstices between words and stanzas, and in 1791 they would have been made of previously breathing, plant-based materials. Leaves of grass—linen, cotton, hemp—recycled from rag and given yet another life as a book. Further intensifying this narrow passage about "birds of passage," two actions of the mouth—swallowing and breathing—create a verbal and spatial resonance between the breathing wood, the speaking mouth, and the avian swallow paused for observation in the greenery.

The Botanic Garden is full of such accidental beauty and formal sleights of hand. There is no rising action to a unifying climax but, rather, waves of narrative action compounded by the movement of other tangentially related narratives. Poetic forms, like human and plant behaviors, are neither essential nor immutable; they are evolving and contingent. Complex designs are not smoothed out for general consumption; rather, they are shown to generate further interference patterns. The poet seems to rush out onto the page and then turn hesitant. When something is asserted—or when the author is speaking on behalf of something that cannot speak for itself—that *something* must be represented with sufficient complexity, even when it requires reader and writer to traverse a confoundingly digressive path. Darwin's interruptive "interludes" (episodic interviews between a Bookseller and Poet) address a series of poetic, cultural, and political issues similar to those addressed in the central text, but their informal nonnarrative structure allows them to treat composition and authorship more directly.

Bookſeller. **Y**OUR verſes, Mr. Botaniſt; conſiſt of *pure deſcription,* I hope there is *ſenſe* in the notes.

Poet. I am only a flower-painter, or occaſionally attempt a landſkip ; and leave the human figure with the ſubjeĉts of hiſtory to abler artiſts.

1.3. First Interlude, *Botanic Garden, Part 2: Loves of the Plants.*

The Poet is addressed as a Botanist and answers as a "flower-painter." The Bookseller wonders if pure (poetic) description will sell and hopes the volume's explanatory prose will salvage it. The Poet parries—but with an apology that aligns him with the amateur world, apart from the "subjects of history." Within another of these digressive passages, Darwin asserts the value of digression as he touches on Homer's use of simile.[1] The poem argues in its own defense that figural language is inherently digressive—and that it lends itself to episodic rather than totalizing patterns.

Darwin's beginnings and endings, in particular, cue us to a world of unresolved and expanding episodes. *Loves of the Plants* opens with an "Advertisement for the present volume." What follows is a "Preface." Then a "Proem" to the "Gentle Reader." Then just before the poem begins, the poet bids us "FAREWELL." In the page between this leave-taking and the opening of the first canto, the poem is preempted by a list of its errors:

ERRATA.
P. 29. l.6, for his, read her.
P. 42, l. last but one, for poetry, read poetic.
P. 87. l. laſt, for fecond, read third.
P. 94. l. 76, for boated, read bloated.

P. 101. l. laft but one, for ifle, read ifles.
P. 132. l. laft but 6, for exoitic, read exotic. (viii)

The end of the text is similarly complicated, sidetracked, all but evaded. In the last few pages of the poem, where a conventional pastoral might deliver a domesticated shepherdess, Darwin swerves into a further rewriting of mythic and literary figures. Potential threats appear—a leopard, a swan—but, as if undoing Leda's fate, *they* are tamed, appearing among the protagonist's ceremonial parade, guarding her steps, gliding along in lateral relation as its social and erotic sphere opens further. A hundred virgins and swains appear, led by Adonis, with the footnoted explanation:

> "l. 388. Many males and many females live together in the same flower. It may seem a solecism in language, to call a flower, which contains many of both sexes an individual; and the more so to call a tree or shrub an individual, which consists of so many flowers. Every tree indeed ought to be considered as a family or swarm of its respective buds; but the buds themselves seem to be individual plants; because each has leaves or lungs appropriated to it. . . . In respect to the male and female parts of a flower, they do not destroy its individuality. . . . The society called the Areoi in the island of Otaheite consists of about 100 males and 100 females who form one promiscuous marriage." (164)

In the poem's last stanza, the procession comes to an end, night approaches, and silence falls—but it is a silence full of further activity and sound: "applauding Zephyrs," "fluttering wings," "murmuring crouds," and "air-wove canopies." Night puts a lyre to his ear and bids "his Nightingales repeat the strain" (165), undoing the end of the canto with the promise of repetition, of unending song.

This final line of the poem is followed by eight pages of "Additional Notes." On the subsequent two pages, Darwin presents his "Catalogue of the Poetic Exhibition," an index of images that reprise the poem's looping movement between romantic narrative, art making, industrial reproduction, and social commentary:

> Tender husband
> Self-admirer
> Rival Lovers
> Coquet . . .
Arkwright's Cotton-mills

Invention of letters, figures & crotchets
Mrs. Delany's paper-garden
Mechanism of a watch . . .
          Mr. Howard and Prisons
          Slavery of the Africans . . .
Turkish lady in an undress
Ice-scene in Lapland . . .
Gnome-husband and Palace under ground
Salt mines in Poland
Statue of Lot's wife in salt
Lady inclosed in a fig . . .
Lady on a Dolphin . . .
          Night (174–75)

The subsequent three pages index the "Contents of the Notes," after which we find an "Index of the Names of the Plants," ending with a capitalized italic "*FINIS.*" Yet after this seemingly definitive end, we find a "Supplement," and on the final page of the four-page supplement is a last instruction to the printer:

Please to place the print of Flora & Cupid opposite to
    the title-page.
The two prints of flowers in small compartments
    facing the last page of the preface.
The print of Meadia opposite to page 6.
Gloriosa opposite to page 13.
Dionoea page 14.
Vallisneria page 33.
Apocynum page 182. (184)

Of course, at the time Darwin's text was produced, printers set type from handwritten originals. After a signature of text was printed, the author could review it for errors, but those errors would be corrected not by costly reset-ting and reprinting but by adding to the next set of pages a list of errors and editorial changes. This conversation between author, printer, and text may be visually peripheral, but it is central to the text's accuracy and coherence. A poem about typology becomes a poem about typography. Plant reproduc-tion meets textual reproduction; art and science converge. The pleasures of composition are both hidden and evident. The instruction "Please to place the print" is followed by

ERRATA.
P. 13 In the second line of the note read *stand up* in-
      stead of *hang down*.
      In the last line of the advertisement put a *comma*
      after the word *leizure*. (184)

A tribute to the fallibility and unendingness of textual production, *The Botanic Garden* begins and ends in error, diversion, and disclosure. To enter or leave the text is to pass through several portals that turn the reader around and disorient the mind in ways that facilitate the reception of what follows. The poem makes its own "virtual" world.

The formal openness of *The Botanic Garden* met me—or I met it—in a world that had acknowledged the compositional reality of "writing beyond the ending" and had accepted, via Deconstruction, the text's resistance to authorial intention. Many years after my initial encounter with Erasmus Darwin, I found myself writing a kind of amped up, revisionary pastoral, and the series of prose poems that began to take shape brought me back to his work. *The Botanic Garden* affirmed my ongoing interest in the generative quality of mistakes, irregularities, and anomalies—what were called "monsters" in the parlance of its time. If irregularities and errors in replication enriched the biological and textual landscape of that work, I thought, couldn't poetic form continue to evolve in relation to the interference patterns of the present? I was concerned with the echoes of pastoral discourse I heard within public rhetoric; there was a rapacious touchiness in asserting America's natural abundance ("Drill, baby, drill") while reiterating its status as a victim under constant threat of attack. This America was figured not as Uncle Sam but Lady Liberty, a woman assaulted by infidels. While multinational corporations held the legal status of individual subjects, the security industry seemed to be driving the country's ongoing expansionism—its unmaking of other nations and their cultural histories under the guise of "nation-building."

Meteoric Flowers unfolds through a series of interruptions, mistakes, and reconsiderations within an intergenerational, cross-cultural, cross-gendered dialogue about domestic and global patterning. For me, the question of where to begin was also a question of how and why to continue in a world saturated with apocalyptic religious rhetoric on one hand and post-postmodern poetic discourse on another: "Heaven's voice has hell behind it. . . . It says we haven't died despite the cold, it sells the green room's sweat and laughter. . . . It says you promised to go on" (3). Apology pivots toward incitement, and the physical world wrestles its way, unprettily, into text: "I'm crawling toward the corn, kicking open the field" (4). Didn't the poetic field have to be repeatedly kicked open? What is the status of the female within the corporatized and militarized forms of "field" work? "She doesn't want to be the dollar sign, split and smirking, living in a desert of bolted-down things" (10). The subject is not only split but is caught in a repeated witnessing of the binaries that define it: "From the couch I see Mary saying yes and no, he and she" (12).

If "pronouns understand their game before we join the histories that betray us" (63), I wondered, how do the bodies to which those pronouns are attached move through those histories? How do they, as political subjects and desiring agents, negotiate form and function, art and survival? Where do these voices reside outside the monologic scroll of the news feed? "If I appear to play the violin, it's only to keep my head on. Everything heavy falls in September, a fire truck lost on polar seas. I see the blueness of our thinking, lit up from behind. Turning to salt, turning to stone, I'm turning into water. When my blood plays cold, just think where my face has been. If I can speak for the entire space station I'd say we've suffered less than most. Maybe this moment is a test of coloration, an ashy mountainside made to look like dawn" (55). Questions of union and disunion, of building and collapse, of contour and coloration are aesthetic problems as well as political ones, ineluctably and reciprocally.

In the process of writing *Meteoric Flowers*, I realized that the idea of a revisionary pastoral had led me to think more broadly about categories, combinations, and the extent to which metaphor harbors both hidden pleasures and encoded violence. Early in the project, I heard on the radio something about a "daisy cutter." The term referred to a weapon system that had been deployed in Vietnam to mow down large areas of jungle into landing strips. In the war with Afghanistan it was being used to kill, disable, and intimidate humans. The power of the euphemism took me aback. Certainly a war that sounded like it was being conducted with garden implements would be more acceptable to the general public. It brought back images from the peace movement of the Vietnam War era: in particular, the protestor placing a daisy into the muzzle of an American rifle. How far was this daisy from Emily Dickinson's Daisy, a woman surrounded by civil war? Was there a hyperlink between her "Master letters" and the masters of war? Between the vocabularies of theology and eros and battle? Had poetry acquiesced to its place within the collateral damage of the global theater? If real bodies were being cut down and going largely unacknowledged, wouldn't the conscious mind of a poem, like Freud's magic writing pad, have to reveal at least a trace of this reality?

I thought Darwin's attacks on slavery and colonial violence were perfectly—not haphazardly, as might be one's first impression—placed in the context of a poem about sexual pleasure and reproductive life and the dynamism of other observable natural processes. Like Darwin, I wanted such losses—the real acts of violence obscured by "daisy cutting"—not to be felt at a distance; I wanted to counteract the ways metaphorical language was being used propagandistically to distance and absolve the voting public. Don't words or figures touch on all sides the generative world around them? Here is what we have made, and here is what we have inherited. Here is what is possible; here are its processes. Here is what has been fenced out; here is what lies just beyond the line: "Suddenly the daisycutter someone was waiting for. I hear the keys like modern ice on its way to hell. We safecrackers have come here for the job, a gasp among luggage. Useless wings. Hook & eye. Assemblage as forgiveness. Get in the car on collaborative ankles. We're rowing like Greeks before those trees turn to treason, erased of all their writing" (54). What are poets but reporters, encoders and interpreters, thieves and "safecrackers"? What do we carry—and what carries us off? With what meaning-makers do we collaborate? Even as poems take on a life beyond the poet, the poet is implicated in the messages the poem carries. Language leads into a place of extremity that offers no assurances of resolution: "Let me just say that I'm hanging from this screen into an icy darkness" (48). If a formal awareness of address is built in to lyric poetry, shouldn't the poet be called into question as much as anyone else? "What do you think of our soldiers, Elizabeth . . . ?" the poem asks (49).

When Darwin wrote *The Botanic Garden*, Britain had recently lost the American colonies but was still the most powerful military and economic power on the planet. Furthering the colonial drive it had fought against, the fledgling American "Union" violently took possession of previously unbounded space—though it maintained (and continues to bolster) within its self-image the defiance of empire that shaped its creation narrative. What now?

About sixty years after *The Botanic Garden* and thirty-five years after Shelley declared poets the "unacknowledged legislators of the world," Whitman wrote that "The United States themselves are essentially the greatest poem" (5). If the "union" were a poem, what would be its formal demands, its patterns? In his preface to the 1855 *Leaves of Grass*, Whitman hopes that America's poems will achieve the status of living, organic, botanical forms; that they will "show the free growth of metrical laws and bud from them as unerringly and loosely as lilacs or roses on a bush, and take shapes as compact as the shapes of chestnuts and oranges and melons and pears, and shed the perfume impalpable to form" (11). What follows this passage is a set of beatitudes that, among other things, claims for poetry the status of scripture and invites the reader to question and investigate—essentially to read and write her world:

> This is what you shall do: Love the earth and sun and the animals, despise riches, give alms to every one that asks, stand up for the stupid and crazy, devote your income and labor to others, hate tyrants, argue not concerning God, have patience and indulgence toward the people, take off your hat to nothing known or unknown or to any man or number of men, go freely with powerful uneducated persons and with the young and with the mothers of families, read these leaves in the open air every season of every year of your life, re-examine all you have been told at school or church or in any book, dismiss whatever insults your own soul, and *your very flesh shall be a great poem and have the richest fluency not only in its words but in the silent lines of its lips and face and between the lashes of your eyes and in every motion and joint of your body.* (11, emphasis mine)

The intimate engagement Whitman demands is a total transformation of the human into a poem and the poem into a human. In his later prose, Whitman's disappointment in American politics and literature is palpable, but he continues to urge present and future readers to rise to the occasion he places before us. We are not meant merely to read across the boundaries of species but to lose the distinction between subjects and objects, reading the lines of a poem as closely as we would a lover's face.

Composition is a form of intimate congress: with the phenomenal world, with other writers, and with everyday language acts. Near the end of *Meteoric Flowers*, Whitman enters: "This I, this me, I'm speaking from a book. That brain that taught me delicious things, forgivable trains, a signal business. I don't want to be tragic, even to the goldleafed bug. I, Walt Whitman, with Texas in my mouth. Dismiss this fantasy in favor of our startled shade. I remembered my tricks and what they did. Even apples aren't free. Our life against the midnight lens: poor Crusoe on Mars. I'm walking through this wall of air to comfort my senate" (74). The capitol at midnight was, for Whitman, a dreamlike vision; the capitol of the capital, housing legislative bodies within the crowded, lonely, and erotically charged city. Within *Leaves of Grass*, he repeatedly looks for his companions, readers, and lovers, his hand against the leaves of his endlessly remade book, a site of literary, sexual, and political risk. A self is made and unmade as it argues and "sings" for an expanded vision of the subject. Whitman's assertion of the possibilities of a poem or "union," is not mere positivism; it is provocation. It is a dare.

Meteoric Flowers was fueled, in part, by a desire to accept that dare—a desire for an expanded and compounded sense of poetic figuration and for what that figuration can reveal. The embodied vision of poets like Darwin and Whitman helped me confront the muddled conditions of the present into which I repeatedly woke. It allowed me to see the sentient, conscious qualities of the green world; the intricate network of figures fanning out within the thigmotropic reach of the poem. To see the undoing within the making of things. To make of these endings a beginning.

Note

1. "Any one resembling feature seems to be with him a sufficient excuse for the introduction of this kind of digression; he then proceeds to deliver some agreeable poetry on this new subject, and thus converts every simile into a kind of short episode" (83–84).

2

"The Oracular Tree Acquiring"

On Romanticism as Radical Praxis

Dan Beachy-Quick

I. A First Glance, through the Ear; or, Music as Vermifuge

In September of 1851 Henry David Thoreau returned repeatedly to "the new telegraph wire" to hear the music in the air. The music sang not only in the air, though the wind blowing across the tense wires gave the "sound of a far-off glorious life, a supernal life" that "vibrated in the lattice-work of this life of ours." The music also resonated in the poles holding the wires up. Then, "I put my ear to one of the posts, and it seemed to me as if every pore of the wood was filled with music, labored with the strain—as if every fibre was affected and being seasoned or timed, rearranged according to a new and more harmonious law. Every swell and change or inflection of tone pervaded and seemed to proceed from the wood, the divine tree or wood, as if its very substance was transmuted. What a recipe for preserving wood, perchance—to keep it from rotting—to fill its pores with music!" (Rothenberg and Robinson 723–24). Thoreau hears inside the vibrating wood the accumulating "prophetic fury"—a prophecy not of words, nor in words, but a harmonious rage whose meaning eludes interpretation. One cannot know if one is damned or saved, being forewarned or being welcomed into the next new world—there is only the fact of the perception itself, a hearing that is also a feeling, and the thoughts there born that find no cure in knowing.

These passages in which Thoreau hears the music "working terribly within" the wood have vibrated themselves into the latticework of my own life (Thoreau, *The Heart of Thoreau's Journals*, ed. Shepard, 60).[1] I have come to think of them not as a Romantic principle (perhaps there is in Romanticism no such thing as a "principle"), but as a Romantic realization.[2] The telegraph wires strung tight between poles carry human words across distances over which the spoken voice of its own power could not cross. The wires carry the words instantly. But it is not those words that create this music, this music that both thrills Thoreau and seems in ways to terrify him. What carries the words makes the music possible, the wires themselves. Here, the Aeolian harp of Romantic fancy takes on a far more startling dimension, in which the wire is our own voice, a tension across which blows that "supernal" music, so it can be heard. One might extend the thought in its astonishing trajectory, that the meaning in the human voice—the meaning strung along not only the telegraph wires but also those wires that are the lines of a poem—has very little to do with what the words spoken or written mean, and everything to do with creating in every line a tension that allows the unheard breeze blowing over the surface of all things (page and world and mind teetering between both) to gain sensibility, to thrill into harmony. "The fibres of all things have their tension, and are strained like the strings of a lyre" (Thoreau 60).

I cannot help but hear, in the tense lyre-string of my own mind, Keats's lines "but here there is no light, / Save what from heaven is with the breezes blown" (Rothenberg and Robinson 308–11), in which the wind carries light from an upper realm to a lower realm, a light that is not wholly light, interweaving the latticework of one world into that of another, claiming inside music, vision. In complete darkness, the nightingale singing ever farther away, Keats names every flower whose scent he can smell, brought to him on this heaven-blown breeze. This is not a vision *of*, but a vision *in*. As with Thoreau's "telegraph harp," Keats's perception creates itself out of a synesthesia, which, rather than one sense evoking the work of another, might here be best understood as perception itself becoming perceptive, hearing that hears, sight that sees, and so the sense itself conducts a thinking, and each sense is for Keats its own mind. Romantic realization erupts out of crisis, that unexpected moment when the conditions of daily life unfold into vaster possibilities. Then it is not enough for the eye to see or the nose to smell or the ear to listen. Then the senses themselves must sense, must rely on powers not simply their own: the ear learns to see, the eye to listen. Deep inside Romantic urgency resides the seemingly modern notion that the poem does not record experience but shows how experience experiences itself, and does so not as an intellectual gesture but as a personal revelation. Here, too, the personal extends into the universal, is implicated intricately outside of itself. A link is formed. Thoreau hears the music he feels. Such music grants the eye not the object seen but the light by which the object may be seen. It is just such music that Thoreau sees when he listens, his ear against the wood, and learns that in all empty spaces music vibrates, not simply occupying absence, but entering absence so as to preserve it. It is music that preserves.

Thoreau's friend, Ralph Waldo Emerson, suggests a similar audacity: "Genius is the activity which repairs the decay of things" (218). Genius is an idea not yet abandoned in Romanticism, but hearkened after in all its ancient oddity. Thoreau goes even further in his suggestion. That music playing itself on the telegraph harp?—it is an ingenious music. If it vibrates in the pores of the wood then it vibrates in the pores of the skin, in the lacunae of the bones—our skin and our bones. The work of writing creates in oneself a musical tension by which another music may be heard. We sing to hear that other singing—a song that cannot be heard save against the music of our own voice. It is this genius that repairs us (this genius always imperfectly other), and repairs not only us, but our relation to the world we sing about.

To hear it is to be changed by it. When Thoreau puts his ear to the post and finds music in every gap, he also establishes a radical metonymy. The telegraph pole extends his ear, resonates not only with the music that fills it, but simultaneously with the ability to perceive that music. It is a moment of profound imagination, as Coleridge writes it: "They and they only can acquire the philosophical imagination, the sacred power of self-intuition, who within themselves can interpret and understand the symbol, that the wings of the air-sylph are forming within the skin of the caterpillar; those only, who feel in their own spirit the same instinct, which impels the chrysalis of the horned fly to leave room in its involucrum for antennæ yet to come" (Coleridge, *Selected Poetry and Prose* 236). The telegraph pole—and the image of a man with a stripped tree springing out of his head (almost absurd in its literalness)—becomes Thoreau's antenna. Every object promises the same extension—not simply an extension of the self, but an expansion of the receptivity of that self to the world whose spiritual instinct realizes that the world entire is an ear-horn, and we but one of the half-deaf who bring our ear next to the object to hear better the song.

It tells us to forget who we are.

II. "What shocks the virtuous philosopher, delights the camelion poet"

In the telegraph pole of the letter *I*—a line that stands up from its slumber, a line perpendicular to the horizon—hides a labyrinth. When I say *I*, I speak this labyrinth. I am inside this *I* I speak, monster and victim indistinguishable, monster and victim both. One can think of the poem as Theseus's thread unspooling itself behind the hero's speculative wandering, but to envision the dilemma fully it must become fully impossible. This impossibility is not the complexity of the maze, this I who riddles itself with saying *I*. What is impossible is that the labyrinth cannot be seen save by the thread coursing through it, the line—these lines of the poem—by which means the maze is meant to be escaped. The line marks the maze, reveals its trap, illuminates (even if in half-light) the intricate riddle. The poem reveals the crisis we do not know we are in, difficult gift. It is a strange form of recognition that forsakes clarity for complexity—self revealed not as what one knows, not (as Keats has it, "my identical nature" [Keats, *Selected Letters* 195]) as a resource of subjective certainty, but as an uncertain quantity whose deepest necessity is being in motion. This labyrinth-self is a self of self-abandonment: self cast into itself as its unforeseen, impossibly unforeseeable, crisis.

Wordsworth's (in)famous definition of the poet's work can now begin to take on its more radical hue: "I have said that Poetry is the spontaneous overflow of powerful feelings: it takes its origin from emotion recollected in tranquility: the emotion is contemplated till by a species of reaction the tranquility gradually disappears, and an emotion, kindred to that which was before the subject of contemplation, is gradually produced, and does itself actually exist in the mind" (cf. Rothenberg and Robinson 160–81, 898). A poem begins in a tranquility its own work ends; it begins in an absence whose end is presence—but here no presence is pure. It is a presence complicated by the fact of itself. The poet places herself in this crisis of herself, a crisis the poem actualizes, conjures into a world, makes real even as it undermines its own reality. This labyrinth-self, this riddle-*I*, is curious prologue to the difficulty of representation, in which the certainty of self is transformed into uncertainty so that the world can be real and simultaneously questionable in its reality. The mind wonders about that world through which it wanders. The poem must become the forest through which it marks a path; the poem must create the distance it crosses. This questionable world—so reminiscent of our postmodern condition that the cutting edge of contemporary thought reveals itself on an antique blade—places poetry, and so the *I* through which the poem comes to be, in a strange relation to world and knowledge.[3] A poem is the fact beneath the fact, not a bedrock foundation but a seismic fault remarkably sensitive to the convective motion of a molten center whose upheavals make possible the very land it shakes.

The mind, too, is a convective process. It is within such molten light that certain audacities of Romantic thought might be seen. Wordsworth's "Poetry is the first and last of all knowledge" (Wordsworth, "Preface" to the second edition of the *Lyrical Ballads* 17) bears relationship to Emerson's similarly volcanic (i.e., generative *and* apocalyptic) insight: "For poetry was all written before time was, and whenever we are so finely organized that we can penetrate into that region where the air is music, we hear those primal warblings and attempt to write them down, but we lose ever and anon a word or a verse and substitute something of our own, and thus miswrite the poem" (Rothenberg and Robinson 907–8). The initial claim in both quotes is one, as Keats might say, that would "shock the virtuous philosopher" (*Letters* 195). Both Wordsworth and Emerson give to poetry a special being verging on impossible being. Poetry—here a general realm, a realm of genius, the genuine field—precedes the poem. Poetry is before and after the poem as much as it is "the first and last of all knowledge." Epistemologies want to explain the labyrinth in which they hide. Poetry exists before knowledge, before the experience that leads to knowledge, an impossible a priori in which experience occurs before itself, a pattern akin to fate, but a fate always flawed by the self who receives its sentence. Romanticism claims poetry as that difficult art that shows us the condition we are in by making that amazed condition apparent. The cost of the gift is being included in the gift's trap, and to fail is to both escape the maze and be lost in it. The drama inherent at the most fundamental level of poetic activity—that is, in the writing of a poem—exacerbates the fault line lurking between *I think* and *I am*. The poem calls into question not only experience, but how experience is experienced. It calls into question the very experience it creates—an experience of itself, its own textual life, but a life never circumscribed by its own limits, by its own language. For the labyrinth of the poem, like the labyrinth of a nervous system, finely attunes itself to the possible existence of another—world or person, world that is a person, that other who is also real.

Emerson sees that the poet must be "finely organized" to penetrate into the poetry that precedes the poem. The poet is a pattern before she is a person. As Thoreau could hear the music filling the pores of the telegraph pole by virtue of being himself filled with holes (what are the senses but proof of our porousness), so poetry takes advantage of what is world in us before it takes advantage of what in us is self. Before self-saying, before personality and talent, we might see ourselves as a smaller pattern (Donne: "I am a little world made cunningly" [248]) within the larger pattern of the world. These patterns seem different, create difference, and so create thought, create knowledge, whose authority thrives in creating hierarchy and category that difference itself reveals and makes possible. But poetry is before knowledge, is written before time; the poem contains the knowledge it creates (a faulty, fault-like construction), occurs in the very time its eternal inclinations wish to repudiate. One might think of two glass disks each marked with a pattern, each rotating at its own speed and in its own opposing direction, unmatching until both rotate in such a way that the patterns align, and through what had been a confused opacity pierces a sudden light. Save it is we who are one of these disks; and the world, the other. There is no outside observer. When the patterns align the light is not seen by us but moves through us, is not knowledge but revelation, is light falling *through* before it falls *upon*, light as that through which sight occurs, a seeing-light, a light through which we see that we see.

But vision ends in or at an object—it is not possible to remain in light's transport, in its conveyance. Destination is destiny; consciousness, a step outside. Something is seen; someone sees it. It is a reductive definition, but perhaps a useful one, to say the poetic process perceives an exterior world the perception of which internalizes, that the mind in its amalgamation of memory and imagination recognizes that world and seeks a language by which to describe it. It is awfully simple, but maybe necessary to say, that the poem is that description. It is just as important to say, and perhaps more difficult, that the poem undermines the stability of the boundary that keeps self and world separate, and simultaneously undoes the ease of its own definitive urge, defining world in order to torment that definition with doubt. Romanticism shows us that we do not doubt *what is not* but must learn to doubt *what is*. The poet writes a poem within which the objects of the world are called back into reality but does so knowing, always and inevitably, that the reality of the world precedes that of the poem. Witness is its own riddle that suspects it must create a world in order to say that the world it did not create is real.

Just such amazed intricacy underlies the Romantic sense of poetry's impossible relation to knowledge and experience. Coleridge's sense of poetic wholeness that "reveals itself in the balance or reconcilement of opposite or discordant qualities" (Coleridge, *Selected Poetry and Prose* 269) includes the illogical harmony in which the reality of the poem precedes its own manifestation of that reality. The poem sees that the past is ahead of it, the past is where it is going—a genuine fate in place of an ingenuous fact, in which every word's work is an attempt to reach back to that first moment of consciousness when word and world impossibly coexisted as one. Shelley hears the beauty of this dilemma when in his "Defence" he writes of the child singing who "seeks, by the prolonging in its voice and motions the duration of the effect, to prolong also a consciousness of the cause" (Rothenberg and Robinson 902–3). The poem, as does the child's song, sings in order to retrieve the world back into consciousness; it is also by the song's being sung that the world is lost.

Recollection in tranquility begins as absence becoming aware of itself. A perceptive nothing. The poet, let us say, is a nothing that sings. The song is a song of presence. The world is what is present. The song is not conscious of the world but presents the world to consciousness. When the singer ceases to sing, when the words are no longer in the air but on the page, when ink bears what breath once bore, then the mind reaches its mute terror: that the world the poem has called into reality has superseded the basic fact of the world's own most basic fact, that it *is*, that it *exists*. The panic inside the poet is that the poem obstructs connection to the very world it sought connection to. Emerson understands that we mar the music we hear by noting it down. That flawed pattern—it is ourselves.

It is me.

I am the place to be abandoned.

III. "Not myself goes home to myself"

Language others us. John Keats, on October 27, 1818, wrote a famous letter in which he describes this primary poetic difficulty:

> As to the poetical Character itself (I mean that sort of which, if I am any thing, I am a Member; that sort distinguished from the wordsworthian or egotistical sublime; which is a thing per se and stands alone) it is not itself—it has no self—it is every thing and nothing—It has no character—it enjoys light and shade; it lives in gusto, be it foul or fair, high or low, rich or poor, mean or elevated—It has as much delight in conceiving an Iago as an Imogen. What shocks the virtuous philosopher, delights the camelion Poet. It does no harm from its relish of the dark side of things more than from its taste for the bright one; because they both end in speculation. A Poet is the most unpoetical of any thing in existence; because he has no Identity—he is continually in for—and filling some other Body—The Sun, the Moon, the Sea and Men and Women who are creatures of impulse are poetical and have about them an unchangeable attribute—the poet has none; no identity—he is certainly the most unpoetical of God's Creatures. If then he has no self, and if I am a Poet, where is the Wonder that I should say I write no more? . . . It is a wretched thing to confess; but is a very fact that not one word I ever utter can be taken for granted as an opinion growing

out of my identical nature—how can it, when I have no nature? When I am in a room with People if I ever am free from speculating on creations of my own brain, then not myself goes home to myself: but the identity of every one in the room begins so to press upon me that I am in a very little time annihilated—not only among Men; it would be the same in a Nursery of children. (Rothenberg and Robinson 904–5)

The postmodern poet has inherited a notion of the Romantic poet as one for whom world and self and other are easily and too sweetly amalgamated into a universal whole, a unity in which difference ceases to exert its pressing difficulty, where clouds throw down their shadows on hills of daffodils, but the weather will pass, and the sun shines equally on each and all. I fear it is our naïveté that accuses them of naïveté. I find in Keats's notion of the "Poetical character" a fearsomeness that predicts Rimbaud's imperative for the poet's deepest life: "But the soul has to be made monstrous, that's the point" (147). But unlike Rimbaud—writing some sixty years after Keats wrote his letter to Richard Woodhouse—who claims that the "first study for a man who wants to be a poet is the knowledge of himself, complete" (147), Keats bears no such notions of the poet possessing, or needing to possess (or being able to possess), a complete knowledge of the self. Romanticism places its poetic brunt at the very crisis where existence of world and self, and knowledge of world and self, are not determined, but undetermined (even undermined) by the poet's work—expression, song—and the self is far from the certain container in which curious perceptions morph clearly into strange facts. For Keats, it is the self that is monstrous: "Might I not at that very instant have been cogitating on the Characters of saturn and Ops?" (Rothenberg and Robinson 904–5). Whereas Rimbaud suggests the soul must *become* monstrous, Keats sees that the soul's nature *is* monstrous, for its nature is not identical. The soul is the other. The soul contradicts simple notions of self, dispels easy notions of essence, for the soul—taken as a reality, a poetic reality—places a manifold and plural anonymity at the fundament of identity.

This sense of soul, being manifold, porous, free floating, rupturing, othering, closely replicates Wordsworth's and Emerson's impossible epistemology in which poetry precedes experience, precedes knowledge. Here too, in Keats, the poet seeks to undo that Gordian knot of self, that which feels "original," and works instead to venture into that which is in common. Language others us because language is what is in common.

Romanticism begins, one could say, in the semiecstatic recognition of the common—semiecstatic only because ecstasy's bliss may too easily preclude the strangely rigorous ethical nature of the experiment. It is an experiment—

I like to remind myself as I like to remind my students—that we cannot assume is over. The germ of that experiment reappraises the language poetry might occur in, as Wordsworth describes it:

> The principal object, then, which I proposed to myself in these Poems was to chuse incidents and situations from common life, and to relate or describe them, throughout, as far as was possible, in a selection of language really used by men. . . . Low and rustic life was generally chosen, because in that condition, the essential passions of the heart find a better soil in which they can attain their maturity, are less under restraint, and speak a plainer and more emphatic language; because in that condition of life our elementary feelings co-exist in a state of greater simplicity, and consequently may be more accurately contemplated, and more forcibly communicated . . . because in that condition the passions of men are incorporated with the beautiful and permanent forms of nature. The language, too, of these men is adopted . . . because such men hourly communicate with the best objects from which the best part of language is originally derived. ("Preface" to the second edition of *Lyrical Ballads* 5)

The latticework overarching the crisis of Romantic epistemology—of experience impossibly preceding experience, and the poem as the expression of that paradox—is a theory of language. That theory (predating the Russian Formalism it is so prescient of) seeks a use that can strip the language, and so the eyes whose habit language forms, of expectation, of easy recognition in which the mind overleaps existence by assuming the reality of what is "real." It is the common that is strange. "Common" here points beyond the class distinction that is the word's brute meaning. That "low and rustic" life is valuable not only because of its honesty, but because that honesty alters the epistemological relation to language's use, brings it not only closer to the earth, but reestablishes primary relation between a speaker and the spoken. A common language bears within it the necessary conditions of its own use. A rustic life chosen as the object of poetic imitation allows access to a language whose meaning is not simply referential in nature, but relational—a work-language whose expressive source erupts from the ground whose command it gives to turn, to plow, to sow, to reap. It is an urgent language whose danger is deeply intertwined with its own mimetic root. The urgency is that the world is real, is material, and though it seems wholly false, merely "romantic," to claim for a word a reality as substantive as that of an ear of wheat, or the germ whose ponderous weight bends the ear back to the ground from which it sprang, it is Romantic to see that language inscribes in the human mind the process by which the wheat grows, is harvested, is ground, is baked into bread. It is just as Romantic to see that language is that yeastlike substance that allows the bread to rise, save that this bread is a metaphorical bread, nonetheless sustaining, in which the unspeakable world rises through words into the world utterable, marking the division of *I think* from *I am*, claiming the division as a connection, forging the livid bond in which opposites coexist. It does so—as Emerson knows when he writes that "every word was once a poem" (215)—not because language functions via sense and reference, but because every word contains in itself the poetic moment of first consciousness, the very moment of the child's song, when a word is not a definition, not a recognition, but a relation in which the reality of the world must be countered by the reality of the self in that world. This real world is dubious. To sing extends reality through the doubt that the song creates; to sing claims inside the real a life that makes of the real a value. Poetry is a human art because it is a living art. I do not mean that it is living because it is still being written. It is a living art because it contains words that are themselves a form of the life they name.

This living quality of language removes Keats from his identical self. It must be so. For Keats realizes—as if instinctually, as if innately—that Romanticism's most radical experiment is not simply a return to a common language, but the understanding that language is what is in common. A poem recognizes in ways the writer of the poem may find uncomfortable that the other is always as real, if not more real, than the self who speaks. The poem calls into doubt the writer of the poem by offering itself to an unknown other who must exist to receive the poem, to warrant the world it bears as a real world, and by doing so, claim herself as real.

Language extends this relational bridge across which the poet cannot help but walk, but she does not walk as herself—she walks across as the other she seeks, for the bridge is a common bridge, and to walk upon it is to put mere identity aside and become more real by becoming anonymous. The self, Romanticism says, is a hybrid creature. It is the choral revelation, when to say I is to speak for All, and the report, as in the old tragedies, is to say what the world is, and what it is in the world that has been done. It is to hear the report, to hear the news. Not the news as Ezra Pound might have it. Not the "news that stay news." But the voices speaking in the wires, the humming wires, whose import is not merely the words they carry, but the wind that blows across those tense lines in the air, that epic wind, whose singing fills the gaps, whose song sings of the world's ceaseless morning ceaselessly, the song that thrills tranquil absence into a humming presence, whose voice can be heard only against the curious fact of our own.

Notes

1. Latticework is deeply significant as an image for my experience of how Romanticism has affected my own poetic practice. A lattice is formed of a grid and so can be thought of as a kind of matrix. Here the opposed interweaving slats that make up the lattice provide a symbol in which, say, the opposed notions of theory and practice are interwoven into a structure whose very integrity depends on the inability to tell one apart from the other. Romanticism, for my own poetic efforts, has undone the ability to give precedence to either theory or practice and instead has shown that the deep formal life of a poem invests itself in confounding easy notions of causality and consequence—a confusion so profound that to pull one slat from the other results in the collapse of the whole structure. Just as important to me, though, and found only by taking Romanticism's encouragement toward the poem as a form of experience in and of itself, is the thought that such a lattice has another, a more important, purpose than simply providing for its structural integrity. It also serves as a form upon which the creeping vines grow, gives a formal life to that which must climb another structure in order to live. It does feel to me that to write a poem is to create just such a lattice—a work that must be concerned with its own formal life in the absurd hope that it will allow another life to continue to grow, an organic one, a flower-life, which when flourishing, makes of the lattice itself a plant. This sense I have of my own poems being not simply a form and a life of their own, but one deeply in service to those previous works that fill tradition, these works I love, and in whose care I tend to see my own writing, has led me to realize that structure is itself alive—as sometimes, as I have seen in my garden, the pea plants twine around themselves to rise.

This Nest, Swift Passerine is perhaps my most radical experiment in such Romantic hopes. One poem might suffice to show the nature of the experiment, though no single method typifies the work.

> *deep within* I *turned from reading*
> the day outside the page
> *a sort of rainbow seemed to obscure it*
> through which the birds flitted
> *with a sort of sleepy heaviness*
> their bright bodies *interwoven with it*
> some *ashy light* in my eyes
> forced me to put down my book
> and my ambitions therein
> *my eyes both night and day*
> and my comfort if comfort it was

> I saw in the pages that closing
> narrowed the whole day into *a minute*
> *quantity of light as if through a crack*
> and I had no way to speak of it
> and then it was done (21)

The italicized lines are taken from Milton's letter describing the onset of his blindness, a letter quoted in its entirety earlier in the poem. The desire is not simply to point at another text. In fact, I might claim that the effort is not allusive at all but aims at a sense of radical inclusion. I mean that "radical" in two distinct ways. I mean it as a form of experiment, a marker of the experience the poem hopes to both offer a reader and accomplish within itself—that is, the poem as it experiences itself, and the deepest reading of which must include the sense that a poem is also always the narrative of language striving to realize itself within itself, consciousness's own parable. I also mean radical as root, and the poem as that which seeks through itself for its own rootedness—and should those roots be found, to pull them up into sight. The radical poem makes of itself a fertile ground, and the tearing up of roots is a violence that is also tradition's necessary compost.

The ground within *This Nest, Swift Passerine* includes Dorothy and William Wordsworth, Keats, Milton, the Baal Shem Tov, Heidegger, Emerson, Thoreau, "The Song of Songs," and Ovid, to mention just a few. The effort is not to prove my own learnedness. If anything, the effort opposes allusion as a sign of intelligence and sees in allusion a deep sense of one's own ignorance, incapacity, incompleteness, and rather than shying away from such evidences of failure, enters into them in order to make that ignorance (as Thoreau might say) of use. The weaving into the poetry I write of those poems I have not written is also a means of questioning what the "original" signifies. I do not believe in the solitary nature of genius; I do not believe in genius as a capacity of self. Genius is that flaw that requires the recognition of another, of many others, and refuses to mark difference as exclusive. I mean to say only that genius is the effort not to distinguish, but to intermingle, intercomplicate, the binding-self from the bounded-other.

In this sense, *This Nest, Swift Passerine* weaves into itself those writings by others that make any sense of the self as subject who says "I" possible in the first place. The poem is as a robin's nest, a spiral that includes all the roving bird finds, be it mud and grass, be it Christmas tree tinsel, be it a receipt from Wal-Mart or a page from *Paradise Lost*, and brings that back to make out of it a home. *This Nest, Swift Passerine* offers itself as just such an experiment (and in more minor ways, the extensive footnotes of this very essay are an attempt to mimic the radical nature of the Romantic experiment—that is, to provide for itself a ground that the thinking must dig down into, and in digging down, bring back up into a more considerate light).

Keats himself traces within his greatest works such *nested* or *latticed* borrowings. One feels in the epic fragment *Hyperion* the deep influence of the three-volume edition of Dante stuffed in his pack on his Scotland adventures (Gittings). In more telling ways, as traced by Helen Vendler in *The Odes of John Keats*, we see the vocabulary of Keats's beloved Shakespeare (and to a similar, if slightly lesser degree, Spenser's "Mutability Odes") iterating itself into the language of the Odes. Again, this is no servile appropriation, but a signal to what degree Keats's perceptive faculty was forged by the reading he did. Shakespeare did not simply offer Keats a language; he *nerved* Keats; he gave Keats new eyes. To the Romantic writer, the words of others, those beloved words, are a nervous system without the body. The poem is proof that no one says "I" alone.

2. As Jeffrey Robinson and Jerome Rothenberg's *Poems for the Millennium, Volume Three* makes abundantly clear, the Romanticism we have inherited cannot be narrowed to a British phenomenon of two (or three, depending on the critic) dominant waves. Romanticism as it is now being reconsidered proves itself dynamic, manifold, and global in scope—unchanging, as Heraclitus might write it, only in its capacity to change. That said, I am concerned with Romanticism in a very typical sense, one that traces its concerns through England—notably via Wordsworth and Keats—and how those concerns find curious transplant in American Transcendentalism.

There is no single definition I aim to adhere to. In many ways, my deep love for the Romantic resides in its refusal of easy definition. The essay that comes closest to expressing my own multivalenced, polymorphous love of Romantic work is likely also the one that first brought me into its influence: Emerson's "The Poet." If only to give a sense of what these aspects of Romanticism are that undergird the higher hopes of this essay, I thought I might quickly reprise some necessary notions from Emerson's work.

The poet ceases to have a primary value as an individual; or, rather, has value as an individual only insofar as that particular subjectivity garners access to consciousnesses not limited to his own. In this sense, the poet not only confronts and enters those others (both people and objects) in order to participate in a mutual naming, but in more radical ways, undermines individuality with a profound sense of poetic anonymity as creative source.

The poet works in order to gain access to those patterns underneath existence that give form to the sensible world, an atomic search for fact. The poet is herself one such fact. This is a work the poet does, but also a work done upon the poet. The poet labors so as to be worthy of receiving the gift, be that gift vision, or be it a glimpse into that music that rectifies discord into sudden harmony.

The poem conducts within itself a search for the necessity its beauty rests on.

Its thinking is this search. Such thinking is multiform, and so too is a poem. A poem demonstrates in its own wildness, its own inability to see to the end of the thinking it is in, "the ravishment of the intellect . . . coming nearer to the fact" (Emerson 220).

Genius is no capacity of self, but otherness brought into the intimate confines we half-mindedly call "self." Genius not only "realizes and adds," (212), it is the furious repair of the world.

3. It is within this crisis of self, this riddle of *I*, that Martin Corless-Smith's work gains one of its radically romantic valences. Corless-Smith is returning to the roots of the Romantic tradition—a poetic gesture not of exhumation, nor of the critic's effort to classify the previously living strand, but rather a method of digging down to the roots so as to revivify them, to show the vitality never left, and to graft his own experiment onto this previous experiment whose organic life never ceased its living. (I think perhaps it is the poet who understands Thoreau's conviction that the "head is an organ for burrowing" [Thoreau, *Walden* 188]; it is the poet who knows one does not graft the fruit of one limb to the differing fruit of another, but grafts at the root, and becomes the plant one is grafted to.) All of Corless-Smith's books prove relevant to this discussion, but his third book, *Nota*, is much on my mind these days. In it, the poet writes: "There are those, including often the self, who you cannot abide—but those, especially the self, that you must" (Corless-Smith, n. pag.). Harsh wisdom. Wisdom that confronts and does not comfort. It also provides not a sentiment, but a suspicion, that Romantic work is anything but "romantic." That is, the work of encounter, of self in enveloping collision with other and with self, is in its erotic trouble dizzying, maddening, and labyrinthine as often as (if not more often than) it is epiphanic. The poem, like the self, might be considered "a field where nothing borders nought" (Corless-Smith, n. pag.), but as a field (location *and* practice), it is also a place of dwelling. In the midst of *Nota*, Corless-Smith places a book within a book: "A Selection from the Works of Thos. Swan (MS. 8911 Worcester City Records Office)." The inserted book purports to be a discovery of another poet's notebooks, filled with notes (on the odd nature of color, etc.) and poems in various states of vision and re-vision. The poems bear enough of a lyric sensibility that the reader suspects Corless-Smith is the poet who wrote them. But the perfection of his mask is its imperfection. For the poems too differ, and one suspects—even as one tries to dismiss—that Swan's poems are truly written by Swan himself. But what is it that "truly written" signifies? Our desire for "authority" proves itself suspicious. That suspicion is Corless-Smith's Romantic inheritance—one that he admirably, necessarily, furthers. This lyric ambivalence also casts light back onto such protomoderns as Fernando Pessoa as profoundly Romantic in their experiment. Indeed, it might be heteronym as polytropic self,

a self that never can unify into the mere self—self as that indeterminate point in which accuracy and inaccuracy are interchangeable—that typifies radical Romantic personhood.

The Romantic poem itself suffers, almost sympathetically, the very crisis the person undergoes. For example, Bin Ramke's poems in recent years include within them notes that guide the reader to texts wholly other than his own. The gesture differs from the allusive in that it does not claim within itself the text it points at, and so any illusion of unity is impossible. The very notion of allusion might in Ramke's recent work be replaced by that of *articulation*, or could be if we move the word from its immediate connotation of clear expression and push back into its etymology. That etymology reveals *articulation* as the art of finding within a body the joints by which it is held together, and *articulation* as such marks within the poem those tense lines by which it is joined together—the very same lines by which it can be torn apart. Ramke's *articulate* poetry is Romantic not exactly in its sensibility, but in its need to mark the vulnerable points of its own insufficiency.

In the fall 2011 issue of *Fence*, Ramke's poem "Articulation" contains within it not only etymologies of "fact," "part," and "cloud," and a poem by Hildegard of Bingen ("Our king is swift / to receive the blood of innocents / But over the same blood clouds / are grieving" [Ramke 160]), but also texts on mereology from a variety of websites: "I draw a rabbit that to you looks like a duck. Have I thereby made two drawings? I write 'p' on my office glass door; from the outside you read 'q.' Have I therefore produced two letter-tokens? . . . There is just one thing here, one inscription, and what it looks (or means) to you or me or Mary or John is totally irrelevant to what that thing is" (Varzi 2008) http://seop .leeds.ac.uk/entries/mereology/ (157).

Ramke's notes and inclusions are not simply indexical. We find ourselves confronting a textual experiment, a tangible demonstration of one aspect of Keats's epistemology: "Now it appears to me that almost any Man may like the Spider spin from his own inwards his own airy Citadel—the points of leaves and twigs on which the Spider begins her work are few and she fills the Air with a beautiful circuiting: man should be content with as few points to tip with the fine Web of his Soul and weave a tapestry empyrean. . . . But the Minds of Mortals are so different and bent on such diverse Journeys that it may at first appear impossible for any common taste and fellowship to exist between two or three under these suppositions—It is however quite the contrary—Minds would leave each other in contrary directions, traverse each other in Numberless points, and at last greet each other at Journeys end" (Keats, *Selected Letters* 92–93).

It is not at "Journeys end" that Ramke leaves us, but more spectacularly, in the midst of the web itself, where the pressure on a single thought brings into awareness one of those "Numberless points" where contrary minds converge. Ramke, in the most humble, most sensitive of ways, locates within his poems those moments of insufficiency that might not be seen by a reader. He points out the wound, he exposes the flaw, those indebted moments in the poem that reveal its own frailty, and shows that poetic unity is not a factor of a single poem's formal cohesion, but something far grander in scale. The unity that matters is the one that can be seen only in the honest admission of any given poem's failure, and through the failure, the next text is found, discovered, wandered toward in such a way that it demands the present book be closed so that another can be opened. Ramke's work affirms not itself, but the larger experiment of which it is but one strand.

We find ourselves now in hindsight's wonders, where the seed of the plant can be glimpsed through its blossom. I can see in Keats's "Ode to Psyche" the young poet's effort to create a bower that does not work in ways entirely different from Corless-Smith's masking. Keats here does not put on a mask but makes of his face one—a hollow whose open eyes are open only, like Psyche's bedroom windows, "to let the warm Love in!" (*Poems* 277). He makes of his face, and the realm behind the face (so mistakenly called mind), that "untrodden region" (*Poems* 277) where Cupid and Psyche can forever consummate their holy love. The poet's face is a form of enthusiasm, wherein the gods dwell. The eyes give the barest hint of the thralldom, a seeming glance outward, and the steady gaze within. We see also the gently latticed ways in which Dorothy's journals become William's poem, which to commemorate, in *This Nest, Swift Passerine* I wrote:

Wm composing in the wood
The vision in his sister's eye

I happened to say that when I was a child
I would not have pulled a strawberry blossom

Caught in the web of Wm's mind
He composed each day in wood

At dinner-time he came in with the poem
Of "Children gathering flowers" (14)

3
Singing Schools and "Mental Equality"
An Essay in Three Parts

Rachel Blau DuPlessis

"Will no one tell me what she sings?"

How is gender represented, constructed, and played through in the literary tradition as we know it? Clearly there are many ways—but there might be some preliminary typology one can construct of these mechanisms, mechanisms that fundamentally rest on the terrain of power-in-culture. This terrain is also the zone of cultural memory. Unless we have literary historical paradigms that involve dialogue, contestation, response, one is limited to monotheistic models of singular figures doing singular things in their singular poetry. Using some materials provoked by the publication of the anthology *Poems for the Millennium, Volume Three: The University of California Book of Romantic and Postromantic Poetry* and beholden to the expansion of the field of Romanticism by the recovery of women practitioners and by attention to the social issues of gender, I will attempt such a—necessarily incomplete—three-part typology. This essay concerns gender tropes and mechanisms, poetic conventions and their outcomes, and the sociality of poetry, as well as thoughts on my poetic practice.

Why use the Romantic era as the starting place? In Anglophone culture, the complexity of women's political rage and social desires, their yearning and forceful analyses of their second-class legal and educational status, their powerful goals for female liberation, their libidinous investments in their liberty and in the liberation of other second-class semicitizens are all vital to the Romantic era. The decolonization of women, sexual minorities, other minoritized groups, and enslaved peoples; the establishment and enforcement of civic personhood for all; the ability to value (not just "tolerate") differences and differentials within communities are all indicators of real modernity—a modernism drawing upon the energies of active Romanticism.

Part the First: Exclusive Manhood as Poetic Power

Trying to establish the contradictory relations of male literary artists and female literary artists in long modernity is an intricate process, a process counterintuitively assisted by an attempt to critically examine—not just to assume—the cultural claims of the hegemonic gender. That is, by exfoliating what Man, Masculine, and Manly might mean in any given poetic community or enterprise, one may uncover the sociopolitical relations of male artists to their representations of women and to their senses of the feminine. Making these processes and assumptions visible may help puncture the regime of cultural inequality.

Ezra Pound (1885–1972) and William Wordsworth (1770–1850) deployed female figures quite purposefully in "Portrait d'une Femme" and "The Solitary Reaper" to block and dissolve the full impact of the creative work of the historical women on whom each particular female figure was based (DuPlessis, *Blue Studios*). That is to say, the poets' placing of a historically attested creative/productive woman inside a poem, and their uses of specific poetic conventions to depict each of these figures, leached the women's historical presence in favor of an abstracted and stereotyped depiction. In the case of the Wordsworth poem, this was a strained, yearning idealization of a distant figure ("Will no one tell me what she sings?"); in the case of the Pound poem, this was a callow deidealization of a person well known to Pound and of whom he was somewhat jealous.[1] These male poets' uses of poetic convention and poetic institutions had the outcome of effacing, unsettling, and otherwise negatively repositioning female agency, female artistic autonomy, and female pleasure in historical women's own artistic production. Of course, as with any cultural product, one might also find fissures and slippages in this system; it was my attention to these moments of contradiction—often around tone—that provoked my anatomy of these works. This myopic close reading strategy infused with historical and biographical information I have called social philology or sociopoesis. Both of these poems rested loosely upon the male poet's urge to reclaim an assumed territory of power. Exclusive male cultural power (a myth in which both Wordsworth and Pound wanted to believe even with some uncertainties) had been implicitly challenged by the two female practitioners whom they depicted.

One poetic claim made around maleness as representative of universal humanness is found in William Wordsworth's "Preface" to the second edition of *Lyrical Ballads* (1800) and in related works like the 1798 "Advertisement," with their rejection of artifice, guile, and cant (*Prose Works* 124). Although females are depicted and sometimes given voice in Wordsworth's experimental poetry, Wordsworth nonetheless insists that poetry is particularly vital when written in the "real language of men" (118, 143, and 150; see also 161 [appendix]). This key phrase is repeated several times in both the earlier and later versions of this document.

The poet as a figure "is a man speaking to men" (Wordsworth, *Prose Works* 138). It is impossible to ignore the repeated evocation of men as a gender in this striking essay at the same time that one "knows"—or does one?—that this is just Wordsworth's forceful manner of delineating his universalized poetics. For in his 1798 "Advertisement," the word "human" is also repeatedly deployed. The goal for poetry is to depict "human passions, human characters, and human incidents" (116). However, this ambiguity of meaning is actually formidable. To say the real language of all human beings is a weaker proposition rhetorically, since only human beings have complex spoken and written language, and since this criterion would assimilate all language uses, all styles. Of course the weight of the proposition falls on the word "real"—authentic, down-to-earth (but not too far down), the way people really speak, nothing "poetic" or gussied up.

Yet even today a good deal of forensic tread is gained for men as a gender in the semantic slide possible between man as male and man as the universalizing, incorporative word for person. Wordsworth appears to be drawing upon the diction of natural rights of man—a political discourse of the first importance—while reaching beyond or under it to a bedrock, arguing that pleasure produced in poetry "is an homage paid to the native and naked dignity of man" (*Prose Works* 140). "Naked" is a nice way to evoke fundamentals. Wordsworth may well be conscious of the force of the term "men," given, for instance, such contemporaneous argument and polemic as the 1792 treatise by Mary Wollstonecraft, whose semantic distinction among women, human, females, and men was certainly one plausible source of the word "human" as applied to all without distinction of sex-gender.[2]

This universalizing term "men" erases class difference as well as gender differentials. As Barbara Johnson once proposed, "the substitution [in Wordsworth's "Preface" as compared to his "Advertisement"] of the expression 'the real language of men' for 'the conversation of the middle and lower classes' acts out an erasure of 'class,' a gesture of dehistoricization and universalization" (92). Because what good is a universal if not all persons have the same access to political, civic, legal, and human rights? What good is it as an ideal if it is not actualized for everyone it claims to be including?[3]

Inadequate poetic diction—always of other poets, of past generations, of other "singing schools" (in the words of W. B. Yeats, "Sailing to Byzantium")—is often the villain of documents in poetics. Or, more to the point, the vil-

lainess. Wordsworth's revolutionary proposition that the languages of poetry and of prose are fundamentally the same does come at a price, a price I
am foregrounding here. In Wordsworth's "Advertisement to *Lyrical Ballads*,"
feminized or class-critical words such as "gaudiness" and the "inane" are used
to characterize the finicky and mannered dictions that impede the depiction
of "human passions, human characters, and human incidents" (*Prose Works*
116). So too his terms "capricious" and "fickle tastes" are resonant with gender implications (124).

It appears that he is making a critique of women's character (a critique
parallel to Wollstonecraft's) without proposing any political or educational
solution to that civic inequality. Wollstonecraft does, of course, propose these
solutions. Wordsworth borrows the fickle/capricious descriptor for women
but does not see these traits as malleable and changeable with changes in
consciousness or education, or as occurring as a result of sociosexual expectations, especially those around modesty, repression, and conformity. He
claims that the centrality of poetic honesty, sincerity, freshness, and plain-
ness, the "spontaneous overflow" (*Prose Works* 126) of "feelings" that have
the force of personal, emotional "powerful"-ness, are enough to overcome
external social forces or interior self-and-social repression.

The incontrovertible forces of urbanization, standardization, and the ra-
tionalization of labor "blunt" people and coarsen them to a "savage torpor,"
a trope evoking class and race or ethnicity. This socioeconomic situation—
he further diagnoses—makes such degraded people demand melodrama
and sensation in their art products. These products in their turn are given
an almost exclusively female, sometimes effeminate, and sourly critical sex-
gender implication. They are "frantic novels, sickly and stupid" plays, "and
deluges of idle and extravagant stories in verse" (*Prose Works* 126, 128). For
these class-based conditions of economic degradation, false—because feminized (and hysterical)—sops have been created. In contrast, Wordsworth will
propose his true ("manly") solutions. Poetry is postulated as one effective
force that can "mend" the sociocultural damage of modernity as he observed
it. Poetry becomes a pastoral-parental force constructed by males—it is a
haven and help to all, ministering to social ills, able to succeed in its mission because it "adopt[s] the very language of men" (130).

That diction in poetry has a political function as well as a polemical one
should not be surprising. Claims for even the plainest diction are an ideological formation. That is, no formal or rhetorical feature is neutral; all are
situational; all participate covertly or overtly in social meanings and debates.[4]

Wordsworth reiterates his gendered proposition, insistently saying "man"
in several contexts. For instance, poetic pleasure depends on good topics

"metrically arranged" in such a way that "the style is manly" (*Prose Works* 146). This remains a remarkable claim—that meter (rhythmic arrangements and related syntactic choices) can be gendered. This may be glossed as a rejection of poeticity, of the far-reaching quirkiness of language itself, expressed in the runaway "caprices" of the signifier ("poeticity" from Jakobson; "caprices" from Wordsworth, *Prose Works* 144).[5] What is feared and scorned is "a motley masquerade of tricks, quaintnesses, hieroglyphics, and enigmas"—any kind of "extravagant and absurd diction," for these lead to and from a "perturbed and dizzy state of mind" (162).

So Wordsworth emphatically rejects any poetic language evoking the feminine, the effeminate, the quirky, the "adulterated," the "perverted" (*Prose Works* 161). This is a historically vital critique of the exaggerated, mannered poetic diction of prior generations and of current poetic fashions. A key target is the Della Cruscans with their heady, erotic sentimentalisms. Yet these strictures, however influential, including on the plain style of Poundian modernism, and however positive—or at least hegemonic—from some of our contemporary points of view, also emphatically rest on powerfully encoded sex-gender assumptions: about passion, about being carried away into reverie, witchery, ecstasy. And they may possibly rest on political assumptions, given that people are made "dizzy" and "extravagant" with the potential for human liberation, the ecstatic and rapturous moment of hope in the revolutionary possibility of the 1790s.

In fact, "rapture" is a word repeated when words almost fail the poet Mary Robinson as she contemplates revolutionary possibility. For Robinson (1758–1800), in a poem against tyranny ("Ainsi Va le Monde" [1791]), the poetic diction and the soaring rhetorical overleaping bolstered and underscored her rapturous political claims. To recall Isobel Armstrong, the affective "gush of the feminine" was a "way of thinking through" "philosophical traditions that led to a demeaning discourse of feminine experience," such as we have seen in Wordsworth (Armstrong, "Gush of the Feminine" 16). Such discourses of rapture had both political and epistemological meanings as ways to both investigate and instantiate "how far the affective *is* knowledge" (16).

Indeed, as Jerome McGann argued in 1996—something I seem simply to have rediscovered here—Wordsworth's "Preface" had, among its other tasks, the charge of responding to Mary Wollstonecraft's analytic essay and to Mary Robinson's feminist polemic and poetical claims. To support his argument, McGann analyzes Robinson's manifesto-cum-poetic text of the poetry of sensibility: *Sappho and Phaon* (1796). McGann notes that "Wordsworth's revisionist 'Preface' to *Lyrical Ballads* (1800) . . . seeks to restore poetry—including the poetry of feeling and imagination—to its 'manly' heritage" (*Poetics of*

Sensibility 99). Wordsworth was explicitly challenged by such proclamations of enlightened, passionate female powers and such rhetorics of sensibility as Robinson claimed in this work. He therefore tried to retrack poetry to a single-gendered zone (102). Wordsworth may have succeeded all too well, but there is no reason to continue to follow him.

What might be a counterclaim, or a modifying one to this Exclusive Manliness of Poetic Power? The repetitive manliness is a claim twinned with a further gendered structure of feeling. The male figure denominated by Wordsworth is "a man, it is true, endowed with more lively sensibility, more enthusiasm and tenderness," with "a more comprehensive soul"—more than what? "More than are supposed to be common among mankind" (*Prose Works* 138). So this "manliness" is the manifestation of a Better Man—this suggesting a potentially antimasculinist argument. The evocation of affect, sympathy, delight, ready response that Wordsworth gives in his portrait can suggest a figure that fuses the best stereotyped behavior of both genders and melds several roles in a new transcendent Romantic Subject. This Subject will leave behind the blunted, turbid sensibility of the one gender and the fickle sensationalism of the other while combining the forcefulness of the one gender and the sympathies of the other. There is a "new man" or "new human" quality to poets—such people heighten and synthesize "passions and thoughts and feelings" general to all humans (142). Wordsworth oscillates between this tender new Subject, with its bigendered emotionality and androgynous newness, and the virile poet underscored by his insistent repetitions of "manly."

This imperial, all-places and all-genders new male-but-beyond-male Subject shows the utopian ease of making a solution to social contradictions by appropriating all affirmative cultural sites. No need to choose; this is an innocently new Imperial Subject who fuses all sex-gender contradictions into himself, and thereby solves them simply by Being. This new universal Subject negotiates within himself the strands of sexuality and gender (perhaps even of class) without ever having to account for political, economic, and historical issues that would confront him were he in fact an embodied, and not an imaginary, female or were he an actively homoerotic person and not simply a man of feeling. This Imperial Androgynous Male Subject becomes the central type of modernist masculinities out of Romanticism—he is oft seen amid the denizens of the twentieth and twenty-first centuries. Both the exclusively Manly and the inclusively Male-but-Androgynous templates for cultural power clearly work in other sociopoetic situations—around the colonizer and the colonized, for instance. And while this Imperial Androgyny has much to recommend it, and while it is a recurrent solution when people think about transforming the sex-gender system—as Virginia Woolf's *A Room of One's Own* also shows—it begs a few questions. What then to do about women poets as Romantic Speaking Subjects, or about nonmanly Romantic Subjects?[6] Can females also be imperial inhabitants of the terrain of poetry, amassing any and all subject positions and deploying them? How can one acknowledge—in poetry and elsewhere—the actual living political and social bodies of gendered people?

Part the Second: Gendered Dialogues, Cultural Power, and "Mental Equality"

Interchanges, dialogues, and contacts between emphatically gendered writers are particularly fruitful zones for examining, with some historical specificity, the larger issues of gender and power in poetic cultures. The longing for social power, the playing with sexual power, the achieving of cultural power are aspects of the story. But importantly, these practices are all intersubjective. They occur between at least two people, both or all of whom have interests and agendas, although they may have unequal abilities to instantiate these agendas for themselves or to be convincing (to later critics) when histories of the interchange get written. To examine even a two-person intersubjective relationship in the making of literary texts weans criticism away from the obviously retro, but still hegemonically powerful, model of the singular male (or more rarely, female) genius. Suppose related male and female poets (or male and male poets, etc.) were analyzed not only as precursors and followers, or as original and epigones, but also as cursors, running alongside each other in intersecting but differently inflected paths. We would then critically value poems of dialogue, along with cultural situations where critics could construct ex post facto dialogues among poems, plus poets staging "answers" to other poetic texts, even exchanges that have been occluded, buried, and hidden. We would value polemical performances of poets in relation to each other and to other cultural materials and social events.

In this period, the lived textures and the mean social outcomes of female inequality gave rise to heartfelt texts of polemical analysis. To overturn gender injustice, one needs inspiring analysis, personal determination, some educational chances, and political leverage with rational men. This complex is what Mary Robinson presents in her essay "A Letter to the Women of England on the Injustice of Mental Subordination" (written in 1798, published in 1799). Robinson's cards are on the table from the first words of this essay: "Custom, from the earliest periods of antiquity, has endeavoured to place the female mind in the subordinate ranks of intellectual sociability. WOMAN has ever been considered as a lovely and fascinating part of the creation, but her claims to mental equality have not only been questioned, by envious and interested sceptics; but, by a barbarous policy in the other sex, considerably depressed, for want of liberal and classical cultivation" (1).[7] This is quite a polemical challenge: "her claims to mental equality" are still in doubt in fundamentalist and most other societies into the twenty-first century.

To approach this challenge within literary criticism, we began with an analysis of male insistences in rhetoric (as with Wordsworth). The investigation of staged dialogue and even disagreements between striving male and female subjects is another way to examine the issues around sex-gender materials. Where gender materials are concerned, some speaking subjects are not particularly triumphalist; they are more riven and fractured, more opportunistic, using whatever tool of subject position comes easily to hand. Mary Robinson, for example, plays with her feminine weakness and charm somewhat coyly and temptingly, as well as insisting on "sociability."[8] As Bakhtin and Medvedev might see it, the more discourses a writer uses, the more "social evaluations"—even conflicting and alternative ones—might be visible in a text.

One may see some of Robinson's analysis in twinned poems—satiric bagatelles, really—about the feminine attention to fashion in both women and men ("Modern Female Fashions" [1799] and "Modern Male Fashions" [1800] in McGann, New Oxford 196, 197). Even a theatrical celebrity, a fashionista, a flamboyant sometime courtesan (consorting with the Prince of Wales)—and Robinson was all these—has chosen to insist on the ridiculousness of women's and men's enslavement to fashion and fickleness. Her matching poems in comic quatrains veer from each other only in the nature of their conclusions. These poems are part of the critique of luxury, the praise of unaffected artlessness ("nature") that are part of the discourse of the time. Yet even if Robinson walked one walk, she was all too capable of talking another talk. It is an amusing hypocrisy, let us say, or, more seriously, an illumination of complex conflicts around how, actually, to be a female. One may still see these conflicts in every modern fashion magazine for women with its pages of makeup and bangles along with its exhortations to success. However, our mockery of her mockery should not be the final word. Robinson uses one of these poems to propose that women have a mind in potentia that should, she exhorts, be activated; men have only claims of seduction and an unjustified power ("reign") that she teases and excoriates.

There are even more intense dialogues in Robinson's oeuvre, ones that stage the practice of "an equal portion of fame" divided between people of both genders (Rothenberg and Robinson 73). No matter that the education and even the speech and writing of one group have been compromised through many ages of prejudice, and are compromised even in the age of revolution by some of the theorists of liberation—Jean-Jacques Rousseau is the notorious example. As Mary Robinson proposes about the female "sex": "She is capable of mental energies," and she is therefore due "mental equality" (Rothenberg and Robinson 73; in the 1799 edition of "Letter to the Women of England"). "Mental equality," a key phrase, occurs at least five times in the essay as a whole.[9] Certainly any female claim or stance of "mental equality" attacks the colonization of mind so notoriously a problem for socially subordinated groups. It is clear that Robinson saw this claim as an ideological shift of great importance for both female and male consciousness. However, "mental equality" (considering yourself an intellectual equal to the socially powerful gender) is a necessary but not sufficient condition for civic, legal, and political equality. In any event, Robinson's concept of "mental equality" fuels my consideration of two sets of poems in dialogue between Mary Robinson and S. T. Coleridge (1772–1834). All these exchanges took place during the final few years of Robinson's life; she died in 1800, at only forty-two years.

During this period, dialogues between male and female poets were a lively mode of practice. A number of female and male cultural figures experimented with poetic exchange in responsive poems, flirtatious and sentimental calls, and allusions to each other's masquerades. These were publicly available in certain periodicals under calculated poetic pseudonyms. Both "Laura" and "Sappho" were Robinson's "names"—ambitious, duplicitous signifiers, as one was a muse and the other was a poet. The tone of this work was yearning, passionate, juiced up, making much of erotic (if apparently chaste) identifications. This work emerges in the Della Cruscan coterie, in which Robinson participated, belatedly but with considerable pushiness and theatrical panache, in several poetic exchanges in 1788 (see Gamer and Robinson). Yes, this work (hers and others') is overheated; yes, various modes of "panting" are noticeable; yes, erotics are just barely sublimated; yes, this is a notably palpitating poetry. One might use the adjective "Keatsian"—though he of course followed this group and drew upon its ethos.

The Della Cruscan coterie offered a pattern book of male-female and female-male poetic exchange and dialogue, evoking mental equality via passionate responsiveness. The first of the complementary poems, Robinson's "Ode to the Snow-Drop" (1797) is answered by Coleridge's "The Apotheosis, or The Snow-Drop" (1798), both originally published in the same newspaper, the *Morning Post*, and therefore perceivable by readers as matching works.[10] Robinson's almost fully natural description of this little flower—certainly a topos of vulnerability and frail but stalwart presence—is then moralized to a depiction of the writer's current plight—or her dramatic claim of having "known the cheerless hour." Robinson's work allegorizes the nature of the snowdrop (that "beauteous gem") as the first flower to appear in barely-spring, blooming in the cold, sometimes emerging through the snow, modest, "weak and wan," living and dying before anything else "verdant" takes hold (*Selected Poetry* 323).

The snowdrop is compared poignantly to the female speaker—lonely, isolated, without companionship. The simple, pathos-laden snowdrop of Robinson's poem gets transported and extended by a whole narrative panorama in the matching Coleridge work. The heroine of Coleridge's poem is an efficient figure, a version of both female poet and female muse. Her name evokes the Petrarchan heroine, Laura, which is, as noted, one of Robinson's poetic pseudonyms. Thus Laura is both the maker of the original snowdrop poem (Robinson) and the inspirer of Coleridge's poem (also Robinson). This figure is both female poet (she carries a harp; she whispers "witching rhymes" to the flower) and female muse (she falls asleep in the course of Coleridge's narrative and does not actually play that harp). The conjunction of the two poems reveals some nervousness on Coleridge's part about the autonomous artistry of a female poet. It also reveals how Robinson's passive and sentimental tropes around loss encourage a kind of pity, which will allow Coleridge to reposition her agency in his poem.

Coleridge's response imagines a female double, friend to the lonely snowdrop, who mimes and sings to the cold little flower, "interpreting" it in parallel gestures. Laura has "breathed" over the flower, with "the potent sorceries of song," wafting it and herself to a sublime and exaggerated realm of sleep, reverie, and dream (Coleridge, *Poems* 356).

The Spirit's eager sympathy [Laura's, animated by a further "Spirit"]
Now trembled with thy trembling stem,
And while thou [the flower] droopedst o'er thy bed,
With sweet inclining sympathy
    Inclin'd the drooping head.

She droop'st her head, she stretch'd her arm,
She whisper'd low her witching rhymes (356–57, from the second and
    third stanzas)

Although the snowdrop is borne into an immortal realm, there is a good deal of "drooping" on the part of the flower and the female poet, these "droopings" an indicator of both the real flower's actual appearance and the female poet's feminine position as she does an empathetic mimicry of the flower. The word leaves an odd tinge over the praise. "Droop" means to sink down from exhaustion, to sink out of sight, to decline in strength or energy, to flag in spirit or courage, to become despondent. It has been underlined by the triple repetition.

The figure of the female poet ends the poem asleep, in a somewhat escapist mode—escaping, that is, the pain and isolation that Robinson had proposed for her heroine in the figure of the snowdrop. In order to sleep, she has sidelined her poet's harp.

> The Harp unhung by golden chains
> Of that low wind which whispers round,
> With coy reproachfulness complains,
> In snatches of reluctant sound:
> The music hovers half-perceiv'd,
> And only moulds the slumberer's dreams;
> Remember'd LOVES relume her cheek
> With Youth's returning gleams. (358, the eighth and final stanza of the
>   poem)

This is a curiously fraught depiction of a female poet, a strange acknowledgment of her powers by a partial dissolution of them. Having sung about the snowdrop and drooped empathetically above the snowdrop, having then been wafted upward to an imaginary realm of bliss, Coleridge's heroine is depicted as (blissfully) asleep—not as creating poetry. The harp "sings" in her stead, but only in a feminine, and somewhat automatic, mode ("reluctant sound"). The harp has no agency, and it "complains" coyly. This is yet another feminine figuration, transferring agency from human choice to a choiceless, will-less object that, because Aeolian—a harp played by the wind alone, like wind chimes—cannot help itself from emitting sound. The sleeper-poet does not even hear this song with any live consciousness (it is only "half-perceiv'd"), and finally, the last lines of the poem return Laura to her past life as sexual object with many gleaming memories of Love (or at any rate, of conquests).

Coleridge's poem is an elaborate, but slightly suspect, compliment to Robinson. Coleridge makes a plethora of female subject positions available to Robinson, both active and more passive ones, both flower and singer, dreamer and poet, poet's song and harp's sound. By the end of his poem Coleridge has slowly peeled Laura's agency from her by his imagined narrative; it is another version of the Pound and Wordsworth situation—turning a functioning female artist into an idealized figure. Yet Laura's power is also considerable; she has cast a spell over the snowdrop, so that the flower is transported to the home of the muses and becomes—temporarily—immortal.

The flower now lives, at least for the length of Coleridge's poem, "mid laurels ever green," where even Love will think it "a blossom from his Myrtle tree" (*Poems* 357). "Myrtle"—mythological tree of Venus—is a tricky allusion to Robinson's sexual and romantic career. Yet the "laurels" are, of course, the leaf and the wreath accorded to fame in poetry. If the narrative arc of the poem dissolves Laura's agency, many stanzas taken individually nonetheless retain and admire that agency. So the poem constructs contradictory, unstable allusions to female sexual charm interwoven with praise of female authorship.

Both the male poet who has engineered this transport as the speaker of the enunciation (the poem as object), and the Laura as speaker of the enounced (the pronouns and characters inside the poem) who has (according to Coleridge) wafted this flower into bliss have an interest in this apotheosis of a feminized flower through the powers of female song. Exaltation of a glorified ideal of feminine pathos allows the male poet still to seek identification with and understanding of the feminine as part of the erotic charge of his career; in fact Ashley Cross argues that Coleridge learned from the "feminine" positions "a poetic authority" compounded of receptivity, sensibility, and empathetic responsiveness that, under Wordsworth's influence, he would "later reject" (50, 51).

The main locus of dialogue and exchange between the two poets is S. T. Coleridge's "Kubla Khan" and Mary Robinson's poem, following his, with its dedicatory title "To the Poet Coleridge" (Rothenberg and Robinson 202–4 and 115–17). In their matching poems, both poets sought to define a Romantic Subject adequate to the toils of sex-gender, both erotic and political. Robinson was responding directly to Coleridge's text, which she had apparently seen in manuscript long before it was published; this is hard to trace, but it is incontrovertible. Robinson's poem "To the Poet Coleridge" is an extended variation of Coleridge's "Kubla Khan," filled with repetition of it and citation from it. Yet the structuring of poems in dialogue within a critical text like this means that one also qualifies older narratives of secondariness, copying, belatedness, and inadequacy in the consideration of female poets.

The dialogues of position and gendered subjectivities that emerge in these matching poems create a very striking conjunction for readers today, particularly as Coleridge's poem has become a necessary classic, while Robinson's is an underknown and underread appendage. We can see, framed by our sense of the gendered stakes of poetic dialogue, that Mary Robinson's response to

Coleridge's "Kubla Khan" is compliment and complement. Her close tracking of his work, constituting an imitation and a reading of it, nonetheless makes one significant revision: she domesticates and even sentimentalizes the male-androgynous whirling singer at the end of the poem, coupling his rapture with her response to that rapture.

And why? What could have motivated her? One might apply Jeffrey Robinson's more general finding and argue that "the poem to Coleridge releases that . . . sense of erotic response to the male poet, not in a subservient way but in order to claim responsiveness itself as an essential feature of a socially visionary, incendiary poetry" (*Unfettering Poetry* 137). That is, Mary Robinson domesticates his male-androgynous figure in order to create "mental equality" in the matching poems. She thereby claims to be able to follow Coleridge into this intricate landscape, to be his companion within it.[11]

She does so writing under the pseudonym "Sappho"—thereby connecting the passionate—here heterosexual—career of that female poet (a career she narrates in her sonnet sequence *Sappho and Phaon* [1796]) to her pleasure in what the Coleridge-figure has achieved.[12] To write her poem, Robinson tracks the lavish fantasy space that he created. Her poem in several stanzas ends every stanza but the final one with a variation of the following quatrain:

> "With thee I'll trace" or "I'll raptured trace" (etc.)
> . . . . the circling bounds
> Of thy rich paradise, extended,
> And listen to the varying sounds
> Of winds, and foamy torrents blended. (Rothenberg and Robinson,
>   115–17)

As a whole, her poem appropriates many descriptors from Coleridge, both words explicitly cited in quotation marks (like "'caves of ice'" and "'sunny dome'") and those implied, like "meander" instead of "mazy" or the "fountain" whose sexual suggestiveness is put forth overtly in such words as "heave" and "panting." Robinson's respondent poem emphasizes that both together, her female speaker (and poet) "with thee" (the male poet), will "wander" the paradise he has created. It makes the visionary landscape available to both and makes the female visitor a boon companion, in awe of the "new creation."

Coleridge's imagined space, among other possible interpretations (exotic Orientalism, for instance), is also clearly a palpitating allegory of sexuality, even of sexual arousal and fulfillment. It is also an allegory of the making of poetry and thereby links the eros of poesis—the longings and identifications in that realm—with imagination and poetic pulse. Coleridge's work is finally a poem about a drug-induced vision; at the end of her life Mary Robinson, like Coleridge, needed drugs for significant pain, and both authors may have had a shared recognition of the fantasies emerging from drug-related trances.

Coleridge's paradise is created literarily via description and textually via rhythm and sound: "With music . . . / I would build that dome in air." Coleridge makes the site's own excess thematic and sensory, by entering this hypnosensual substratum. His poem is neither nonsense nor perfect sense. When Coleridge says "and here were . . ." and then lists the features of the landscape, one might be able to intuit "hear," a way of making place present via sound. This is why at the end one moves between ear and eye so promiscuously: "and all who *heard* should *see* them there [my italics]". This is why the response to seeing the "flashing eyes" of the final figure is an outcry in sound: "Beware! Beware!"

The Coleridge poem repeatedly evokes paradoxes, which may be tied to sexuality or to the liberation of nature given the supernatural fantasy that the poem unleashes. He creates a landscape of contradiction. The pulsing descriptors are barely anchored by a patriarchal leader. In Khan's command to build this park, the two words "stately" and decree" are the last vestiges of the somewhat tamed, somewhat domesticated, somewhat hierarchical power of the figure. There are "walls and towers . . . girdled round" and gardens as nice and lucid as a medieval miniature. The only destabilizing moment is the presence of "caverns measureless to man" in the first stanza.

"But oh!" the shift in the tenor of the poem after this introduction! An amazing plethora reigns. First, the landscape is liberated from nature. The mazy motion of an old river, the periodic pulsations of a geyser, the cleft of a chasm, and rocks thrown up in the gush all arguably emerge from different natural geographies and geologic forces, not easily found together in nature.[13] Second, several evocative female and feminized figures populate Coleridge's landscape, either in simile or in allusion. These are shadow figures: a cleft in the earth where one might find "a woman wailing for her demon-lover" brought into being by words alone, by the force of poeticity (in Roman Jakobson's term). There is also a dark "damsel"—an Ethiopian figure—playing an instrument, not necessarily here in this vision, but perhaps somewhere else, in another, receding vision.

The imaginary temporalities and "geography" of Coleridge's paradise are so intertwined that it is impossible to tell what is where, what emerges from what, and why. For example, can a mazy (that is, geologically old) river coexist with a (geologically new) volcanic spurt of a geyser? Are the "caverns measureless" the same as the "caves of ice"? And—to be perfectly flat-footed about this, how come the ice does not melt under the "sunny dome"? Does the dome of pleasure enclose all of this or is that dome just another feature inside the fantastic space? Outside and inside, hot and cold, spurts and placidity—it is a world only semireadable in its own space and time. And is the geography anyway a consequence of the song sung by the Abyssinian maid whose song inspires the poet ("I") suddenly named twice in the final stanza? Female and male—inspiration and inspired—which is which?

The final stanza also enacts the remarkable pronominal displacement of this "I" to a "he," a quick shift of subjectivity from first to third person. This is the whirling, ecstatic poet-dancer, encircled by onlookers. Coleridge's speaker addresses these onlookers as "you"—another pronominal shift from an implied "they" to a "you," third to second person. These multiple pronouns (accelerating at the end of the piece) are dizzying, until ending in the insistent "he."

> And all who heard should see them there,
> And all should cry, Beware! Beware!
> His flashing eyes, his floating hair!
>   Weave a circle round him thrice.
>   And close your eyes with holy dread,
>   For he on honey-dew has fed,
>   And drunk the milk of Paradise. (Rothenberg and Robinson 204)

Plethora, connections beyond logic are set forth in a rhythmic charm and quickening pulse potentially endless. The poem can end only with an enclosing quatrain rhyming *abba*, with the completion of a circle ("thrice" being a figure of closure), with the biblical evocation of "honey-dew," and with the stabilizing but ecstatic word "Paradise." Yet finally it is difficult to surmise whether the final quatrain is a containment of the ecstatic figure or an incitement to it.

The figures in Coleridge's poem are all females in some kind of artistic or sexual rapture with the exception of the figure at closure, a ramping up in an effeminate figure called "he," whirling in an ecstatic dance, who summarizes both the sexual and the poetic rapture and becomes the apotheosis of the bigendered or feminized male poet. This is another version of that New Romantic Subject about whom Wordsworth wrote, yet one whose trance state is far from the temperate balance that Wordsworth suggested for his fused male figure.

It is this pulsing, passionate dancer whom Robinson transposes in her poem. He is no longer the self-pleasuring, poetically isolated, awe-ful figure with "His flashing eyes, his floating hair!" Coleridge's figure was a male daimon, and possibly (if one wanted narratively to fix this poem) the demon-lover for whom a female figure might well wail. Robinson excluded the singularity of this figure in favor of what seems weaker: an erotic "*invitation au voyage*," addressed to the writer, a passage that signifies on his tropes and praises him as the object of the song of the nymph, who is repeating his own song, in an intertwined dialogue of poetry. And she overtly writes the singing female figure into her final stanza, as linked to him but causing her (Robinson's) responsiveness to his song, mediated by this female singer.

> And now, with lofty tones inviting,
> Thy nymph, her dulcimer swift-smiting,
> Shall wake me in ecstatic measures
> Far, far removed from mortal pleasures;
> In cadence rich, in cadence strong,
> Proving the wondrous witcheries of song!
> I hear her voice—thy "sunny dome,"
>   Thy "caves of ice," aloud repeat—
>   Vibrations, madd'ning sweet,
> Calling the visionary wand'rer home.
> She sings of thee, oh favoured child
> Of minstrelsy, sublimely wild!—
> Of thee whose soul can feel the tone
> Which gives to airy dreams a magic all thy own. (Rothenberg and Rob-
>   inson 117)

She domesticates this figure by having the nymph with her dulcimer call "the visionary wand'rer home" rather than, as the watchers do in the Coleridge poem, by standing in awe of his autonomous whirling, as he twirls farther and farther away from their world. Robinson makes an equality of these raptures: "she sings of thee." Furthermore, while this "nymph" is repeating, for the third time, in quotation marks, the distinctive phrases by Coleridge ("sunny dome"; "caves of ice"), she situates her minstrelsy in the temporal present of the poem, both repeating his phrases and re-creating him. In Robinson's poem, the Coleridge figure is uniquely positioned to "feel the tone" of her (the nymph's and Robinson's own) "wondrous witcheries of song"—by this last phrase reminding Coleridge of his compliment to her. For Robinson, as Coleridge described her, had, in the snowdrop poem, produced "the potent sorceries of song" and the "witching rhymes."

The Robinson poem is considerably less familiar to us and, while it is a supple and attractive work, it is not the cultural equal of the Coleridge poem. It is clear, however, that Robinson is a fascinating and skillful poet. But neither judgment is to the real point. Robinson has attempted a very notable *détournement* in her response to Coleridge: she has attempted, of Coleridge's ecstatic work and in response to it, to produce a "balance of raptures" between the female figure and the male figure, both poets, and both engaged with the intellectual and passionate feeling that poetry offers (McGann, *Poetics* 71). In that task, this poem, complementary and complimentary both, offers an example of a female poet proposing and producing and claiming "mental equality" in the cultural realm.[14] She is a woman speaking to men and to women. Poetry made by a man speaking to men characterizes only one singing school even if it is plausible that there is a distinct difference between Coleridge and Wordsworth on the topic of female practitioners.

Further, the typology presented here is not yet obsolete. We are still in the literary period marked by the dialogue between Coleridge and Robinson, marked by the insistences of Wordsworth. This is a period in which gender and sexuality are overt and covert in the making of poems and poetic careers. One may see examples well into our time: monogendered insistences in framing a cohort by losing a major female influence (cf. Charles Olson and Frances Boldereff) and complicated dialogue between gendered poets (cf. H. D. and Pound; Eliot and Moore; Pound and Zukofsky).

Part the Third: "Mental Equality" and Queering Gender

Speaking from a position of female authorship, as if I am an allegory, I will remark that Je est un author. Un autre. Une other. I am in both feminine and masculine subject positions and I can or may enter these (as best I can) at will, but in society I may be framed by one. Mastery is a struggle not to be limited and caged by gender, and truly to claim mental (cultural) (civic) (social) equality. Yet this stance may (have to) continue to use gendered tropes to talk about cultural power, because gendered tropes construct a powerful cultural legacy that must be acknowledged and faced. This is a queer position, to try to move beyond binary gender ascriptions (but not beyond gender), to claim the power of various modes of gender transformation and mixing to walk away from stereotypes of feminine and masculine in the cultural compact while aware of their saturating power.

And from that author position (inside gender as a system, drawing on both genders, living inside one apparent gender), I have invented my particular act of "mental equality." It is certainly not unique to me (as the work of Mary Robinson shows), but it is insistently present in my recent work. I have variously taken up key works or materials of Dante, Pound, Oppen, Coleridge, Wordsworth, Pope, Mallarmé, Zukofsky, Eliot, and Ingeborg Bachmann in various individual cantos of my long work called *Drafts*. These poems address their concerns, use their forms, or consider their methods and conclusions. In all cases these are posthumous dialogues—one of the poets is dead—that attempt to articulate gendered concerns among other concerns. My Pope poem is an antifundamentalist, profeminist polemic in rhyming couplets; my Oppen and Zukofsky poems have moments of gender critique, as does my work with Eliot's "The Waste Land"; my Dante poem talks about girls, women, and poetic vocation. Others of these torqued texts revisit the powerful political urgencies and arousals of the long twentieth-century fascism, endless war, ecological disaster, economic injustice.

Je est that kind of other to myself as a conceptual act of disturbance and cultural recalibration, of "confiscation, superimposition" (Fitterman and Place 23).[15] I am them as female author, which has been a mere simulacrum of authorship throughout history. It is hard to set this aside, and callow not to recognize the seepage of former assumptions. Look at the reception career of Mary Robinson, the ways she is variously seen as occasional, half-baked, inadequate. The question of mental equality is still in play, still in struggle. Taking the sweep of literary history, "I" am a fake become ghost become real. For now, that history is marked by the shadow of me and others like me. I am a female writer with a set of interlocking differentials or position, access, potential for dissemination and reception, if not production. I am a particular writer—privileged in language and semiprivileged in country of national origin, critical in politics, secular in my skepticism. I am this mix of hegemonic and emergent in relation to even the critical edges of that culture in which I am also saturated, and through which I have expressed my longing. Or part of that longing. Through which I have also expressed and exposed my resistance.

If all culture must begin again from the ground up—the premise of Romanticism as well as modernism and feminism, then as a consequence, I am called to torque texts. I am, in fact, driven to torque texts. I torque texts for many reasons, to extend them, to deturn them, to criticize some of their premises, to position myself in dialogue with them. This strategy is more than the use of allusion or citation. It addresses the power of these texts within our cultural tradition and some of the meanings of that power. It addresses the potential power a woman author may also claim—we can again call this "mental equality." I am now an author entering the territory of a queer struggle to move beyond binary, hierarchical gender. Addressing prior texts critically and sympathetically is a conceptual strategy of ethical, political, formal, and cultural interrogation.

Torquing texts or textual appropriation is a specific strategy of cultural citation that, instead of citing from a plethora of materials (as in Marianne Moore, T. S. Eliot, Melvin Tolson, or William Carlos Williams), chooses to engage with one text, overwriting, digging into it, excavating it, twisting it to other uses. The social basis for this and the ethical-political aura produced might depend on the measuring of a distance, historical or social, and on the channeling and examination of the impact of that text, as well as the achievement of a critical relation to that text and its uses. Especially if this text has hegemonic force, my citation, allusion, and recontextualization, my playing with now-classic statements, all have the effect of suspicion, a wary reckoning of temporal, historical, and social distance between the original of the torqued text and the authorial agent doing the torquing. It is also an act of empathy and curiosity—what is there, in that text; what remains vital in it?

Torquing texts, overwriting, responding to the work of others, revisionary seeing—this is, in fact, culture as we know it. Everyone rewrites everyone, everyone repaints, re-etches everyone. It is the claim intellectually and affectively to take ruthlessly from culture whatever is needed. This is a fact and it is everywhere—call it influence, appropriation, stealing; call it borrowing, refashioning, subversion by trumping; call it allusion, citation, quotation; call it critique, imitation, adaptation, refashioning; call it transmission, allusion, and versions. Why am I insisting particularly on the importance for myself as a female author in accomplishing this act repeatedly? Because it expresses a desire for, and a performance of, "mental equality," to cite Mary Robinson. It claims agency in the making of culture and trumps or transcends the more passive position that some cultural criticism would still uphold as the proper position of the female within poetry.

And this, in turn, has to do with my acknowledging the long, long history of ambivalence to female agency in culture despite the powerful existence of female practitioners through many centuries, and despite a long history of attention to them, particularly in feminist reflection and criticism. For the cultural position of female figures is repeatedly iterated—even in the most current theories. Here is an example. Giorgio Agamben's essay "An Enigma concerning the Basque Woman" speaks about a story by the contemporary Italian writer Antonio Delfini that has an apparently incomprehensible citation of a Basque poem in it. "The Basque woman appears through the sweetness of an unknown language and she disappears in the ungraspable murmur of words in a foreign language" (Agamben, *End of the Poem* 120). This

is, of course, precisely the situation of "The Solitary Reaper" and Wordsworth revealing his gendered cultural frustration that he cannot get at her
song (DuPlessis, *Blue Studios*). Agamben proposes that this kind of female
is "the symbol of the language of poetry" linked to maternal speech, speaking in tongues, and a symbol of "that which is so inner and present that it
can never be remembered." I want all that, too. Who wouldn't? But I want to
be not only the symbol of the language of poetry for someone else, but the
bearer of it, the maker of it, me along with my peers, other women writers
who have existed inside this tempting, devastating cultural ghetto.

For Agamben, "[Dante's] Beatrice is the name of the amorous experience
of the event of language at play in the poetic text itself. She is thus the name
and the love of language, but of language understood not in its grammati-
cality but, rather, in its radical primordiality, as the emergence of verse from
the pure Nothing" (*End of the Poem* 58). This is a brilliant (and familiar . . .)
argument on an epistemological limb jutting out over an abyss; the female
figure is that which produces something (language) from Nothing (the void)
by virtue of maternal generosity and generativity. Such an argument is attractive by its evocation of poetic bliss, a primal pleasure in sound, in rhythm,
in "the affective gush," to cite Armstrong. And of course it curiously ignores
Beatrice's role as intellectual in heaven, her exaltation as Dante's teacher and
mentor. But just thinking of this situation of poetic bliss as generated by
women and only by women is problematic. Let this trait be known as pan-
gendered—Coleridge claimed its power and so can we.

For let us postulate that women do not want only the homage that Agamben accords them; it is too close to what they are given, or endowed with by
male power to begin with—all those changeable affective tricks that Wordsworth so deplores. Can we separate traits or stereotypes of masculine and
feminine from actual men and women? Let everyone have both and all have
and both claim all—all of what is wanted in poetry. Let everyone have the
imperium of claim. So—when we talk of any woman writer we must talk of
judgment, creativity, intelligence, and drive not only of mythical generativity
and generosity. What about her social intervention? What about her social
generosity? Let her be an agent! And if she is these things, she may also suffer
loss, grief, sorrow, inadequacy, rage, those losses and extreme emotions from
which Agamben chivalrously tries to protect his female figures by claiming
such a female figure was primordial and not historical.

Put female and male back equally in historical and cultural time. Let
both be confused, let both be devastated!—not representing the Ideal, but
living and acting in the Real. This is why I am intolerant of this endless ro-

manticizing of Her power, the Power of Her. In those time-honored moves, she is dehistoricized. No!—it is enough! I want the female in history, as the maker. I do not want her outside history and time. Can female people not be agents, driven to help remake our collective culture? Only, as I have argued, through "mental equality," civic and cultural equality, and dialogue, and only by queering and drastically destabilizing and rethinking all gender ideas. That is one importance of claiming the agency to write again the texts that we know, in historical time as we know it, thereby to construct—to provoke—texts and sociocultural possibilities that we do not yet know.

Notes

This essay incorporates some sentences from *Purple Passages: Pound, Eliot, Zukofsky, Olson, Creeley, and the Ends of Patriarchal Poetry*, University of Iowa Press, 2012 and two paragraphs from the essay "Torquing Texts" from *I'll Drown My Book: Conceptual Writing by Women*, Rachel Blau DuPlessis and Les Figues, 2012.

1. I only recently came upon Jeremy Prynne's socially exacting philological masterwork *Field Notes: "The Solitary Reaper" and Others*, an even closer reading of this poem in a full social panoply of materials. There is some overlap in certain of our conclusions—mine in the essay in *Blue Studios*: "The switch of emotional values produces a deep *impasse*, in which a strong commitment to write women back into the world from which they have been marginalized comes into conflict with the traditional gender role of the working male poet as the active comptroller, even as implicit oppressor of women almost invisible (though not here inaudible) in their relegation to archaic tasks" (Prynne, *Field Notes* 79).

2. See, for instance: "One cause of this barren blooming [women as socially and intellectually enfeebled] I attribute to a false system of education, gathered from the books written on this subject by men who, considering females rather as women than human creatures, have been anxious to make them alluring mistresses than affectionate wives and rational mothers" (Wollstonecraft, *Vindication*, 7). Mary Robinson made similar analyses in 1798–99.

3. Adriana Craciun catalogs the "investment" in the idea that poetry be masculine, the "literary aggression toward women readers and writers expressed by canonical male poets" in the context of an argument about the feminizing, queering, and sexualizing of poetry and the poetic career in this period (159–68).

4. "Language is created, formed, and constantly generates within the bounds of a definite value horizon" (Bakhtin and Medvedev 124). "When the poet selects words, their combinations, and their compositional arrangement, [she/he]

selects, combines, and arranges the evaluations lodged in them as well" (123). "The poet does not select linguistic forms, but rather the evaluations posited in them" (122).

5. Roman Jakobson defines his term as follows: "Poeticity is present when the word is felt as a word and not a mere representation of the object being named or an outburst of emotion, when words and their composition, their meaning, their external and inner form, acquire a weight and value of their own instead of referring indifferently to reality" (378).

6. The first sentences of this paragraph and its general argument are also found in *Purple Passages* (DuPlessis 195), with thanks to the University of Iowa Press.

7. The current "mental subordination" of women is a bar to universal progress and to "universal knowledge" (M. Robinson, "Letter to the Women" 3). It involves a kind of enslavement of women to passivity and compromised agency (4). The strange term "sociability" is, as I read it, like a portmanteau formation, combining ability and sociableness—women's potential for mutual friendship and genial conversation. All page numbers are from the hypertext link to the original edition.

8. Judith Pascoe argues that "Robinson's alternate identities are not . . . an effort to seize a masculine authority but rather an effort to explore the possibilities of a multiply constituted female one" (260).

9. "In what is woman inferior to man? In some instances, but not always, in corporeal strength: in activity of mind, she is his equal" (M. Robinson, "Letter to the Women" 17).

10. Ashley Cross gives a subtle account of their bond (with special focus on the Aeolian harp imagery), seeing the "dialogue between genders" as a crucial critical position, a critique of the separatist romanticisms of earlier feminist work; I echo this (Cross). Robinson's somewhat complicated libertine reputation was eventually to complicate Coleridge's cool and "admonitory" relationship with Robinson's daughter, after her death. See both Griggs and Stelzig for an apt and pertinent review of the whole relationship. The word "admonitory" is Stelzig's evaluation of the Coleridge letter to Robinson's daughter (121).

11. Her poem is also a recapitulation of English prosody, in metrics and line allusions, according to the cunning reading offered by Daniel Robinson, presenting a history of English meters and prosodies from the folk ballad, through Chaucer, the Renaissance sonnet, the couplets of the eighteenth century, and finally the romantic ballad (D. Robinson). Thus the poem becomes a sampler of Mary Robinson's poetic mastery.

12. Jeffrey Robinson tracks the various meanings of her use of this "heteronym" of Sappho (*Unfettering Poetry* 68).

13. This might well be why Shelley alludes to Coleridge's poem in his much more accurate account of Alpine geography and geology in "Mont Blanc: Lines Written in the Vale of Chamouni." See: "Thy caverns echoing to the Arve's commotion, / A loud, lone sound no other sound can tame; / Thou [Dizzy Ravine] art pervaded with that ceaseless motion, / Thou art the path of that unresting sound" (Allison et al. 616; lines 30–33).

14. Jeffrey Robinson further suggests (pers. comm. 22 April 2012) that Mary Robinson's *Lyrical Tales* (1800) is her attempt to respond, as in a dialogue, to Wordsworth and Coleridge's *Lyrical Ballads* (1798).

15. The sentences here draw on, and sometimes vary, my brief note in Bergvall et al. With thanks to Les Figues Press. I also use some of this thinking in the preface to DuPlessis, *Surge*.

4

A Deeper, Older *O*

The Oral (Sex) Tradition (in Poetry)

Jennifer Moxley

> He who thought that in all creative work the larger part was *given*
> passively, to the recipient mind, who waited so dutifully upon the gift.
>
> Walter Pater, "Wordsworth"

Jonathan Culler admits in his essay on apostrophe that the poetic *O* is an embarrassment, "embarrassing to me and to you" (*Pursuit* 135). It is so by virtue of being "the pure embodiment of poetic pretension," which "proclaims its artificial character rather too obviously" (*Pursuit* 143, 152). This shameful trope, wedded to Romanticism, has been "too often denied" and framed out of "the most radical and experimental works of our time"[1] by modernism and its inheritors; from Pound's discomfort with Whitman's pathos, to Olson's excoriation of what Keats called the "Egotistical sublime."[2] Yet, as the editorial insights of *Poems for the Millennium, Volume Three* show, Romanticism was a project with a "boundary-breaking impulse," radical by virtue of its formal innovation, political dissent, and yes, its embarrassing *O* (2). In fact, the critical silence identified by Culler around this trope may betray the *O* as the most radical inheritance Romanticism bequeathed our ironic age.

In its apostrophic appearance the *O* calls forth presence, yet it is also an example of ecphonesis, a figure of pathos that expresses an emotional outburst. In both functions the *O* can, in some poems, mark something far more threatening than an unwelcome blush brought on by poetical conceit. By echoing a nonlinguistic human sound often associated with sexual arousal and orgasm, the *O* can evoke embarrassment of a slightly different character than Culler's "poetic pretension"; and to go even further, the poetic *O* may, all prudish discomfort aside, put us in an uncomfortable proximity to the sound of the body's dissolution, and by analogy, death.[3] The passivity necessary to undergo this kind of dissolution is remarkably similar to the passivity that many poets believe to be at the heart of poetic inspiration. Both point to a necessity in poetry of a *radical receptivity* to the other. Enthusiastically embracing the emotional *O* of their Romantic inheritance, John Wieners and Robert Duncan—two gay male poets from the innovative poetic tradition as framed by Donald Allen—evince this receptivity in their poems, as did their predecessors, Whitman and Crane, through the figure of oral sex.

Why oral sex? The fact that poetry is first and foremost an oral art is a commonplace as well as a central tenet of the New American Poetry. When we locate the poem in the voice and the throat, it is not so very far to take a further associative step to sex acts so located. *Inspiration*, traditionally figured, is also matter of this anatomical region given its etymological root in the Latin *inspirare*, "to breathe into, or blow upon." As Rilke put it, stressing the boundary-dissolving nature and cosmic implications of inspiration, "Breathing: you invisible poem! Complete / interchange of our own / essence with world-space" (*Ahead* 463). In the tradition that places the source of the poem outside of the poet's ego, that mysterious creative event that Plato called divine inspiration, Whitman "translation," and Rilke and Spicer "dictation," the poem's success depends on a radical receptivity to the other—whether that other be a metaphoric Muse, Martian, voice from the dead, unconscious mind, or unnamed cosmic force.[4] The poet who is seduced by inspiration soon realizes that the resultant poems can "say just exactly the opposite of what he [or she] wants . . . to say" (Spicer 6). This "practice of outside" implies a deep passivity, insofar as the poet must, as Pater said of Wordsworth, "wait dutifully upon the gift" (39). The poet must acquiesce to an external stimulation of the mind that will allow her to, as Duncan put it, "commune with creation, with the divine world; that is to say . . . the most *real* form in language" (*Selected* 3). Furthermore, this radical receptivity may allow the poet to experience her own limits and by extension death *not* as a negation of identity, but rather as a threshold, past which she can view her connectivity to others and to the totality of all things. To quote Duncan again: "For in our *common* human suffering, in loss and longing, an intuition of poetic truth may arise" (*Selected* 4; emphasis added).[5]

In Freud's account of the stages of childhood sexuality, the oral stage (breast sucking to the autoerotic pleasures of thumb sucking) is the most primal. The *orality* of sexuality, therefore, made manifest through the *orality* of poetry may have the paradoxical effect of replacing the complex system of signs that is language with a primal sound, a deeper, older O.[6] The poetic O becomes a hole through which we, like Alice in Wonderland, can fall into a seemingly endless system of alternate signs, each quavering with the possibility of an unforeseen connectivity between ourselves and the larger totality to which we belong.

Yet I do not mean to imply that any time a poet turns to the topic of oral sex we are necessarily in the presence of so radical an affect. The celebratory and universalizing vision formulated above is the outgrowth of a poetic that, as I have said, locates the source of the poem *outside* of the poet and embraces a radical receptivity to the other. Such a vision cannot be made manifest should the poet feel denied access to a "commun[ion] with creation" because, for example, of gender inequities. In such a case the result may be a very negative or selfish association with orality, which can manifest through portrayals of oral sex as damaging and painful. In such cases, the resultant poetic register may show symptoms of oral repression, what happens when, according to Freud, the "erotogenic significance of the labial region" is denied: the child feels a "disgust at food" and can experience "hysterical vomiting" (*Three Essays* 48). In order to illustrate the above, as well as its opposite, I shall now begin a journey through a series of words relevant to my theme that contain the O in its humbler, lowercase form, beginning with the vulgar slang term for fellatio—blowjob. Contemporary poet Catherine Wagner's poem "De Profundis Clamavi, or Did I seek," from her book *My New Job*, illustrates symptoms of oral repression in its portrayal of a blowjob:

Fallacious = fellatio + delicious

but is delicious
cut grass and oysters

Beachy Head,   if unpleasant

against the rear throat,

the gag reflex you learn to control
in high school

Terrify all comers. (39)

In the poem's opening we learn that "The fucking isn't interesting." The conclusion, quoted above, continues this line of sexual misery with the anagrammatic wordplay of "Fallacious = fellatio + delicious." To think of fellatio as delicious is fallacious. If it is *not* delicious, are we to assume it is disgusting? The poem settles this question by moving to lines that refer, albeit in a cryptic way, to cunnilingus: "but is delicious / cut grass and oysters." Wagner then cheekily evokes "Beachy Head," which is a chalk headland on the English coast known for being a place where young girls in their misery cast themselves into the sea, as well as a celebrated poem by Romantic-era poet Charlotte Smith. If we recall the apostrophic opening of Smith's "Beachy Head": "On thy stupendous summit, rock sublime!" we can see how Wagner's double entendre with the word "head" reaches its own horrific sublimity. Wagner's poem argues that "Head" is "unpleasant" because it violates our physiognomy. The throat was not meant to have things shoved into it repeatedly. Nevertheless a blowjob can be endured with the right training: "the gag reflex you learn to control / in high school." Unlike Freud's theory of repressed orality leading to "hysterical vomiting," here the repressed orality leads to disgust with receptivity to the other. While there is no vomiting in Wagner's "De Profundis Clamavi, or Did I seek," the nausea provoked by the theme is palpable. Wagner's last line, "Terrify all comers," has a double edge. If we assume the poem's speaker to be female, Wagner seems to be saying that all women who choose to perform fellatio must overcome a sense of terror. But the poem also implies that men who are brought to orgasm by blowjobs—"all comers"—are also at risk. Given the gender anger infusing this poem, it is easy to take her meaning as a warning: having your cock sucked may put you at very great risk (doubling of the phrase "at risk").

Given Wagner's poem, we might ask if *fellatio*'s pleasures are reserved for men—both gay and straight. Can the O of a blowjob be an image of radical receptivity to the other when the poet is a woman? Laura Mullen's sonnet "Late Spring (1973)" explores the complexities of this issue. It describes a scene of woman-to-man fellatio set against a backdrop of sociopolitical issues. Mullen's tone feels measured when compared to the affect typically unleashed by the O. Yet it is belied by the touching nature of the scene she describes. I shall quote the poem in its entirety:

> I am kneeling in the soft red earth,
> Giving a boy a blow job in the privacy
> Of a lemon orchard. Dark leaves, bright fruit.
> He had some weed he'd shared; I wanted him
> To love me. "Watergate": is a new word;
> We're coming to the end of our involvement
> In Vietnam and we've secretly committed
> To having our way with the Chilean government.
> I close my eyes. I've learned to swallow it.
> We already know we'll need to be passionate
> About "the environment." Subdivisions long
> Ago replaced those groves. We hold each other
> Close when I rise to kiss him, to pour back out
> This gob of tangy seed I kept in my mouth. (114)

The speaker has not trained to suppress a "gag reflex" but "to swallow." Is this training against nature, endured only because the girl "wanted him / To love" her? Mullen does use sexual language throughout to describe invasive political policy: we are at the "end of our involvement" with Vietnam, we are "having our way" with Chile. Yet the poem's closing lines offer a radical alternative to reading relationships only through the negative lenses of breakup or rape. Mullen describes a scene of connectedness between two people, setting their tender Eros apart from the sexualized politics of government strong arms. In doing so, she leaves open the possibility of receptivity to the other, even against a backdrop of nefarious politics and "subdivisions" that destroy "bright fruit." After the boy has been brought to orgasm the girl stands up to kiss him and they "hold each other / close." He has given his penis to her mouth, she has given her mouth to his penis, and finally, joined by their mutual receptivity, they hold each other and she "pours"— a gentle word, connoting a libation—his semen back into his mouth, completing a circle of exchange that begins when he "shared" his weed. Mullen's focus on the connectedness of the lovers after the boy's orgasm shows us that by learning "to swallow," the girl has also learned to take the other fully and completely within herself, an optimistic reading somewhat troubled by the fact that the girl in this poem has not actually swallowed, because the semen remains in the cavity of her mouth. Why? Perhaps that we may see the importance of her final gift, the "gob of tangy seed," which further dissolves the boundary between them by putting the boy in the girl's position as someone who swallows the semen of men. The "tangy seed" also connects the lovers to their environment, to the lemon orchard, which, because bulldozed long ago, stands in for a lost Eden. Mullen's poem manages to allude to Adam and Eve and yet subvert the negative characterization of oral sex as spilled seed. She also provides an image that serves as a metaphor for the interchange between Muse and poet.

The sexual arousal represented through the Os of the blowjob in Mullen's poem shows a radical receptivity to the other and mirrors the mental arousal that takes place during poetic inspiration. Inspiration is also connected to the word "blowjob" through a charming if false etymology.[7] To provoke his or her O and connect with a totality beyond the individual voice, the poet must be willing to be *blown* by the Muse. Yet seeing oral sex as analogous to poetic inspiration is not without its problems. If the poetic O is in fact orgasmic, representing par excellence the inspired poet, then the giver of oral stimulation takes the active role of Muse, the receiver the passive role of poet. This matches Spicer's "dictation" as well as all other accounts that place the poem's source outside of the poet's control. Yet it should be noted that in this model the Muse must also practice a form of *radical receptivity*. The giver of oral stimulation—whether fellatio or cunnilingus—must be willing to *receive* the other into his or her mouth and to have his or her own voice temporarily stifled in order to unleash the O of the receiver. The circularity of the final image of Mullen's poem provides a helpful analogue: having received, you can then give back. The semen in the girl's mouth stands in for the poem, which comes from an "outside," and to an "outside" returns.

The specter of the stifled voice returns us to Romanticism, and to the Romantic ode in particular, a form that foregrounds apostrophe and that poets such as Wordsworth and Shelley used to stage an intense drama about the failure and reaffirmation of the poet's voice (*New Princeton* 857). Wordsworth's "Intimations Ode" is the most celebrated example, and while not traditionally read as having anything to do with sexuality, much less orgasmic apostrophes, its pastoral setting and insistence on the connection between the poet's loss of voice and his inability to "feel the gladness of the May" do hint at an erotic subtext. Sexuality in the pastoral mode is often anarchic, partaking of the kind of voluptuousness oral sex represents, free of the repercussions and responsibilities that accompany reproduction (Poggioli 13).[8] In Wordsworth's "Ode," the poet's voice is stifled by "a thought of grief," provoked at the hearing of joyous birdsong as well as by the sight of lambs bounding as "to the tabor's sound." These May Day activities remind the poet that he can no longer see the "celestial light" that bathed the earth during his childhood, and therefore can neither feel joy nor celebrate that joy in song. The paradox here is that the poet *is* singing all the while. Three-quarters of the way through the "Ode" the poet's crisis ends with the revelation that Nature safekeeps our knowledge of transcendence, even if we have forgotten it: "O joy! That in our embers / is something that doth live, / That nature yet remembers / What was so fugitive!" (Wordsworth, *Oxford Authors* 300; lines 132–35). The poet realizes that his own "first affections" and "shadowy recollections" provide a permanent conduit for his soul to the "immortal sea." Through Nature's transmission of memory and poetry the poet can recapture and understand, profoundly this time, the eternal truths and the interconnectedness of all things. The poet is then able to celebrate and sing the surrounding springtime atmosphere:

Then sing, ye Birds, sing, sing a joyous song!
   And let the young Lambs bound
   As to the tabor's sound!
We in thought will join your throng,
   Ye that pipe and ye that play,
   Ye that through your hearts today
   Feel the gladness of the May! (171–77)

By choosing to write "We in *thought* will join your throng," Wordsworth's ecstasy remains an intellectual one (174; emphasis added). Nevertheless, the intention to join in with the piping and playing of the pastoral scene is sincere.[9] The final lines of Wordsworth's "Ode" give credit to the heart for threading the poet back into the weave of nature's joy: "And oh ye Fountains, Meadows, Hills, and Groves, / Forebode not any severing of our loves!" (190–91).[10] Wordsworth brings the "Ode" to a close with these celebrated lines:

> Thanks to the human heart by which we live,
>   Thanks to its tenderness, its joys, and fears,
>   To me the meanest flower that blows can give
>   Thoughts that do often lie too deep for tears. (203–6)

The word "blows" in the "meanest flower that blows . . ." is an archaic form of the word "bloom," meaning to be in flower, to blossom. The Muse blows into us and we blossom, with thoughts that lie "too deep for tears." A deeper, older *O*. We hear in this line a sound beyond emotion coming up from the very depths of the throat, or perhaps from the genitals, from the moment when the body shatters, the moment in which the *O* is released. Wordsworth's "Ode" connects the power of the poetic voice directly to our power to be able to "play the pipe," to "feel the gladness of the May," in other words, to feel sexual joy. Wordsworth's decision to link this ability to "immortality" is startling and fresh, but also the key to what makes the "Ode" so moving, for the poet's immortality is an immortality for all, an immortality born of our connectedness to the totality, to the limitlessness of all things.[11]

Shelley's "Ode to the West Wind" also stages the loss of the poet's voice—caused this time by a "heavy weight of hours" that have "chained and bowed" the poet. From its very first line, "O wild West Wind, thou breath of Autumn's being," Shelley evokes an anarchic force that leaves no doubt concerning the source of the poem. It comes from *outside*. As Ann Wroe explains, he "addresse[es] the wind . . . as a force far beyond him: a revolutionary agent, a force of history. Necessity itself" (276).

Shelley chooses to be blown by a tempestuous autumn wind to match his revolutionary spirit. He tells this wind that he is "one too like thee" (579, line 56). The first three sections of the poem ally the wind with the cycle of life and death, represented by dead leaves and seedpods, the rage of an autumn storm, and a fall seascape. This census of the wind's far-reaching effect works to endow it with an almost supernatural power. When in the fourth section of the poem the poet entreats the wind to help him overcome his loss of voice, we accept the wind's ability to do so without question. He admits that he is "less free" than the wind, which he renames in an emotional outburst that makes full use of the potential unleashed by a deftly wielded *O*: "thou, O uncontrollable!" (line 47). The poet then implores the "uncontrollable"— and "impetuous"—wind with this astonishing request: "Make me thy lyre" (line 57).

Though the poet asks the wind to play upon him as though he were a lyre, the more metaphorically appropriate instrument is the Aeolian harp. An Aeolian harp *is* played by the wind, and it is well known that it was used as a metaphor for poetic inspiration during the Romantic Period. The wind, like the Muse or giver in oral sex, is active; the poet, who has told us in a previous stanza that he has "fallen upon the thorns of life" and wants to be lifted in the manner of a "wave, a leaf, a cloud," is passive. He needs the mighty harmonies of the wind to draw "a deep autumnal tone" from him: a deeper, older *O*. This sound, though in the minor key, will be "sweet though in sadness." Why sadness? The poet has plaintively asked: "what if my leaves are falling"? This returns us to the images of dead leaves that yet lead to new life at the start of the ode. With the lines "Be thou, Spirit fierce, / My spirit! Be thou me, impetuous one!" (61–62) we see just how radical Shelley's receptivity is. He is willing to risk his autonomy in order to bond with this other, this impetuous wind, so that "in the most thrilling way, they would absorb each other" (Wroe 277). The deeper, older *O* that the wind draws out of the poet will scatter the seeds of the poet's words through his lips and into the world: "Drive my dead thoughts over the universe / Like withered leaves to quicken a new birth" (lines 63–64). The seed-words pour through Shelley's lips, prefiguring Mullen's "gob of tangy seed," the gift returned in thanks for being blown. They will become "The trumpet of a prophecy." Shelley desires the consequences of his words, the revolutionary actions they might spawn. Unlike Wordsworth, he does not join the throng "in thought" but asks for bodily transformation, to give himself up to an uncontrollable, impetuous force. The risk in such radical receptivity is great: "This power controlled him utterly. It pushed him to the boundaries of life, through death, to whatever was beyond" (Wroe 276).

Shelley's radical receptivity to the dark autumnal wind reminds us of the risk we take in giving ourselves over completely to the other. He knew, as did Dante, that we must go all the way down into Hell if we intend to come to the border of our limits and catch a glimpse of the limitless beyond. Going down is, as Jed Rasula reminds us, "an Orphic obligation."[12] Though the connotation was probably unintended, one cannot help but hear in Rasula's phrase the *O*s that echo in the slang for cunnilingus: to go down on. Thus we arrive, simultaneously, at the *O* of Orpheus and, once again, at the *O* of oral sex. Fear of the female genitalia as a dark, mysterious, and potentially dangerous region, such as the *vagina dentata* ("toothed vagina") of folklore notwithstanding, the "going down" in this instance refers primarily to journeying to the Underworld of classical mythology. Orpheus is the most famous poet to make such a journey, ostensibly for the love of a woman. The basic outline of the story is well known: Eurydice dies from snakebite, after which Orpheus, bereft at her loss, follows her to Hades. There he charms the denizens of the Underworld with his lyre. Hades and Persephone return Eurydice to Orpheus on the condition that he not look at her until they reach the upper world. In most versions, Orpheus does look back, killing Eurydice a second time and losing her forever. After this tragedy he laments her loss with a song so beautiful it charms the trees, rocks, and animals. In Ovid's version of the myth, it is at this point that Orpheus gives up women altogether, angering the Thracian women who will eventually murder him in a violent *sparagmos*:

> complaining
> The gods of Hell were cruel, [Orpheus] wandered on
> To Rhodope and Haemus, swept by the north winds,
> Where, for three years, he lived without a woman
> Either because marriage had meant misfortune
> Or he had made a promise. But many women
> Wanted this poet for their own, and many
> Grieved over their rejection. His love was given
> To young boys only, and he told the Thracians
> That was the better way: *enjoy that springtime,*
> *Take those first flowers!* (236)

Having failed to go down successfully, Orpheus is blown by the north winds and finally resorts to blowjobs. Scholar Kaja Silverman sees one of the sources of Western misogyny embedded in this story. According to her, the moment Orpheus looks back at his wife and must watch her pulled down to Hades a second time is the moment that "makes death real to him" (5). The reality of his own finitude, made palpable through Eurydice, is intolerable to the poet. In this reading, his turning away from women is actually a turning away from an acceptance of his own death, in an "attempt to rid himself of his mortality by feminizing it, and since this projection renders women repugnant to him, he transfers his desire to young men" (5).

Silverman's reading asserts that, unlike Shelley, whose call for the west wind to sweep him through "life, through death, to whatever was beyond,"

Orpheus failed to be radically receptive to the other. By fearing and then subsequently feminizing his own death, he actually destroys his poetic gift. His severing of his connection to Eurydice's fate, and indeed to the fate of all living creatures, causes his music to fail him. The rocks and beasts that he once controlled through the power of his music no longer fall under his spell. Instead they are "reddened" with the blood of the poet (259). Fearing the passive reception of death's caress, Orpheus loses access to his song.

Rilke's "Orpheus. Eurydice. Hermes" also represents the two lovers as fatally divided (*Ahead* 55). Orpheus is portrayed as a selfish singer so obsessed with his art that his lyre has "grown into his left arm." As he takes Eurydice out of Hades he devours the path in "large, greedy, unchewed bites," unmindful of the possibility that his wife may have a smaller stride than he does. Eurydice, accompanied by Hermes, follows as though in a dream. Rilke portrays her as a woman who has become an individual through the severance of her role as a desired, sexual being. She is "filled with her vast death"; "her sex had closed / like a young flower at nightfall," and she was no longer "that man's property" (57–59). When Orpheus looks back she does not even see him, nor does she seem upset as she turns and walks back into Hades with steps "uncertain, gentle, and without impatience" (59).

Rilke wrote "Orpheus. Eurydice. Hermes" in 1904, inspired by a stele from the fifth century BC that he had seen in Naples. When contrasted to the universalizing Orphic vision of his 1922 masterpiece *Sonnets to Orpheus*, the failure of the hero-poet in this earlier poem to accept what Duncan called the "intellectual adventure of not knowing"[13] becomes all the more stark. The *Sonnets to Orpheus*, which Rilke wrote down "in a single breathless act of obedience" to "the most enigmatical dictation," foreground Orpheus's role as psychopomp, his relationship to nature, and his *sparagmos*, or dismemberment. Rilke threads these three themes into an ecstatic and praise-filled poetic sequence that "speaks pure oneness" (*Letters 1910–1926*, 327; *Ahead* 491). The Orpheus of the *Sonnets* is inherently transgressive; he "obeys" by "overstepping" (*Ahead* 419). His song is directly linked to his knowledge of the mysteries of death, for "Only he who has eaten / poppies with the dead / will not lose ever again / the gentlest chord" (427). His "metamorphosis / in this and that" is a gift to us, for, as Rilke writes directly to the poet-god: "Only because you were torn and scattered through Nature / have *we* become hearers now and a rescuing voice" (419; 461). Orpheus is returned to his earlier classical and subsequent Neoplatonic role as a poet, prophet, and priest with a deep knowledge of the mysteries. He is a far more powerful presence than the failed lover of "Orpheus. Eurydice. Hermes." This is the Orpheus of Orphic doctrine, a central tenet of which is that "everything comes to be out of the One and is resolved into the One" (Guthrie 75). This Orpheus is the primal *vates*, whose claim for the power of his art is grand indeed. This Orpheus *has* transcended his own limits and moved past the threshold, and in doing so has shown us the interconnectivity of all things. Like the apostrophe—which seems almost to mark his continued presence in that moment when, threatened by market capitalism and industrialization, the Romantic artist withdraws from the public to become "a special kind of person"[14]—the Orpheus of Rilke's *Sonnets is* the Romantic *O*, a "pure embodiment of poetic pretension" (Culler, *Pursuit* 143).

The universalizing vision and presentation of death as a part of life rather than its undoing in Rilke's *Sonnets* recalls the visionary poet of Whitman's *Song of Myself*, with the difference that Whitman is forthright and, indeed, provocative in his sexualizing of the Orphic vision of "oneness." Whitman's narrator often comes by his knowledge "that there is really no death" through a body that "is no callous shell" but has "instant conductors all over" it (32, 55). The voice in ecstatic utterance is everywhere present throughout *Song of Myself*. It appears as an act of speech: "I hear the sound I love, the sound of the human voice," as well as through the bodily apparatus of mouth, throat, and tongue in lines such as "The orbic flex of his mouth is pouring and filling me full," and "I act as the tongue of you, / Tied in your mouth, in mine it begins to be loosen'd" (53, 54, 55, 84). The organ Rilke foregrounds in the *Sonnets* is not the mouth but the ear. Apart from the Eros of listening to the *O*s of the other, the sexual potential of the ear may not be immediately apparent. Yet Rilke's celebrated opening apostrophe, "A tree ascended there. Oh pure transcendence! / Oh Orpheus sings! Oh tall tree in the ear!" manages to turn the entire earth into a listening ear as well as serve as a displaced image of sexual receptivity and penetration (*Ahead* 411). Rilke espoused the belief that the "deepest experience of the creative artist is feminine," here allegorized as a *radical receptivity* to the other through the ever-open organ of the ear (*Letters 1892–1910*, 181). In sonnet I.II a little girl makes a bed inside the poet's ear, further feminizing Rilke's Orphic vision to rhyme with his belief that when the (male) poet speaks it is as "though a woman had taken a seat within him" (*Ahead* 413; *Letters 1892–1910*, 181).

It is common to feminize sexual passivity and by extension the *radical receptivity* that, according to Rilke, is part of the creative act. When it is a man who chooses to "play the passive part" in sex, he is "placed in a situation characteristic of womanhood" (Freud, *General* 193). Freud calls this masochism, which he equates in men with "an expression of feminine nature" (192). In poems such as "Feminine Soliloquy," New American poet John Wieners willfully embraces "the passive part," dressing his male voice in masochistic stereotypes of degraded female experience. But, as I have argued elsewhere, Wieners still manages to endow such supposedly pathetic social positions—such as the torch singer, outdated movie queen, or cocksucker—with power and selfhood.[15] In his "A poem for cocksuckers" the giver of fellatio *is* the Muse. Nevertheless, this poem must be read in full cognizance of the fact that, as Catullus LXXX shows, to be called a "cocksucker" is an insult of longstanding provenance:

> Why Gellius,
> are your pretty red lips,
> always so pale-white?
>
> Early morning,
> or rolling out of bed
> mid noon, white lips.
>
> Not to spread gossip but,
> (if word on the street is true,)
> your lips have been getting
> a work out,
> strained on massive cocks
>
> The confession's proclaimed
> by the victor's thighs
> in whey on those lips. (85)

Gellius is insulted for having repeatedly given sexual pleasure to other men in a fairly selfless way. The recipient of those favors is the "victor," Gellius the victim. Catullus is in keeping with classical (and indeed, many contemporary) notions of sexuality by believing that there is no benefit or dignity to the passive role in sex. Defiantly, Wieners dignifies the role of giver. No one is fellated in Wieners's "A poem for cocksuckers," yet the "fairy friends" are indeed the eponymous dedicatees. Wieners uses the third-person plural—until the final line—to build a dialogic frame that includes the reader:

> Well we can go
> in the queer bars w/
> our long hair reaching
> down to the ground and
> we can sing our songs
> of love like the black mama
> on the juke box, after all
> what have we got left. (*Selected* 36; lines 1–8)

Thus we as readers, like the cocksuckers of the poem, begin at the end of our rope: "after all / what have we got left" (line 8). The lyrical necessity of song as healing agent enters through the figure of the "black mama" (line 6). Though Wieners adored and identified with Billie Holiday, the particular singer to whom he may refer is less important than the mood he evokes of torch singing, a mood, according to the poem, conjured by midcentury "queer bars" ("A poem for cocksuckers" was composed in 1958).[16] Torch songs teeter at the edge of their protagonists' desperation.

The second stanza introduces the "fairies," who "giggle in their lacquered / voices & blow / smoke in your eyes" (lines 10–11). The word "lacquered" introduces the image of brightly painted fingernails, though it is applied to the voice. A "lacquered" voice may be a polished voice, or one that is shiny and artificial. It has a layer of enamel over it, contrasting it to the presumably raw sound of the "black mama." Through a strategic use of enjambment Wieners gets two senses of the word "blow," the first sexual, the second describing an attitude of performative social defiance, to "blow / smoke in your eyes" (lines 11–12). He then suggests that we "let them," an entreaty made in full acknowledgment that a more typical response might be one of homophobic violence. Wieners's gentle suggestion also echoes a line from the love poem "The Ivy Crown" by William Carlos Williams: "Children pick flowers. / Let them" (125). The allusion underscores the innocence inherent in an act of minor transgression committed by a socially powerless person that finally hurts no one.

The poem then makes the startling assertion that "it's a nigger's world." The world referred to here of course is the world of "queer bars," of fairies, and of cocksuckers, a world beneath contempt (as indicated by the offensive slang term "nigger"). Following this characterization of the situation as negative and hopeless, the poem takes an unexpected turn. It leaves the dark bar and moves to a pastoral, springtime scene:

> and we retain strength.
> The gifts do not desert us,
> fountains do not dry
> up there are rivers running,
> there are mountains
> swelling for spring to cascade. (lines 14–19)

From the dark bar the poem moves into a space of abundance, evidenced through the use of such words as "gifts," "fountains," "swelling," and "spring." These words are also suggestive of erotic pleasure and poetic power. Wieners (or rather, the cocksuckers) have taken us into a Wordsworthian space. It exists, this power, this tumescence,

> between
> the powdered legs &
> painted eyes of the fairy
> friends who do not fail us
>   in our hour of
>   despair. (lines 20–25)

The Romantic legacy of a *radical receptivity* to the other and the risk of bodily dissolution inherent in the O are all brought to bear in "A poem for cocksuckers." This is not surprising from a poet who was compared to John Keats by his contemporaries, and who, in poems such as "Ode on a Common Fountain," deliberately employed Keatsian affect (47).[17] In the moment when the voice is at risk, "what have we got left" but the support of the cocksuckers, those who, because they "do not fail us," unleash a cascade of spring.

In the final lines the poem switches to the first person: "Take not / away from me the small fires / I burn in the memory of love." The move from a space of seeming sexual degradation to an assertion of personhood is a move Wieners often makes.[18] He entreats us to allow this homage to the cocksuckers, and to leave him to perform his small rituals, not to love but to its memory. In Wieners the cocksucker—the giver in the oral sex act—*is* Muse, a Muse trolling in regions akin to Eurydice's Underworld, where we expect social degradation and the stifling of song, not spring's abundance and the unleashing of the voice, of the deeper, older O. Yet we do find it, and "The gifts do not desert us" (15).

Robert Duncan also connects oral sex with the unleashing of the voice but does so in a different setting, and to different effect. In "Night Scenes" we can see his indebtedness to the Romantic heritage in his comfort with emotional registers evoked by the O. In the first two sections Duncan describes discrepant night scenes, from urban streets suffused with the threat of police violence to an erotically infused domestic bedroom that is safe enough to engender the dissolution of identity. These shifts allow Duncan to juxtapose the atmosphere of sexual repression that permeated San Francisco in the early sixties with an argument against that repression, made through the evocation of scenes illustrating the creative power of his sexuality.[19]

"Night Scenes" begins with the "moon's up-riding," the light of which Duncan connects to that of cars speeding through darkness. He goes on to describe the "neon-glow" of "merchants and magickers," soon to travel back to their quiet neighborhoods, "towards deserted streets where morning breaks" (*Roots* 5–6; lines 1, 4–6). But this comforting scene of routine is disrupted by a "whale-shark dark" that "pushes up a blunt nose of loneliness" (lines 10–11). The shark represents the shadow of night's darkness under which men out seeking sex may hide but also may be put at risk. The darkness

> shakes
> the all-night glare of the street lamps
>   so that for a moment terror
> touches my heart, our hearts, all hearts
>   that have come in along these sexual avenues
> seeking to release Eros from our mistrust. (lines 12–17)

Moving from "my heart" to "our hearts" and finally to "all hearts," Duncan draws a line between his own experience and that of all creatures who have sought the trust needed in order to be open to the other. The word "mistrust" disrupts this line. It is followed by an ominous transfer of sexual cruising onto police-car cruising, continuing the atmosphere of ambient threat: "Our nerves respond to the police-cars cruising, / part of the old divine threat" (lines 18–19). The words "old divine threat" conjure the destruction of Sodom, so eloquently countered in Duncan's earlier poem "This Place Rumord to Have Been Sodom."[20] The barriers to Duncan's queer Eros are ancient and formidable, but its power may be more so. The words "old threat" lead the poet to a thought about the purpose and connection between all things, here referred to as a *design*: "How in each / time the design is still moving" (lines 19–20). This "design" is "shared" through "identity" between the "*here-and-now* and *eternity*" (*Selected* 8). It is now that the poet is ready to cry out, to exclaim his *O*:

> O, to release the first music somewhere again,
>   for a moment
> to touch the *design* of the first melody! (lines 24–26)

The primal sound of the deeper, older *O* is the "first music," and the "first melody." His desire to "release" and "touch" it implies either that he has lost touch with it, or that it has been lost altogether. The first melody has been smothered by the disorder, the severing between persons brought on by the authoritarian atmosphere. How can the poet now reach it?

    In contrast to the urban night of the poem's opening, the second section of "Night Scenes" is set against an idealized, pastoral backdrop and borrows heavily from Shakespeare's *The Tempest*:

Where the Bee sucks, there, the airy spirit sings, suck I!

. . . .

In a Cowslips bell, I lie—at the ledge

youth spurts, at the lip the flower
    lifts lifewards, at the
four o'clock in the morning, stumbling,
    into whose arms, at whose
mouth out of slumber sweetening (lines 55, 58–63)

Ariel's song of sucking leads directly to the charged sexual language of youth "spurts" and the "flower" that at the touch of the "lip" "lifts lifewards," connoting a penis growing hard and erect in response to fellatio.[21] H. D., whom Duncan claimed as one of his masters, uses similarly charged language in "Hymen," a poem in which a bee with "honey-seeking lips" "clings close and warmly sips," hoping to see the "stern petals drawing back."[22]

"Night Scenes" then describes a scene of great tenderness. After "stumbling / into whose arms" the speaker actually becomes Ariel and awakens the sleeper with a kiss, "so that I know I am not I / but a spirit of the hour descending into a body / whose tongue touches / myrrh of the morgenrot" (lines 64–67). "Myrrh of the morgenrot" is a pagan-sounding way to say "sweetness of the dawn," which doubly describes the dawning of an erection filled with blood and semen. The metamorphosis into Ariel dissolves the identity of the lover, which is further conflated with the other when the kiss moves downward: "but we see one lover take his lover in his mouth, / leaping. Swift flame of / abiding sweetness in this flesh" (lines 70–73). The ambiguity of who is the giver and who the receiver in this act of fellatio dissolves the boundaries between the two men. We may assume that the speaker, who stumbles in and wakes his lover, is the active party, but the opposite might be argued as well. The next few lines preserve the ambiguity:

Fatigue spreading back, a grand chorale
of who I am, who he is, where we are,
    in which a thin spire of longing
perishes,   this single up-fountain of a
    single note around which

        the throat shapes! (lines 73–78)

The bee/lover who begins as the *giver* of fellatio, once swallowed into the flower changes places. The "up-fountain" recalls the moon's "up-riding" in the opening line of "Night Scenes." Like the moon's white light, the semen rises, pushing the "single note" into the throat, a primal note that can release that "first music." There is a premonition of this music in lines that—echoing "my heart, our hearts, all hearts"—build a connectivity between self and other, dissolving fixed identity boundaries: "grand chorale / of who I am, who he is / where we are." In the moment of orgasm, the "thin spire of longing / perishes," and the song once lost is recovered.

In "Night Scenes" Duncan draws a direct line from oral sex to song and by implication to the inspiration provoked by something *outside* the body acting upon it that leads to poetry. Identity falls through the emotional vector of the O and is transformed into a thing with permeable boundaries: "I know I am not I." Integrity breached, a *radical receptivity* to the other ensues. Through this receptivity an "intuition of poetic truth may arise," but not only—there also may arise an intuition of the larger truth that is the design of our existence as part of a totality in which the poem and poet participate.

On the American side of the British Romantics' O, Wieners's and Duncan's inheritance came by way of Walt Whitman and Hart Crane. It did so in defiance of the academic elevation of Eliot's "impersonal" poetics, and Pound's interdiction against any "emotional slither" that might prove embarrassing, such as Whitman's tendency toward exclamations like the following: "O I perceive after all so many uttering tongues!"; or his famous "barbaric yawp," an unrefined American version of the Romantic O if there ever was one (68, 124; lines 119, 1333).[23] Whitman was not, to use his language, "afraid of the merge" and, as mentioned above, does make repeated references to the orality of both sexuality and language. There are two scenes in particular in *Song of Myself* that affirm the fact that the "myself" referred to in the title is not a solipsistic and closed vehicle but does, indeed, "contain multitudes." First, an unambiguous description of all-over-body oral lovemaking:

I mind how once we lay such a transparent summer morning,
You settled your head athwart my hips and gently turn'd over upon me,
And parted the shirt from my bosom-bone, and plunged your tongue
    to my bare-stript heart,
And reach'd till you felt my beard, and reach'd till you held my feet.
    (lines 87–90)

Like the rolling rhythms of Whitman's generous lines, which will not linger over anything so perversely focused as end rhyme, the genitals become just a passing stop on the polymorphous landscape of the poet's body. In this next example, the primacy of the mouth over the eyes demotes the image in favor of the voice and promotes the oral sensuality of the tongue by drawing a connection between the body and the book:

> My voice goes after what my eyes cannot reach,
> With the twirl of my tongue I encompass worlds and volumes of
>   worlds. (lines 564–65)

Hart Crane, Whitman's great modernist inheritor, wrote his six-poem sequence "Voyages" (which includes five instances of the poetic O) about a love affair between himself and a sailor. Scholar Thomas Yingling argues that this poem "creates multiplicities of intersubjectivity" (91). In other words, it is a poem in which self and other, in a radical and mutual receptivity expressed through sex, become one. This connectivity, this "love," allows the poet a vision of the "great wink of eternity," made manifest through the sea, and then through love itself (102). As Crane's biographer, Paul Mariani, writes, "Love, he had come to understand, was greater than death, greater than the annihilating sea, for it was love alone that allowed us to open ourselves to life's greatest mysteries" (154). For Crane, there is something transgressive in both this discovery and the sex that leads to it. He calls his lover "O my Prodigal" (35; line 14). We see this sense of transgression in "Voyages V":

> "There's
>
> nothing like this in the world," you say,
> Knowing I cannot touch your hand and look
> Too, into the godless cleft of sky
> Where nothing turns but dead sands flashing.
>
> "—And never to quite understand!" No,
> In all the argosy of your bright hair I dreamed
> Nothing so flagless as this piracy. (38; lines 13–20)

With his strategic placing of line break and comma, Crane pulls two meanings out of the lines "Knowing I cannot touch your hand and look / Too." The first describes an exquisite ecstasy of disbelief in the possibility of touch; the second, more metaphysical, reading prepares us for the piracy to come:

an image of eternity that offers no connectivity or motion, only the flashing of "dead sands," deserts by any other name. Sticking to nautical metaphors in honor of both the setting of his poem and his lover, Crane comes up with the surprising line "the argosy of your bright hair." An "argosy" is a kind of merchant ship. But I do not think Crane wants us to see his lover's hair as a ship; he was, rather, in love with the sound of that word, as well as with the thought that this "bright hair" promoted his own piracy. The clear vision and dominance of the hair in the poem leads me to conjecture that it is being seen from above, as Crane finally has the courage to *look* as his lover fellates him in the moonlight. From this experience Crane learned that, "such love compels and terrifies, for even in love's orgasmic completion he tasted his own mortality. After all, what timebound creature could look upon the fact of rapture such as this and live?" (Mariani 154).

The intensity provoked by this moment, indeed by the entire dense linguistic surface of "Voyages I-VI," matches the intensity of the Romantic O in its most powerful iterations. By doing so it may indeed be, as Culler believes, "the pure embodiment of poetic pretension." Not the pretension of artifice or false emotionality, however, but a pretense of a rather more metaphysical bent: that of the poet who claims access to transcendence by way of obliteration of the self and a radical receptivity to the other. This O is no trope to be taken lightly; it is rather a deeper, older O born of reciprocal sexual joy and the acceptance of death that binds us to all things.

Notes

This essay was originally given as a talk at the Naropa Summer Writing Program on 17 June 2010, under the title "Headnotes: The Other Oral Tradition." My new title is adapted from *The Inferno* by Eileen Myles (233).

1. Introduction to Rothenberg and Robinson, 1.

2. Allen, "Projective Verse," in *The Poetics of the New American Poetry,* 147.

3. What Leo Bersani calls "Freud's somewhat reluctant speculation . . . that sexual pleasure occurs whenever a certain threshold of intensity is reached, when the organization of the self is momentarily disturbed," and "emerges as the *jouissance* of exploded limits." Bersani equates this "radical disintegration" with humiliation and masochism, but if we discard the necessity of a defended ego there is no reason not to view this same disintegration as a positive event, leading to a feeling of oneness and connectivity similar to that described in mystical experience.

4. For Plato, see *The Republic* and *Ion.* For Rilke, see *Letters 1910-1926,* 327. For Spicer, see *The House That Jack Built,* 1-49; for how dictation informed Duncan's poetics, see Johnston, 49-98.

5. My argument here is much indebted to Kaja Silverman's *Flesh of My Flesh*. Though I did not encounter this book until months after writing the initial version of this essay, the resonance of some aspects of her thesis proved invaluable to refining my own. That said, Silverman's investment in the relationship between the individual to the totality rhymes with much that Robert Duncan articulated in the 1950s and early 1960s: "This presentation, our immediate consciousness, the threshold that is called both here-and-now and eternity, is an exposure in which, perilously, identity is shared in resonance between the person and the cosmos" (*Selected* 8).

6. "She groaned. It was a teeny way she sounded when she looked at art, but this was a deeper older oh. She was a woman. One by one the women I knew who seemed to be girls, or men, or just strangers—when all their muscles tensed then released, and they said oh it was like the deepest voice they had" (Myles 233).

7. "A false etymology—but are any etymologies really 'false'?" (Joris 2).

8. It was Joshua Corey who, after hearing my talk at Naropa, informed me of the centrality of "nonreproductive" sexuality in the pastoral.

9. Wordsworth's "Ye that pipe" recalls the French slang term for blow job, *faire la pipe*.

10. It is worth noting that the *Norton Anthology of Poetry* reproduces a different version of this line, more in keeping with my essay but perhaps less authoritative. In the *Norton* it is thus: "And O, ye Fountains, Meadows, Hills, and Groves," etc.

11. It has been said that Henry Vaughan's "The Retreat" may have served as a model for Wordsworth's "Ode" (Pater 58). In Vaughan's lovely poem, however, the "O" leads only to longing: "O how I long to travel back / And tread again that ancient track," and no transformation of the nostalgia for a lost Eden is envisaged.

12. Referring to "Spicer's fixation" with Jean Cocteau's film *Orphée*.

13. *Fictive Certainties*, 39. This was Duncan's term for Romanticism and is in many ways analogous to Keats's concept of Negative Capability.

14. R. Williams 36.

15. Moxley.

16. See, for example, the poems "Billie," "Gardenias," and "To Billie Holiday's If I Were You" (*Selected* 130, 180, 181).

17. See Robert Creeley's preface to John Wieners's *Cultural Affairs in Boston*.

18. See Moxley.

19. Election of morality-crusading mayor George Christopher occasioned a crackdown against "any public display of homosexuality" (D'Emilio 182–84).

20. *Opening of the Field*, 22.

21. Duncan, perhaps inspired by H. D., often compares male genitalia to flow-

ers; see, for example, "Passages: The Torso" from *Bending the Bow*: "for the torso is the stem in which the man / flowers forth and leads to the stamen of flesh in which / his seed rises" (64).

22. H. D. also made a direct connection between her "overmind" or visionary state and her genitalia: "I first realized this state of consciousness centered in my head. I visualize it just as well, now, centered in the love-region of the body" (*Notes on Thought and Vision* 19).

23. For Eliot on impersonality see "Tradition and the Individual Talent" (*Selected* 21); for Pound on emotional slither see "A Retrospect" (*Literary Essays* 12).

5

The Construction of *Poems for the Millennium, Volume Three* and the Poems It Engendered

Jerome Rothenberg

In the course of assembling volume 3 of *Poems for the Millennium*, I was engaged in two—at least two—companion works. This wasn't at all strange but fit, maybe too neatly, into a view that I like to put forward—that the composition of large structures like the *Millennium* volumes is inseparable from my other activities as a poet and that this would hold true for other poets engaged in what Robert Duncan, I believe it was, spoke of as the construction of a "grand collage" and as "a poetry of all poetries," a type of work practiced in one form or another by many a modern or postmodern poet/artist. Looking back at my earlier works, the first of the anthology/assemblages, *Technicians of the Sacred* (1968), was paralleled by first experiments with "total translation" as a form of composition from oral sources, but also by the beginnings of *Poland/1931* as an exploration, I wrote, "of ancestral sources of my own in a world of Jewish mystics, thieves & madmen." The follow-up, *Shaking the Pumpkin* (1972), an anthology of American Indian texts, was also a catalyst for *A Seneca Journal*, while *A Big Jewish Book* (1977) continued the work of *Poland/1931* and led to first experiments with *gematria* and other forms of traditional aleatory procedures. In the same vein I wouldn't separate *Revolution of the Word* (1974) as its American counterpart from *That Dada Strain*, both celebrations of our Dadaist and modernist predecessors.

Romanticism, as Jeffrey Robinson and I came at it, was a catalyst for us as well, much as it was for those who came before us. In Robinson's case, though his primary life's work has been as a devoted and innovative scholar of British Romanticism, he has accompanied the scholarship as such with an ongoing series of original poetry texts drawn or collaged ("spliced") from the work of poets, both Romantics and moderns/postmoderns, who were central to his studies and enthusiasms. For myself, what I had to overcome was my own prejudice against fixed forms—shared with many in my generation—

in order to see anew the challenges to form and content that were set in motion by the Romantics and a number of others who had preceded them. As a matter of nomenclature Jeffrey Robinson and I began to talk between us about "experimental romanticism," although I'm not sure that phrase came into the actual writing.

With that as our target, experiment and transformation appeared both in aspects of Romantic writing that were largely subterranean and, even more surprisingly, I thought, at the heart and core of the Romantic project. An aspect of this, from my side at least, was that the Romantics and those we called the postromantics began to feel like contemporaries, less like magisterial figures and more like fellow poets with whom we could enter into a free and easy discourse. In large part, if this doesn't sound too arcane or abstract, we rode on Jeffrey Robinson's recovery of the "fancy," salvaging it from Coleridge's otherwise brilliant and long-lived dichotomy of fancy and imagination. The two terms—fancy and imagination—have otherwise been historically synonymous, whereas Coleridge made imagination not just his "shaping spirit" but a binding spirit that reconciled and thereby froze deep conflicts of image and idea. In relation to this "the fancy" appeared as a secondary or degraded or trivialized faculty, an arena of "mere" image making and escape, rather than a liberatory force—for play and invention—the field par excellence of the experimental and visionary.

In this sense I would think of imagination qua fancy less in Coleridge's sense as reconciliation and closure than in Keats's definition of "Negative Capability" followed immediately by his criticism of Coleridge: "Several things dovetailed in my mind and at once it struck me what quality went to form a Man of Achievement especially in literature and which Shakespeare possessed so enormously—I mean Negative Capability, that is when a man is capable of being in uncertainties, mysteries, doubts, without any irritable reaching after fact and reason—Coleridge for instance would let go by a fine isolated verisimilitude caught from the penetralium of mystery, from being incapable of remaining content with half knowledge." Or Whitman in an equally famous passage: "Do I contradict myself? Very well then I contradict myself, (I am large, I contain multitudes)." I would as well speak of imagination as of fancy, the good-of-it being, always, in the meanings, not in the nomenclature—an acknowledgment in any case of their fluidity, both before and after Coleridge, with the invocation of the one often sliding curiously into an invocation of the other.

I thought of all this again in the process of working through a series of poems that I was composing alongside the major work of construction or assemblage that Robinson and I were engaged in. The series in question (fifty poems in all) was my response to Goya's *Caprichos*, a work of imagination or fancy that we included in *Poems for the Millennium*, both as a touchstone of an emerging romanticism and as a forerunner of the expressionist and surrealist side of a modernism yet to be. The images that Goya gave me helped, as with other forms of ekphrastic writing, to launch a succession of my own images and fancies, an interaction across space and time that I've often tried to practice. In the opening poem, for example, I begin with Goya's well-known self-portrait, a figure slumped over a table on which are written the words "El *sueño de la razón* produce monstrous." From that and from the bats and owls that fly around him comes the following, not a literal account of Goya's image but a journey into places where the Fancy leads me on my own:

The Sleep of Reason
    for Clayton Eshleman

Words imprinted on a sign
by Goya   glowing
white against a surface
nearly white:
the sleep of reason
that produces monsters.
He is sitting on a chair
his head slumped
resting on his arms
or on the marble table,
pencil set aside,
his night coat open
thighs exposed.
All things that fly at night
fly past him.
Wings that brush an ear,
an ear concealed,
a memory beginning
in the house of sleep.
His is a world where owls
live in palm trees,
where a shadow in the sky
is like a magpie,
white & black are colors
only in the mind,

the cat you didn't murder
springs to life,
a whistle whirling in a cup,
gone & foregone,
a chasm bright with eyes.
There is a cave in Spain,
a fecal underworld,
where bats are swarming
among bulls,
the blackness ending in a wall
his hands rub up against,
a blind man in a painted world,
amok & monstrous
banging on a rock.

In the course of which I became aware, as I should have earlier, that *caprichos* as a term was most commonly translated as "fancy" or "fancies," which after Coleridge at least would effectively conceal what Goya was unleashing here. Yet it is precisely in his "caprichos" that Goya shows us the fancy as "a power, not a work . . . a struggle, not a thought," as Lorca wrote of that related or perhaps identical power he called *duende*. In Lorca's case too the word in question went back to an earlier source that belied the characteristics that he ascribed to it—a hobgoblin or imp to start with and a driving force among those flamenco singers and dancers from whom he took it. Dramatized by Lorca as engaged in a fierce creative struggle (chthonic, even demonic, in his telling), it also released, as he described it, a sense of unprecedented formal and visionary transformations: "The duende's arrival always means a radical change in forms. It brings to old planes unknown feelings of freshness, with the quality of something newly created, like a miracle, and it produces an almost religious enthusiasm."

It is this force or something very close to it that Jeffrey Robinson captures in his aforementioned description of "fancy," with perhaps a greater emphasis on the transformative or experimental side of the process, as well as the playfulness of the original folk presences that in no way diminish the power of what's at work or play here. The search on this side of romanticism is less toward resolution, then, and more toward struggle and conflict, with a resultant *liberatory* thrust (the adjective is Robinson's), a newfound openness of form and thought. In the process Goya's caprichos operate at white heat, burning away appearances to let new worlds emerge, kept hidden otherwise by "mind-forged manacles" in Blake's words and inherited conventions of the "really real." For me at least the convergence of Blake and Goya is essential to their time and to the times that lead from them to us.

With this in mind and having plunged into the *Caprichos* as the construction of *Poems for the Millennium* got under way, I moved toward the following conclusion in my terms and, I hope, in theirs:

Coda, with Duendes

Duendes sound a last
hurrah   they squeeze
a bellows, scrub a dish
with greasy hands,
a whisper
in an ear bent down
to listen.
No one sees them.
Over every duende
falls the shadow
of a greater duende.
Holy moly!
Is this not a black sound,
Mister Lorca?
Pissing olive oil
I isn't what *I* seems
to be   a poor
partaker
barrel overturned,
the wine *I* swigs
gone rancid.
There is now an end
to everything.
What is flesh
they suck no more,
they drive the foul caprichos
out of sight.
Caprichos, Goya, Lorca,
all my duendes,
locked into a cage
at dawn, evading
sleep & dreams,

those whom they leave
behind them, fathers
raising arms
to heaven,
screaming through
their empty
mouths   like caverns
black holes
where all light
is lost.
Now is the time.

If this, then, was my interplay with Goya and Lorca, the discourse and engagement with romanticism was linking—deliberately on my part—with still other aspects of the poetry I was then composing. At the turning of the century and the millennium I had written and published a long series of poems—*A Book of Witness* (2001)—in which I explored, among other matters, the first-person voice as integral to the poetic act of witnessing, even of prophecy—by the poet directly or with the poet as a conduit for others. I mean here a first person that isn't restricted to the usual "confessional" stance but is the instrument—in language—for all acts of witnessing, the key with which we open up to voices other than our own. There was in all of this a question of inventing and reinventing identity, of experimenting with the ways in which we can speak or write as "I." In the course of putting that identity into question, I brought in occasional and very brief first-person statements by other contemporary poets—very lightly sometimes but as a further way of playing down the merely ego side of "I." The continuity with the first two volumes ("modern" and "postmodern") of *Poems for the Millennium* seems to me obvious, no less the relation to Romantic poetics that I had still to explore.

Shortly before Jeffrey Robinson and I started on our Romantics project, I was beginning a new series of poems—*fancies* perhaps in the sense of Blake and Goya—in which the operative thrust was to suppress the "I" as it had emerged in *A Book of Witness*, and to let world and mind interact absent direct first-person intervention. The title I gave it, *A Book of Concealments*, was drawn from a medieval Jewish work, *Sifra diSeni'uta*, from which I also drew, as with *A Book of Witness*, occasional and very brief statements or phrases but without further citation. The idea of *concealment*, in contrast to that of *witness*, had many implications and was a driving force behind the work as such. Not least of course was the concealment of the singular first-person pronoun, as if that in itself might counter what Charles Olson had called "the lyrical interference of the individual as ego," a challenging if dubious directive in the first place.

Midway through the work and with volume 3 of *Poems for the Millennium* already underway, I dedicated a poem to Michael McClure, with whom I had an ongoing discourse about Romanticism and Romantics as those entered into the poetry and poetics of our own time. The poem's title, "A Deep Romantic Chasm," drawn from Coleridge's seminal and truly fanciful "Kubla Khan," led me to consider using the Romantic poets in *Millennium* as I had used the modern and postmodern poets in *A Book of Witness* and to break down in other ways the barrier between the poems in *Concealments* and the large assemblage I was simultaneously composing. In the process I separated a group of poems under the title "Romantic Dadas" and had those published as a limited edition artist's book, but all remained integral to *A Book of Concealments* and were included as such in the final publication. The result is that the last third of the book has a score or more of such insertions, as in the following, with the Hopkins reference noted in the margin and the title taken from a Seneca Indian ritual source:

The Brain Turned Upside Down

To count time from
the future,
having the end
in view,
this is a sore reminder
of another world,
another chance
to come into the open air,
out of the darkness.
The brain turned upside
down, they told us,
gathers no moss.
No clash of symbols
half as painful
as discounted
time, ready
to plug us
one by one.
A star most spiritual,

preeminent,(G.M. Hopkins)
of all the golden press,
where what is dark
is not obscure,
leads rather
to another light,
a revelation
of the end of all.
For this things fly away,
the distance between
one & one
becomes a universe
no one will track.
The time to view the stars
grows scarce,
the farther we look.
A walk across the street
reckons infinity
& more.

Looking back now I can only surmise that the work of assemblage and that of original composition were, for me at least, deeply co-dependent. Certainly the poems in both *Concealments* and *Caprichos* (later published as a single book) would have been different were I not engaged then in the construction of *Poems for the Millennium*. By the same token I needed just that sort of engagement to feel myself in an active exchange with those poets whom Jeffrey Robinson and I were weaving into our larger composition. It is something like this that I found years ago in Pound's construction of "an *active* anthology," and the use of the word "active" in the title of the present volume again brings that thrust to mind. Whatever it is that goes to create a *canon*—a word and concept we could well do without—or to perpetuate it through a canonical anthology or series of such, an active and thereby transformative idea of anthology, as of our lives in general, is by far the greater work to aim at.

The fancy (as capricho and duende) demands nothing less of us.

6
Copying Whitman

Bob Perelman

Prefatory note: In what follows, the pertinence to Romanticism lies less
in the subject, Whitman, than in my approach. While a case can be
made for Whitman as in some sense romantic (identification with the
world; expanded class sympathy; political urgency of self-expression),
as likely a case can be made for him as modernist (thoroughgoing formal
iconoclasm; his claim that *Leaves of Grass* is "experimental" [657][1]). But
categorizing such a sui generis phenomenon as Whitman is no easy
matter—and certainly not to be accomplished by such a piece as this.
No, the romanticism in what follows lies in its refusal of critical distance. While I copy Whitman I seem to be replacing his claims of immediacy with *mine*. Whitman repeatedly claims that he is present in his
writing—"Who touches this touches a man" (611); "It avails not, time
nor place—distance avails not, / I am with you" (308); here I am claiming that, copying his words, I am writing them. Thus I mostly avoid, in
what follows, typographic conventions that would indicate quotation.

A few times I've turned into an anti-Bartleby of sorts and typed out the work
of other writers. I do it both for pleasure and to practice, somehow or other,
the craft. In this case I opened up the Library of America *Whitman* in the
middle and starting typing the last section of "Passage to India," which I
hadn't read for decades.

At the very least, it was typing practice, which I always need. I have a fantasy of typing quickly, accurately, effortlessly, with the fluency of someone
like Kerouac (120 words per minute), the impossible ego ideal. To have no
conscious interference, but simply to allow the impulse to be articulated in
sequentially appearing letters on the screen, the words gathering to say what
they, unbeknownst to me before that extending moment, actually are say-

ing—the analogy is with music, feeling it under your fingers as you're hearing it.

The scratchier truth is that, after all these years, I'm a fairly lousy typist, better than I was back before there were computers, but hardly reaching mediocrity in my better stretches. This forces me to think and rethink, assert and reframe, typing a few strokes and then lifting my fingers off the keys as I stare at the cursor blinking from its little rut of error. It's a toss-up whether I then abandon incipient formations whose beginnings lie on the screen in mistyped botches, or delete a bit, back up, and soldier on. The overall activity of my typing/writing is a mix of keystrokes, staring, thinking, deleting, starting over, getting frustrated, giving up, and printing up the offending draft onto the distancing paper, which I later hover over with a pencil or pen before going back to the keyboard.

It strikes me that such a practice is closer to Neal Cassady than to Kerouac. Cassady, the story goes, would never correct typos; rather, he would change what he was writing to match the typed letter. It's not an account that makes perfect sense, but schematically it makes for a useful pairing: Kerouac's truly fluent keystrokes disappearing into instant transcription at one end and, at the other, the lunging, stuttering Cassady, each crashing keystroke an intention-twisting blow. I don't give over my initiative to typos to that extent, but my spotty typing must be a formative cause of what I write (what gets written).

Beyond this literal (letteral) level, typing out the work of others is a kind of old-fashioned compositional practice borrowed from painting, where it used to be a standard part of the initial curriculum. Even now, I occasionally see people in the more relaxed museums with their easels, copying.

I wouldn't have thought of applying that exercise to writing except that I read somewhere that Robert Louis Stevenson, in the limbo between rejecting the family business (lighthouse lenses) and becoming an author, copied out passages from writers he admired. In a commonsense way, this sounds hopeless. Yes, copying is "writing" in the purely physical sense, but isn't it the opposite of "writing" in the sense of writing-something-new?

Robert Louis Stevenson wanted to *be a writer* (to be the originator of words typesetters would then copy, printers then make copies of, people then read). He didn't want to merely *write* (physically).

Copying has drastically different imports. Certainly it is drudgery: think of the outsourced keystrokes that underlie much published writing. Not knowing the language being typed, some say, makes for faster, more accurate typing, which in turn makes for cheaper commodity costs. Knowing what you're copying can make it worse, as with Farrington, the copyist from *Dubliners* ("Counterparts"). Here, Joyce makes clear the rage copying can provoke. First, via the copyist's slow attention (he really needs a drink), we get a glimpse of some of textuality's little pleasures: The man returned to the lower office and sat down again at his desk. He stared intently at the incomplete phrase: In no case shall the said Bernard Bodley be . . . and thought how strange it was that the last three words began with the same letter.

But quickly the onus of the business reasserts itself:

The chief clerk began to hurry Miss Parker, saying she would never have the letters typed in time for post. The man listened to the clicking of the machine for a few minutes and then set to work to finish his copy . . . He was so enraged that he wrote Bernard Bernard instead of Bernard Bodley . . . His body ached to do something, to rush out and revel in violence.

Alienated copying. It's a specter whose all-too-physical manifestations (ennui, rage, carpal tunnel) the contemporary environment for writing is designed to banish, thoroughly, and at the smallest level. The cut and paste functions in word processing, macros, the basic correctability of computer files—but these niceties do little against the onslaught of the endless keystrokes.

At another extreme there is reproducing the sacred text, where, in theory at least, the copyist is transmitting and thus sharing the verbal embodiment of divine power.

A distinction that is intriguing to apply here comes from the historian of rhetoric Mary Carruthers, who begins *The Craft of Thought* with Paul Gehl's contrast between orthodoxy and orthopraxis. Orthodox believers seek orthodoxy, which is "to reproduce the experience of learning from the teacher, whose teaching lives on in authentic texts"—letter-perfect copying of the Torah, say. With orthopraxis, on the other hand, the believer wants "to achieve an immanent experience of the divine equivalent to that of the founder, usually by following a devotional practice presumed to be similar." Carruthers goes on to elaborate the subtle interplay of orthodoxy and orthopraxis, noting that they "often co-exist in the same religion." But we can also consider these notions without nuance so that they become polarized, highly portable emblems: orthopraxis/orthodoxy: spirit/letter, writing/copying, innovation/convention, new/settled.[2]

When we move from religion to art, we can see that orthodoxy with its stability and familiarity is very often exactly what needs to be overcome to achieve orthopraxis. Make It New. And then again, orthopraxis is firmly attached, Möbius-strip fashion, to orthodoxy. (When "Make It New" becomes the orthodoxy, the orthopractic need is to make "Make It New" new.)

Stevenson could be imagined as engaged primarily in an orthodox pursuit when he was copying something out, getting the words right, accurately reproducing a bit of doctrine. But it also seems plausible that he was learning a craft via rehearsal of some of its parts, like learning a scale, a passage, a complete mood—in other words, hoping that orthodoxy might become orthopractic, that he would partake of some kind of direct transmission of the authorial spirit whose letters he was reproducing.

I write you. (To anticipate the Whitman to come.) In some backward transitive sense, with subject and object changing roles. What had been "You write, I copy" becomes "I write your writing" becomes "I write you" which eventually reads "I write."

Who touches this book touches a man, to quote the text of Whitman. My first inkling of writing, age twelve. Thus for me, in that bodily experiences of words are never fully erasable, Whitman is perpetually adolescent. And thus, according to my idiosyncratic use of the term, romantic. Romantic suggesting adolescent, semantically and historically promiscuous, impervious to strict definition, its always-ersatz appeal ever rediscovered (by adolescents and the young-at-heart). To avoid unuseful ambiguity here, I should say that this is not meant as a put-down, but as a critical expansion of the definition.[3]

At the beginning of this note I wrote that I copied to practice, somehow or other, the craft. But much of the craft in my case seems to involve interruptive thinking. Reading spilling over into rehearing in the midst of barely serviceable typing.

To repeat, what follows is what happened when I typed some half-good thing from a writer I care about permanently: the last section of Whitman's "Passage to India."

I opened the Whitman in the middle without thinking, as a form of *sortes Virgiliani* (Virgilian lots, making a book such as Virgil or, later, the Bible prophetic when opened at random—in this case, *sortes Whitmani*).

Come to think of it, this procedure splits the difference between orthodoxy (stable text, printed book, authoritative edition) and orthopraxis (need for the new, accurately open to the present).

To repeat, what follows is that typing, but with some editing (interrupting the interruptions, retyping the thinking and rethinking the retyping), editing but aiming for the whole flavor of reading and writing mixing. Both are irreplaceable motions of any transcription.

But they're different operations, writing, reading.

And then there's transcription. What of the trans-? Something is going between things, but what of the between? What is between *what*? Reinscribing goes across *what*? Via what? Doesn't the trans- invoke some continuum, some condition bordering both things but common to neither? Neither reading nor writing, that is. (Here I'm playing dodgeball with the coalition-politics of *wreading*.)

∿

Okay. Now to type out the whole thing. Section 9 of "Passage to India," type the monstrous koan out to its ignoble end. Material progression to immateriality (to give away the plot).

Passage to more than India!
are thy wings plumd indeed for such far flights?
O soul, voyagest thou indeed on voyages like these? "Voyagest thou indeed on voyages" nobody but Whitman.

Note the lettristic, transhistoric synchronicity:
Whitman: Vietnam. Vietnam: Whitman. Whitnam. Vietman.
Disportest thou in places like these?
I got it wrong. It's not "these," not "O soul, voyagest thou indeed on voyages like these," but "O soul, voyagest thou indeed on voyages like those."

"Those," not "these," means it's not here, not felt, not a live report. "O soul, voyagest thou indeed on voyages like those" means those voyages are over; he's just thinking about feeling it. Lots of poetry is like that. Thinking about feeling something.

But it's not as if feelings are transparent. For instance, why, copying Whitman, am I suddenly conscious of the desire to read those old compilations, Scaliger, etc. Why? Why set up those antique spaces? If you copy "those" enough times it becomes "these"? That's one theory.

Soundest below the Sanskrit (sans crit, poesie pure—but who doesn't, at some level, hate puns?), and the Vedas?
Then have thy bent unleash'd.

Type that to get into head:

Then have thy bent unleash'd.
Then have thy bent unleash'd.
Then have thy bent unleash'd.
Then have thy bent unleash'd.

Then have thy bent unbent —
Then have thy bent unleash'd.
Thy bent, have unleash'd.
Then have, then have.

Unlearn'd, thy bent has thee.
Learn thy bent.
Learn, unlearn, unleash.
Unleash'd when unlearn'd.

Learn thy bent lest thy leash stay taut. True enough. Type that into head, into the sensing and sense-making neural configs.

Whitman, walking Basket, decides to let him off his leash. The large poodle immediately runs away. Stein, furious, has to get another Basket, then another, and another. (See the biographies.) All of this is in the continuous present, but still, it gets *annoying* when it happens over and over and *over* . . .

Passage to you, your shores, ye aged fierce enigmas!
Passage to you, to mastership of you. (Whitman's writing during the not-yet-finished transition from slavery to postslavery. Think of other aimless gestures of reconciliation. Todorov, the love the conqueror must feel for the conquered. Rape, conquest, pillage as history's Happily Ever After, dear dear Other, will we ever reach postslavery?)

Passage to more than Whitman's India.
Passage to Afghanistan. A package from Pakistan: for you.

Passage to you, to mastership of you, ye strangling problems! Ye fucking in-
competent parallel parkers taking up two spaces! Ye goddamn Verizon voice-
outsourcing, throwing up verbal baffles from India under the nom de voix
of Frank Fernandez!
Passage to India!
Passage to you, to mastership of you, ye strangling problems!
You, strew'd with the wrecks of skeletons, that, living, never reach'd you.
Actual other dead bodies. Whole lives, trained sensoriums, gene pools, bad
habits, loving aspirations and just shouldering the load, dig the graves and
you have to find someplace to put the dirt, the tree-names of streets supposedly reminding you of home. Actually dead. Got nowhere. Never reach'd.

Passage to more than India!
O secret of the earth and sky!
Of you O waters of the sea! O winding creeks and rivers! Whitman the ma-
terialist: all water is actually in the end *wet*.
Of you O woods and fields! of you strong mountains of my land!
Whitman the nothing-but-autobiographer. Real woods. Real fields. Not "Elegy
in a Country Churchyard."
Of you O prairies! of you gray rocks!
O morning red! O clouds! O rain and snows!
Sometimes it's Of, sometimes it's O. When the secret is most salient, it's Of.
When the surface sense is, it's O.
O day and night, passage to you!

O sun and moon and all you stars! Sirius and Jupiter!
Passage to you!

Passage, immediate passage! the blood burns in my veins!
We leave the vocative, now it's a demand for immediate access. It's orthopractic: Make It So (= Make It New's elder sibling). Give me my ticket. My language is my credit card. My language is worth the world. Whitman is writing with his body again. That's why you've got to hand it to him. But, still,
we each get only one body.

Away O soul! hoist instantly the anchor!
Consider instantly Whitman and word order.

What is problem his?
Cut the hawsers—haul out—shake out every sail!
Have we not stood here like trees in the ground long enough?

Whitman, in 1878, about ten years after "Passage to India," wrote this:

THOUGHTS UNDER AN OAK—A DREAM

June 2.—This is the fourth day of a dark northeast storm, wind and rain. . . .
I have now enter'd on my 60th year. Every day of the storm, protected by
overshoes and a waterproof blanket, I regularly come down to the pond,
and ensconce myself under the lee of the great oak; I am here now writing
these lines. . . . Seated here in solitude I have been musing over my life—
connecting events, dates, as links of a chain, neither sadly nor cheerily, but
somehow, to-day here under the oak, in the rain, in an unusually matter-of-
fact spirit.
    . . . .But my great oak—sturdy, vital, green—five feet thick at the butt. I
sit a great deal near or under him. Then the tulip tree near by—the Apollo
of the woods—tall and graceful, yet robust and sinewy, inimitable in hang
of foliage and throwing-out of limb; as if the beauteous, vital, leafy creature
could walk, if it only would. (I had a sort of dream-trance the other day, in
which I saw my favorite trees step out and promenade up, down and around,
very curiously—with a whisper from one, leaning down as he pass'd me, We
do all this on the present occasion, exceptionally, just for you.) (816)

Have we not stood here in the ground like trees long enough?
Have we not grovel'd here long enough, eating and drinking like mere brutes?
But has Whitman not been the poet of happy eating and drinking?
Have we not darken'd and dazed ourselves with books long enough? "books"?
"screens"? I'm fine either way.

Sail forth—steer for the deep waters only,
Reckless O soul, exploring, I with thee, and thou with me,
For we are bound where mariner has not yet dared to go,
(How they say it now on the reruns is "to boldly go where no man has gone
before.")
And we will risk the ship, ourselves, and all
—, even the ratings because *all* literature is reruns eventually!

O my brave soul!
O farther farther sail!

O daring joy, but safe! are they not all the seas of God?
O farther, farther, farther sail!

So we reach bombast at the end, bombast, bombs bursting in air still the national pastime. Jets drones and smart payloads—what are a few civilians between allies?—cheaper than ground forces, and no local casualties to fill the withering hometown papers.

Notes

1. All Whitman quotations are from *Walt Whitman: Poetry and Prose* (New York: Library of America, 1982), page numbers in parentheses.

2. Mary Carruthers, *The Craft of Thought* (Cambridge: Cambridge UP, 1998), 1.

3. I discuss this in "That Deep Romantic Chasm," a review essay on Jeffrey Robinson's *Unfettering Poetry: The Fancy in British Romanticism*, in *European Romantic Review* 22.1 (February 2011).

7

"A Spark o' Nature's Fire"

Robert Burns and the Vernacular Muse

Nigel Leask

> . . . to encourage the experimental exploitation of the unexplored
> possibilities of Vernacular expression.
>
> Hugh MacDiarmid, 1923

> We have rather neglected the importance of the speech basis ("the
> current language heightened," in Hopkins's phrase) in the excitement of
> developing an eclectic or synthetic Scots.
>
> Edwin Morgan, 1962

The spoken language, like the weather, is part of the local climate in which a poet breathes and writes, and it is just as resistant to prediction or system. This essay sets out to claim Robert Burns's vernacular "revolt against literature" as a harbinger of the "active Romanticism" addressed by the other essays in the present volume. Burns's intrinsic importance and influence lay in his challenge to the class-based imperative of "standard English," although in Scottish literary studies this is usually construed as the stirring of a quiescent national culture in the wake of the 1707 Act of Union between Scotland and England. It is indeed important to acknowledge the *national* (as opposed to merely regional) animus of Burns's vernacular diction at a time when the Scots language was severely attenuated, at least in its written form. At the same time, my present argument seeks to explore the wider global ramifications of his poetry in challenging "poetic diction," the credit for which (as a hallmark of Romanticism) normally goes to William Wordsworth. I will be exploring the tension between Burns's naive pastoral persona as "heaven taught ploughman" and the self-conscious artifice of his poetry, suggesting that the role of pastoral was at once *enabling*, to the extent that Burns's poetry represents the stirrings of "active romanticism," a powerful driver in the direction of vernacular modernism, but also potentially *limiting* to the extent that it was taken to uphold a ruralist and linguistic nostalgia in the century that followed.

Modern European poetry, born of the emergence of vernacular literature from the Latino-Classical heritage, embodies the partial victory of localism and the spoken language over the political and scribal imperium.[1] Yet from the early 1500s onward, this "vernacular drift" was arrested in favor of pre-scribed standard languages and—in the nineteenth century—hedged in by the formation of national canons of literature.[2] Here the local and the na-tional coexist, sometimes in synergy, sometimes in tension. Edmund Spen-ser's praise of Chaucer as "the well of English undefiled" was an early attempt to consecrate the vernacular in national and ethnic terms, but like all such attempts depended on a system of exclusion, as well as of inclusion. Janet Sorensen argues that, "in constructing national subjects in their relation-ship to hearing, speaking, reading, and writing one particular version of the language, the 'standard' language also constitutes them as belonging to the nation on differing terms" (67). Literature as a written medium, in associa-tion with the school system, thus had a crucial role to play in constructing the subject's point of entry into the body politic. A later instance of the ar-rest of vernacular drift was the consolidation of poetic diction in eighteenth-century Britain, well exemplified in the language of Thomas Gray's "Elegy in a Country Churchyard." The "Elegy" is a poem whose "reformist" aspi-rations are evident in its lament for the obscurity of the common dead in a hierarchical society that lacked (as William Empson famously noted) "ca-reers open to talent" (Guillory 94). Nonetheless, as John Guillory writes of the poem, "Gray was concerned to develop a . . . 'poetic diction,' which rep-licated *within the vernacular* a distinction like the distinction between classi-cal and vernacular literacy." That is to say, the poem's pastoralizing common-places disingenuously urged the bourgeois reader to identify with the cultural values of aristocratic *otium* under the pastoral disguise of "mute inglorious Miltons," thereby attaining classical literacy "at a *discount*" (120).

Fine as this is, Guillory overlooks the fact that many of eighteenth-century Britain's "inglorious Miltons" were far from being "mute": however much the language of English court, city, and university formed the gold stan-dard of the new poetic diction, a tradition of eighteenth-century "peasant" and "dialect" poets pursued a more heteroglossic idiom responsive to col-loquial speech, often under the aegis of a newly literalized pastoralism (see Goodridge). Running against the torrent of enameled eclogues (prompted mainly by Pope's juvenile *Pastorals*) that saturated eighteenth-century po-etry and song, this most artificial of genres in the neoclassical canon also provided a linguistic resource for vernacular poets. Ultimately prompted by Theocritus's use of Doric dialect in his *Idylls*, Anglophone readers remem-bered Spenser's use of the vernacular in *The Shepherd's Calendar*. Pope had grumbled in his *Discourse on Pastoral Poetry* that Doric might have had a "beauty and propriety in the time of Theocritus . . . [but] the old English and country phrases of Spenser were either entirely obsolete, or spoken only by people of the lowest condition."[3] Pope here associates the vernacular with laboring-class speakers and seeks to defend the interests of a neoclassical standard for literature (Davis 12).

Ironically disguising his allegiance to the "golden age theory" of the "ancients," Pope's *Guardian* 40 essay adopted a reductio ad absurdum in provincializing Arcadia: "I should think it proper for the several writers of pastoral, to confine themselves to their several counties." To this end, he quoted an antique "pastoral ballad" in the "the Somersetshire dialect": "Cicily. *Rager, go vetch tha kee, or else tha zun / Will quite be go, bevore c'have half a don. /* Roger. *Thou shouldst not ax ma tweece, but I've a bee / To dreave our bull to bull the parson's knee*" (Davis 59; Thomas Crawford 75–76). For all its satirical intentions, this provided an opening for vernacular pastoral, especially in John Gay's more extended parody *The Shepherd's Week* (1714). It was only a short step from Gay's mélange of archaisms and dialect words (plucked from various English counties) to Allan Ramsay's ingenious employment of Scots "Doric" as a "realist" pastoral idiom. Ramsay's equation of Scots with Theocritean "Doric" gave a new cultural dignity to the attenuated Scottish poetry tradition that he sought to revive in *The Evergreen* (1724) and in his own poetic works, which crossed cultural boundaries by drawing on popular songs and chapbook verse. Ramsay sought a more representative "British" poetic in the wake of the 1707 Union, promoting the interests of Scottish language, literature, and culture against a homogenizing classicism. In the preface to *The Evergreen* he criticized the *Northern Poet*, who set his pastorals in Arcadia, for "the *Morning* rises (in the Poet's Description) as she does in the *Scottish* Horizon. We are not carried to *Greece* or *Italy* for a Shade, a Stream, or a Breeze" (Ramsay 4: 236). The importance of Ramsay's localism as a precursor of Romanticism was evident to earlier critics like W. J. Courthope, J. W. Mackail, and J. E. Congleton, although as Murray Pittock points out, more recently such claims have fallen on deaf ears (32, 47).

The language issue was especially complex in eighteenth-century Scotland, where the development of written Scots had been curtailed by the Kirk's adoption of the King James Bible in the wake of the departure of the Scottish court for London in 1603, followed a century later by the Anglicizing influence of the 1707 Treaty of Union. This "headlessness" meant that Scots vernacular poetry took a distinctive trajectory in the verse of Allan Ramsay, Robert Fergusson, and Robert Burns: at once *local*, given the absence of any central Scottish standard, but also *national* to the extent that it was self-consciously *Scottish* as opposed to regional or demotic English. Burns's poetic manifesto is energetically stated in "Epistle to Lapraik," published in his 1786 Kilmarnock volume:

> What's a' jargon o' your Schools,
> Your Latin names for horns an' stools;
> If honest Nature made you *fools*,
>   What sairs your Grammars?   [serves]
> Ye'd better taen up *spades* and *shools*,   [shovels]
>   Or *knappin-hammers*. . . . [hammer for breaking stones]
>
> Gie me ae spark o' Nature's fire,
> That's a' the learning I desire;
> Then tho' I drudge thro' dub an' mire
>   At pleugh or cart,   [plough]
> My Muse, tho' hamely in attire,
>   May touch the heart. (1: 87; lines 61–66, 73–78)

Burns here characteristically sprinkles his verse with colloquial Scots (and Anglo-Scots) diction, while at the same time signaling his modernity by appealing to a pre-romantic cult of "natural genius." The "ploughman poet's" attack on the Latinate "jargon o' your Schools" illuminates the connections between English poetic diction and the classical literacy that it has not so much *rejected* as internalized. Yet paradoxes abound here. Gray's "Elegy," as we have seen the gold standard for the century's new poetic diction, was one of Burns's favorite poems, quoted as an epigraph to "The Cotter's Saturday Night." Moreover, as Burns's editor James Kinsley reminds us, his homage to spontaneous orality and his disavowal of literary learning ("Gie me a spark o' Nature's fire") contains allusions to both Pope and Sterne (Burns 3, 1059). As Christopher Ricks argues in his fine essay on Burns in *Allusion to the Poets*, "we sell Burns short if we begrudge him his skill with allusions" (51). Far from simply rejecting English poetic diction in favor of demotic speech, the Scots vernacular revivalists pursued an *alternative* art-language for poetry, albeit one more open to orality and the rich native song tradition.

Breathing new life into the Scots literary tradition, Burns followed Ramsay (and Fergusson) in frequently eschewing polite Augustan couplet verse in favor of older Scots verse forms like the "Christ's Kirk," "Cherry and Slae," and especially the "standard habbie" employed in these stanzas from "Epistle to Lapraik."[4] The "habbie" is indeed the heavy workhorse of Burns's poetry, although there's nothing "heavy" about the aerial sound patterns and rhetorical ingenuity he achieves at his best, unmatched by any of his precursors

(Dunn 58–85). The homiletic emphasis of the habbie's short line "they *gang in* Stirks, and *come out* Asses, / Plain truth to speak" (Burns 1: 87; lines 69–70),[5] is one of the many devices Burns employs to convey a sense of spoken idiom. Although use of this stanza by earlier poets in the Scottish vernacular revival (including Sempill of Beltrees, after whose elegy on the piper "Habbie Simson" the hallmark stanza is named) focused on comedy and satire, Burns often deployed the form in a more sentimental and sententious manner.

While the Edinburgh novelist and critic Henry Mackenzie initiated the view of Burns as a "heaven-taught ploughman" by downplaying his conscious artifice, Scotland's answer to English laboring-class poets like Stephen Duck or Mary Collier, Francis Jeffrey (the leading reviewer of the romantic age, although hardly an obvious proponent of Scottish nationalism), took a different tack, insisting in an 1809 review, "[Burns's] Scotch is not to be considered as a provincial dialect, the vehicle only of rustic vulgarity and rude local humour. It is the language of a whole country,—long an independent kingdom, and still separate in laws, character and manners . . . Scotch is, in reality, a highly poetical language" (Low 186–87). Jeffrey here rather wishfully evokes Scots as a unified national language in order to distinguish Burns from "regional" writing in plebeian English dialects. The often-competing claims of class, region, and nation are already strongly marked in the vernacular revival of the eighteenth century. Accordingly, Burns was rapidly consecrated both as Scotland's national poet and as a "peasant poet," despite the fact that he was a well-educated Ayrshire tenant farmer and therefore not really a "laboring class" poet at all. In 1828, Thomas Carlyle wrote (with a snub to the literati of the eighteenth-century Scottish Enlightenment) that largely thanks to Burns, "[Scotland's] chief literary men . . . no longer live among us like a French Colony, or some knot of Propaganda Missionaries: but like natural-born sons of the soil, partaking and sympathising in all our attachments, humours, and habits" (Low 372).

Due to the immense popularity of Burns's poetry, as well as the novels of Walter Scott, by this date Scots was the only form of nonstandard English to have won limited acceptability within the "English" literary canon. Even in a century of intense Anglicization, writing in Scots retained a liberating instability in relation to the proprieties of standard English: to quote the modern novelist William McIlvanney, it did (and still does) resemble "English in its underwear, it always undercut pretentiousness" (247). Or as Daniel Bell, a character in James Hogg's novel *Three Perils of Woman* (1823) put it, "ye maun mind that I write Scots, my ain naiteve tongue; and there never was ony reule for that. Every man writes as he speaks it, and that's the great advantage of our language ower a' others" (Hogg 42). Here its informality, based on the very *absence* of a national standard, is taken to enable writers in Scots to retain a proximate relationship to ordinary speech of a kind barely available to their English compeers. And certainly, if one (flippant) definition of a language is "a dialect with a navy," then imperial "North Britain" was never going to evolve a distinct standard whose relation to English was equivalent to that of Portuguese to Spanish, or Norwegian to Danish. But the instability of Scots provided an opportunity as well as a limitation for subsequent writers both within and outside of Scotland. Divested of its national animus, but not its embodied, demotic energy, Scots provided a model for English laboring-class poets like John Clare, as well as subsequent writers of the manifold "varieties of English" in North America, the Caribbean, and other British colonies past and present. As twentieth-century Australian poet Les Murray put it, the example of Scots poetry helped undermine the "mandarin centralism" of standard English, so that "the capital of the world is anywhere a good writer is writing" (Crawford, *Devolving* 301).

Recent focus on "the Scottish invention of English literature" as an academic discipline has perhaps diverted attention away from the important contribution of poetry in Scots to "active Romanticism" (Crawford, *Devolving* 16–44; Crawford, *Scottish Invention*; Jones). The eighteenth-century Scottish institution of university lecture courses in "Rhetoric and Belles Lettres" proposed an inverse relationship between linguistic propriety and the spoken Scots tongue: mutatis mutandis, this was an argument that also proved influential in new college rhetoric courses in the American colonies (Crawford, *Devolving* 16–44). Adam Smith, who more than any other single individual invented "college English," argued that "we in this country are most of us very sensible that the perfection of language is very different from that we commonly speak in . . . the further one's style is from the common manner it is so much the nearer to purity" (42). Smith's friend David Hume appended a list of "Scotticisms," or incorrect "provincial" usages, to his 1752 *Political Dictionary*, and other literati like Sir John Sinclair and James Beattie followed suit (Basker 81–95). For many Scottish, Irish, and North American writers, literary English possessed the cultural capital of Latin in the old canon. Edmund Burke (an Anglicized Irishman) complained of the prose style of the Edinburgh historian William Robertson that "he writes like a man who composes in a dead language, which he understands but cannot speak," although the brilliancy of Burke's own style was attacked for its "Hibernian" excess (Bentman 220).

The act of "deterritorialization" involved in establishing a national language (or its literary equivalent, a "poetic diction") is well exemplified in Dr. Johnson's *Dictionary* (1755), which excluded the usages of provincial English, Irish, American, and other Anglophone language users as well as Scots. Sorensen underlines this "idea of a national 'nobody's language,' detached as it would be from any group in particular, [which] provides a basis for imagining national fellows" (96). In poetry, the Augustan synthesis of classical and Miltonic models had found one of its most distinguished exponents in the Scottish poet James Thomson, whose digressive philosophical poem "The Seasons" remained at the top of the eighteenth century's bestseller list as *the* exemplar of "British" poetry in the georgic mode. While retaining broad Scots speech throughout his adult life in London, Thomson nevertheless satisfied Adam Smith's desideratum that "it is the duty of a poet to write like a gentleman," untainted by the demotic language of the streets and byres (A. Smith 230).[6]

In refusing to settle for a poetic diction of the sort associated with Pope and Gray, endorsed by Adam Smith, and aspired to by Scottish poets like Thomson, James Beattie, and Thomas Blacklock, Burns sent out confusing signals to many contemporary readers, a point to which I will return below. The Scottish literati often associated Scots with the old society and manners predating the 1707 Act of Union, regarding Anglicization as a fundamental article of "improvement" (Sorensen 138–71). At the same time, Scots was not without its champions in the shape of men like James Adams (an Englishman) and Alexander Geddes, both, incidentally, Roman Catholic priests. Adams criticized the application of a Southern English standard to Scotland given that "there was a pure classical Scots spoken by genteel people, which I thought very agreeable; it had nothing of the coarseness of the vulgar *patois* of the lower orders of the people" (Jones 20). This "Scottish standard" of course represented another bid to arrest "vernacular drift" without resorting to an imported paradigm. In a long digressive poem written in Scots and addressed to the Fellows of the Society of Antiquaries of Scotland, Alexander Geddes was less damning about the spoken vernacular, finding in the speech of the common people the vestiges of a purer idiom that he dubbed "Scoto-Saxon":

> For tho' tis true, that Mither-tongue
> Has had the melancholy fate,
> To be neglekit by the great,
> She still has fun an open door
> Amang the uncorruptit poor,
> Wha be na weent to treat wi' scorn
> A gentlewoman bred and born;
> Bot bid her, thoch in tatters drest,   [though]
> A hearty welcome to their best. (Geddes 444)

Nonetheless, despite Geddes's radical politics, Scots vernacular is here presented as "a *gentlewoman* bred and born," and the poem ends with a plea for establishing a national Scots (based on the lexicographic research of the antiquaries) that will return the language to polite usage in the place of "mimic sud'ren dialect" (Geddes 449). The poem closes by hailing Robert Burns as the great hope for a Scottish poetry revival, although Geddes warns him to "Bewar of indolence an' pride; / Nor cast thine aiten [oaten] reed aside: / But trim, an' blaw it mair an' mair; / An' court the Muses late an air [early]" (453).

Caledonian Antisyzygy?

Although these apologetics fell largely on deaf ears, Burns's achievement was in itself sufficient to rekindle enthusiasm for the "articulate energy" of the ancient Scots language as it was still spoken by the majority of the population. This qualifies the dominant story of marginalization related above, for Burns's contemporary popularity in Scotland (as well as in England, Ireland, and America) shows that even the many linguistic "improvers" among the Edinburgh literati were willing to countenance poetry (and especially song) in Scots when licensed by a naturalist aesthetic and the generic allowances of "Scots pastoral." Nevertheless, the disagreement about Scots that I have been discussing was later absorbed into a broader Romantic critique of an "inauthentic" and fissured Scottish culture that would resonate a century later in the writers and critics of modernism. Ian Duncan has recently argued that Burns's romantic biographer John Gibson Lockhart was the first to characterize Scottish literature as split between a cosmopolitan rationalism and an authentic, but unreflective, "true voice of feeling" expressed in the Scots language (Duncan 60; C. Craig 82–118). The Germanophile Lockhart drew here on Schlegelian notions of cultural fragmentation, just as twentieth-century critics made common cause with T. S. Eliot's idea of "disassociated sensibility" to analyze the split at the core of the Scottish psyche, which (borrowing a rebarbative term from G. Gregory Smith) they diagnosed as being afflicted with the "Caledonian antisyzygy" (G. Smith; Carruthers 11,15).

Modernist poets quickly lined up on either side of the "antisyzygy." Hugh MacDiarmid (1892–1978, pen name Christopher Murray Grieve), the leading Scottish poet of the twentieth century, complained about "the dooble tongue—guid Scots wi' English a' hamstrung" (Watson 172) and sought to purge the English contaminant: a return to pure Scots (or "Lallans")[7] might promote "the experimental exploitation of the unexplored possibilities of Vernacular expression" (MacDiarmid 19–20). MacDiarmid's Scots was "synthetic" to the extent that, despite his receptivity to the spoken language, he freely admitted to plundering archaic diction from Scots language diction-

aries, albeit in the experimental spirit of modernism: "We have been enormously struck by the resemblance—the moral resemblance—between Jamie-
son's *Etymological Dictionary of the Scottish Language* and James Joyce's *Ulysses*.
A *vis comica* that has not yet been liberated lies bound by desuetude and
misappreciation in the recesses of the Doric: and its potential uprising would
be no less prodigious, uncontrollable, and utterly at variance with conventional morality than was Joyce's tremendous outpouring" (MacDiarmid 20).
Ian Hamilton Finlay memorably described MacDiarmid's project as a dead
language "animated by some freak electric energy," paying it parodic homage in his pioneering 1961 collection *Glasgow Beasts*, which blended Scots
musical-hall idiom with the Japanese Zen poetry of Shimpei Kusano (Finlay 24). MacDiarmid's famous slogan "Not Burns—Dunbar!" underlines his
deeply ambivalent and often contradictory views of the former poet (compared to his reverence for the medieval "Makar" Dunbar), although his attitude to the twentieth-century Burns Cult can be summed up in one word:
loathing. In a 1931 essay, "English Ascendancy in British Literature," Mac-
Diarmid made common cause with the Ayrshire poet when he wrote, "Burns
knew what he was doing when he reverted from eighteenth-century English
to a species of synthetic Scots and was abundantly justified in the result" (62).
Yet elsewhere he accused Burns of being a typical Scot of his age, "insipis-
sated with English influences . . . his use of the vernacular was exiguous—
eked out with English . . . most of his work rings psychologically false" (62).
Despite his fascination with rural Scots idiom in the early lyrics published
in *Sangshaw* (1925) and *Penny Wheep* (1926), MacDiarmid was also alert to
the historical limitations of Burns's example in adapting "an essentially rustic tongue to the very much more complex requirements of our urban civilization" (MacDiarmid 10; Riach 201). Yet as Dorian Grieve has shown, for
all his admiration for Joyce's *Ulysses*, he had himself little interest in the sort
of literary neologism beloved of other modernist writers (25).

More recently the Glasgow poet Tom Leonard (b. 1944) has developed
elements of MacDiarmid's diagnosis while rejecting both the idea of "synthetic Scots" and its nationalist and class-based premises. Leonard pointed
out that the "proletarian urban dictions" that arose in the aftermath of the
industrial revolution earned the contempt of many of the Scottish middle
class who, following standardizers like Adams and Geddes, sought to consecrate an authentic "Scottish dialect" of the kind they assumed was written
by Burns. Leonard quotes one commentator writing about the working-class
speech of urbanized Renfrewshire in 1933: "It is not Scots at all, but a thing
debased beyond tears. It is a mongrel patois due to lower class immigration
from Ireland, from Lancashire mills, and the meaner streets of Glasgow. . . .

Regret it as we may, the Doric of Renfrewshire is not only dead, but in an advanced state of putrefaction" (xxiii).[8] Such bourgeois disdain is clearly another expression of "vernacular arrest": according to such a view, as Leonard continues, working-class speakers "have lost the right of equality of dialogue with those in possession of Queen's English, or 'good' Scots" (xxiv). Rejecting any kind of linguistic standard in favor of the liberating instability discussed above, Leonard's experimental poetry mobilizes the resources of urban Scots speech and "aligns [itself] with William Carlos Williams in the struggle to find fresh and subtle expression in the kinetics and phonetics of words on the page," often with violent, comic, and surprising effects (Watson 170).[9]

Modernism, however, also saw a revival of the eighteenth-century animus *against* Scots in the reaction of other writers to MacDiarmid's program, which they rejected as utterly quixotic. The Orcadian poet and critic Edwin Muir (1887–1959), for example, remarked in 1936 that "the curse of Scottish literature is the lack of a whole language, which finally means the lack of a whole mind" (9).[10] Influenced by Coleridge's idea of an organic culture, Muir asserted that "when we insist on using dialect for restricted literary purposes we are being true not to the idea of Scotland but to provincialism, which is one of the things that has helped to destroy Scotland. If we are to have a complete and homogenous Scottish literature it is necessary that we should have a complete and homogenous language." For Muir only two such languages existed in Scotland, Gaelic and English, so paradoxically (unless Gaelic should regain its early medieval currency, an unlikely event), Scotland could only "create a national literature by writing in English" (111). Muir's dismissal of "provincialism" has recently been challenged by Robert Crawford, who argues that poets like Larkin, Douglas Dunn, Seamus Heaney, Tom Paulin, Tom Leonard, and Les Murray form part of "an international grouping of writers whose work may be seen as inheriting something from the demotic side of the essentially provincial movement which was Modernism" (Crawford, *Devolving* 298). Another internationalist with strong local roots, Glasgow poet Edward Morgan (1920–2010) likewise sought a poetic idiom for "Scotch English" that would move toward "more truthful naturalism and freer manipulation." As quoted in the epigraph to this chapter, Morgan feared that MacDiarmid and his followers had "rather neglected the importance of the speech basis ('the current language heightened,' in Hopkins's phrase) in the excitement of developing an eclectic or synthetic Scots."[11]

The progressivist assault on the use of Scots vernacular was furthered by the Left-Leavisite critic David Craig, whose widely read *Scottish Literature and the Scottish People* (1961) associated the "reductive idiom" of eighteenth-century Scottish vernacular verse (as well as the "poor man's defensive pose," which he discerned in the poetry of Allan Ramsay and Robert Burns) with "the old constricting habits" of unimproved agriculture (82).[12] Following Muir, Craig found the verse forms and diction of Burns's poetry (compared, say, to the rural poetry of the English George Crabbe) to be "incommensurate with the wholeness of experience," although he undermined his case by erroneously describing Burns as "a crofter" and "a primitive peasant tilling for subsistence crops" (79, 95, 100, 141). Writing in the late 1950s, when Scotland was about as "British" as it ever would be, Craig sought to "deprovincialize" Scottish writing, albeit from a socialist and internationalist, rather than a nationalist, perspective. Burns's poetic voice was "remote from the centres of power"; he had been condemned "to write . . . without a share in the full resources of wealth, goods, power, opportunity, or range of jobs available in his country, one whose privation was to the advantage of those who were in power." Without doubt, this was genuinely felt, although Craig's criteria would exclude many of the greatest writers in world literature. Citing Maxim Gorky's *My Apprenticeship*, he urged that "concern for the better development or fulfilment of people born into such conditions, is likely to be the core of literature produced by working-men" (80, 88). Although Craig accurately described the failure of the Burnsian/Scots poetic model to develop in the very "British" and imperial climate of the nineteenth century, the limitations of his argument are now starkly evident, summed up in Murray Pittock's comment that "because Burns is a sophisticated writer, writing in Scots is always a poetic option for him, not an educational necessity" (147). But Craig was by no means the first (or last) critic to be taken in by Burns's "pastoral" persona.

With hindsight it is evident that the modernist theory of the "Caledonian antisyzygy" created a distorted understanding of Burns's achievement, to the extent that in seeking to suture together a divided Scottish self, he was accused of creating an impure mix. A fundamental misapprehension is evident here. For a start, as North American critic Carol McGuirk rightly indicates, misguided concentration on Burns as a Scots dialect poet simply "encourages critics who are not themselves Scottish enthusiasts to presuppose a regional range for his achievements and [thus] to ignore Burns" (xvii). In fact, far from writing exclusively in Scots, Burns deftly switched between Scots, Anglo-Scots, and English; many of his most celebrated poems (famously "To a Mouse" and "To a Mountain-Daisy") were couched in the contemporary idiom of sensibility, and many of the songs are written in English with only a "sprinkling" of Scots diction. Take a famous example, the startling shift of register evident in the first two stanzas of "To a Mouse":

Wee, sleeket, cowran, tim'rous *beastie*,
O, what a panic's in thy breastie!
Thou need na start awa sae hasty,
   Wi' bickering brattle!
I wad be laith to rin an' chase thee,
   Wi' murd'ring *pattle*!   [spade used to clean the plough]

I'm truly sorry Man's dominion
Has broken Nature's social union,
An' justifies that ill opinion
   Which makes thee startle
At me, thy poor, earth-born companion
   An' *fellow mortal*! (Burns 1: 127; lines 1–11)

Burns's narrator apologizes to the mouse for the fall from grace embodied in the progress of civilization (notably in this case the "improved" agricultural economy) but reassures the "tim'rous beastie" that he's willing to spare the life of a "fellow mortal," even if his less sentimental brethren would have destroyed it with "murdr'ing *pattle*" (line 6).

Although a devotee of the "Caledonian antisyzygy" might see the poem as hopelessly split between diverse linguistic registers, it is a tribute to Burns that his apology retains a colloquial lightness of touch and does not sink under the freight of its allusion to Pope's *Essay on Man* at lines 7–8. Later, at line 15, he adopts another register in writing "A *daimen-icker* in a *thrave* / 'S a sma' request: / I'll get a blessin wi' the lave, / An' never miss't!" (lines 13–18). "*Daimen icker* in a *thrave*" is a previously unrecorded vernacular phrase from Ayrshire, referring to the portion of the farmer's corn "requested" by the mouse as a form of charitable gleaning. (The poet, who cannot have expected even Scots readers from outside Ayrshire to understand this, glosses the densely colloquial and agricultural idiom as "an ear of corn now and then.") Burns's "code-switching" in this poem, and elsewhere, is actually closer to what Robert Young describes as "intentional hybridity" than cultural schizophrenia: "contestatory activity, a politicized setting of cultural differences against each other dialogically" (22). Once again we see Burns fulfilling Edwin Morgan's desideratum of writing a form of "synthetic Scots" that does not lose touch with the language as currently spoken. In this respect his poetry is far from being conservative and backward looking, especially considering its engagement with the English Augustans and the contemporary idiom of sensibility. Unfortunately, though, it cannot be denied that his consummate success often deterred skilled followers, and much subsequent poetry written in Scots was easily subsumed into the "Kailyard," the purely nostalgic and parochial Victorian version of Scottish pastoral against which MacDiarmid and other modernists railed.

Burns and the *Copia Verborum*

Burns's 1786 "Kilmarnock" volume *Poems, Chiefly in the Scottish Dialect* was a runaway success, being avidly purchased and read by readers from all social backgrounds, from Edinburgh as well as Ayrshire and the southwest of Scotland. Perhaps the best key to understanding Burns's poetic language is not so much the famous preface to Kilmarnock as an anecdote reported by the Edinburgh man of letters Dr. Robert Anderson of a 1787 conversation with the poet, written after Burns's death. The poet here reviews his linguistic toolkit with extraordinary technical fluency, employing the term *copia verborum*:

> It was, I know, part of the machinery, as he called it, of his poetical character to pass for an illiterate ploughman who wrote from pure inspiration. When I pointed out some evident traces of poetical inspiration in his verses, privately, he readily acknowledged his obligations and even admitted the advantages he enjoyed in poetical composition from the *copia verborum*, the command of phraseology, which the knowledge and use of the English and Scottish dialects afforded him; but in company he did not suffer his pretensions to pure inspiration to be challenged, and it was seldom done where he might be supposed to affect the success of the subscription for his Poems. (Burns 3: 1537–38)

In the Kilmarnock preface, Burns described himself as a *literal* rather than a *literary* pastoralist: "The following trifles are not the production of the Poet, who, with all the advantages of learned art, and perhaps amid the elegancies and idlenesses of upper life, looks down for a rural theme, with an eye to Theocrites [*sic*] and Virgil" (iii). In Anderson's anecdote, he allows the mask to slip for a moment, although not without expressing some concerns for the damage such candor might do to his subscription list. He underlines the fact that, rather than struggling with an "impoverished" or "restricted" idiom, the Scots poet who commands both "the English and Scottish dialects" in fact enjoys a peculiar advantage over others limited to standard English poetic diction alone. As Jeremy Smith argues, Burns's *copia verborum* ("abundance of words") signifies a language that "contains sufficient vocabulary for all registers (i.e., elevated, plain, demotic)," and his particular skill was

"to shift from one register of language to another in accordance with the social situation of his language" (76, 84).

The myth of the "heaven-taught ploughman" carried the day, however,
and the poet's literary learning remained concealed to the majority of his
contemporaries. Evident in the (generally disappointing) early reviews, however, is an extraordinary lack of consensus about his "experimental" use of
Scots. The debate was largely polarized between what I will term "naive" and
"skeptical" views of Burns's language. The Edinburgh novelist and essayist
Henry Mackenzie (principal champion of the "naive" view) regretted that the
poems' "provincial dialect" rendered them difficult of understanding, which
shows him accepting Burns's "realist" claim in his preface that the poet "sings
the sentiments and manners, he felt and saw in himself and his rustic compeers around him, *in his and their native language*" (Burns, *Poems Chiefly*
iii; my italics). (It is a paradox, of course, and one completely passed over
by Mackenzie, that the preface needed to make its case in standard English
in the first place.) Although Burns's claim had a profound influence on romantic vernacular theorists, especially Wordsworth, those who accepted the
"naive" view that Burns "wrote as he spoke" ran the risk of confounding the
"heaven-taught ploughman" persona with the various literary personae and
the experimental range and literary heteroglossia of the poems themselves
(Bentman 240). This ultimately supported David Craig's damaging judgment
that the Scots poetry of Burns and his peers suffered from a "reductive idiom"
and "limitation of range," reflecting the realities of a rustic, provincialized
outlook and a "disintegrating culture" (13, 74, 82). A clever, postmodernist
version of the naive thesis is resurrected, to sophisticated effect, in Jeffrey
Skoblow's recent study of Burns's "dooble tongue": Skoblow privileges a performative and oral Scots "vulgate" as a kind of "troth-speech" (rekindled in
the poetry of contemporary Scots poets like W. N. Herbert), which always
transcends the appropriative schemes of "standard English" exegesis (183).

The "naive" view may have obstructed appreciation of Burns's experimental ambitions, but the opposite "skeptical" view, fully cognizant of his literary
artifice, has problems of its own. Echoing Pope's criticism of the "antique"
diction of Spenserian pastoral, James Anderson (writing, like Mackenzie, in
1786) attributed the difficulty of the poems to the fact that they were "faith-
fully copied from . . . the ancient Scottish bards," and he recommended that
in future Burns employ a "measure less antiquated" (Low 74). This view was
later reiterated by John Logan, who complained (in a February 1787 letter to
Mackenzie) of "a kind of Imposture not infrequent among poets of convey-
ing Modern ideas in a dialect of Antiquity" (Low 79). Later, Robert Southey
denied that Burns's diction had the least relation to spoken Scots, designat-

ing it (with reference to the antiquarian forgeries of Thomas Chatterton) as "a kind of Rowleyism, composed of all the Scotch words they can collect" (Low 169). An element of this view survives in Raymond Bentman's modern judgment that "the 'Scottish' poems are written in a literary language, a sort of 'designer Scots' which was mostly, although not entirely, English, in grammar and syntax, and, in varying proportions, both Scottish and English in vocabulary" (Bentman 239).

"Burns wrote some poems in pure English, most of them in neoclassical style, but he wrote no poems in pure vernacular Scottish" (Bentman 239). Salutary as is the "skeptical" view of Burns's language to the extent that it opens up the poetry to a modernist spirit of experimentation, it is potentially misleading to the extent that it cuts the ligature with the spoken—and regional—demotic. In the absence of any Scots standard, it is hard to know what "pure vernacular Scottish" might have looked like on the printed page, for the Kilmarnock poems were undoubtedly the closest many of Burns's contemporaries ever got to that elusive quarry. As many critics have pointed out, the poetic diction of the Kilmarnock poems is drawn from a wide range of sources: English-language poets like Pope, Thomson, Gray, Goldsmith, and Shenstone, as well as Scottish precursors, from Montgomerie and Sempill to Ramsay and Fergusson; it also ranged over an extensive linguistic gamut, from Anglo-Latinic macaronics and the rhetoric of sensibility to the homely Scots proverbs of Ramsay's collection. At the same time, the preface's claim that the poems imitated the "native language" of the poet's "rustic compeers" demands serious consideration as a function of the volume's overall plan. To this end, many of the Kilmarnock poems flaunt a rural Ayrshire dialect (evoked in "Epistle to Davie, a Brother Poet" as "hamely, *westlin* jingle") (Burns 1: 65; line 6), highlighted by the poet's own word list in the glossary to the poems. Burns's regional identification as an "Ayrshire bardie" was an important theme of poems like "The Vision" (his muse "Coila" is named after his native Ayrshire baillieric of Kyle), as well as "Epistle to Willie Simson," and as we have seen, several of the poems deliberately employ elements of strong local dialect (e.g., the use of "*daimen-icker* in a *thrave*" in "To a Mouse.").

"Pure vernacular Scots" would have been hard to distinguish, because, as David Murison writes, "almost nothing in Ayrshire dialect had been recorded [before] 1786 when the Kilmarnock edition appeared." Nevertheless, Burns's verse correspondent (and fellow Ayrshireman) Willie Simson later insisted that "the Glossary to Burns' poems, gives a good idea of the Provincial Terms in Ayrshire" (Murison, "Speech of Ayrshire" 222, 226). As Murison points out, Burns's Scots vocabulary (employing over two thousand words) is highly eclectic, drawing from a wide number of Scottish dialects; but his rural poems do feature a number of words from the poet's native Kyle, words like *crunt, daimen, gloamin shot, ha bible, icker, jauk, kiaugh, messan, pyle, raucle, rockin, roon, fhangan, thummert, wiel, winze, wintle* (Murison, "Language of Burns" 63). If Kilmarnock's glossary sought to render local terms intelligible to Edinburgh readers, the expanded 1787 glossary included general Scots terms, indicating Burns's ambitions for the Edinburgh volume south of the border, as well as in North America and the colonies. His poetic employment of local demotic speech was therefore an integral part of Burns's "synthetic Scots," but it also signaled his local status as an Ayrshire poet, a necessary precondition for his subsequent apotheosis as Scotland's national bard.

Conclusion

This essay has argued for the importance of Burns and Scots language poetry in establishing an experimental model for subsequent vernacular poets in the Anglophone world. But I have also traced some of the problems attendant upon rejecting what Tom Paulin calls "the polished urbanity of Official Standard" (xix), especially the danger of simply inverting the hierarchies of linguistic propriety by enshrining an equally exclusive counterstandard, often in the ideological interests of sentimental nativism. In Burns's case, this was all the more problematic given that he wrote on the cusp of urbanization and the industrial transformation of Scotland, even if rural language and experience continued (and continue) to be of great importance to Scottish culture. Burns's modernist heirs were both inspired by his achievement as a vernacularist and poet of "synthetic Scots" and repelled by the Kailyard tradition that sought to enshrine a nostalgic, ruralist, and ultimately petit bourgeois version of Scots vernacular against urbanism, immigration, and the realities of twentieth-century working-class life. (Some even fell into the trap of confusing the "restricted idiom" of the Kailyard with its Burnsian source.)

One important aspect of Burns's importance for "active Romanticism" is his still underacknowledged influence on Wordsworth's "poetical experiments" in *Lyrical Ballads* and other poems. Space prevents any detailed account of this, beyond noting that part of the problem lies in the depth at which Burns's poetry and example were assimilated by the Lakeland poet. Wordsworth generously acknowledged the fact in his poem "At the Grave of Burns," written in the habbie stanza: "whose light I hailed when first it shone, / And showed my youth / How verse may build a princely throne / On humble truth" (Wordsworth 1: 558, lines 33–36). It is worth noting, however, that whereas the advertisement to the 1798 edition of *Lyrical Ballads* declares the linguistic model for its poetic "experiments" to be "the language of conversation in the middle and lower classes of society," the 1800 preface (composed *after* reading Dr. Currie's 1800 edition of Burns, with its introductory "Observations on the Scottish Peasantry") specifies "low and rustic life" as the social locus of "the real language of men in a state of vivid sensation" (Wordsworth and Coleridge 7, 245, 241; Leask, *Robert Burns* 292–98). I have argued elsewhere that in pursuing this critical goal, Wordsworth needed to devise an alternative language for poetry (impossibly) using a rural lower-class vernacular based neither on Scots nor on any English regional speech (Leask, "Burns, Wordsworth" 202–22). As an English poet, Wordsworth obviously resisted writing in Scots, although he showed little interest in experimenting with Lakeland dialect, despite the impressive efforts of local poets like Josiah Relph and Robert Anderson. This perhaps supports John Guillory's view that Wordsworth's bid to emulate "the real language of men" was really a disguise for another kind of "poetic diction": "like Gray, he wishes to produce a different language [for poetry]—but by simplification rather than complication" (127).

Wordsworth's increased focus on the exemplary figure of the poet (rather than the rustic) in the 1802 preface already represented a swerve away from Burns's influence, anticipating Coleridge's account of poetic language in his 1817 *Biographia Literaria*. Coleridge substituted his own canonical notion of a "lingua communis" in place of the preface's "real language of men in a state of vivid sensation," as well as returning to a conventional poetics of pastoral (Leask, *Politics* 68–74). Tellingly, Coleridge explicitly raised the specter of Burns in objecting to what he now regarded as the mistaken theory of Wordsworth's 1800 preface, a rite of exorcism designed to restore Wordsworth to the English poetic mainstream, despite his "vernacularist" delusions about imitating "the real language of men." Recovering the rubric of Mackenzie's "Heaven-taught ploughman," Coleridge insinuated that Wordsworth erred in mistaking Burns, an *exceptional* denizen of rural life, for an *exemplary* one: "[We] find even in situations the most favourable, according to Mr Wordsworth, for the formation of a pure and poetic language; in situations which ensure familiarity with the grandest objects of the imagination; but *one* BURNS, among the shepherds of *Scotland*, and not a single poet of humble life among those of the *English* lakes and mountains; I conclude, that POETIC GENIUS is not only a very delicate but a very rare plant (Coleridge, *Biographia Literaria* 269–70).[13] It is ironic that the author of experimental poetry like "Christabel" and "The Ancient Mariner" should have here sounded the death knell of the vernacular strain in Wordsworth's active

Romanticism, while at the same time contributing to the "monumentalization" of Burns as a figure of tragic exception in the emerging canon of British poetry.

Notes

See MacDiarmid 19–20, Morgan 36.

1. Partial, because in many cases (as, for example, the "Scoto-Latin tradition"), Latin played a vital role in the development of national literatures (Crawford, *Apollos* xiii–liii).

2. John Kerrigan suggests that the "English canon" is largely a product of nineteenth-century revisionism, which occluded the Celtic nations (1–90). Tom Paulin follows modern linguists' preference for the term "vernacular" over "dialect" on the grounds that the latter term "marginalizes regional speech and privileges Standard English" (xi).

3. Davis 12.

4. The hallmark six-line stanza of "To a Mouse" and "Holy Willie's Prayer"; three iambic tetrameters rhyming *aa*, followed by a dimeter, rhyming *b*, another tetrameter rhyming *a*, and a concluding dimeter rhyming *b*.

5. "Stirks" are young bullocks.

6. Smith's remarks on poetry quoted in *The Bee*, May 11, 1791.

7. Burns uses "Lallans" to describe the vernacular speech of Lowland Scotland, but it now generally signifies the variety of literary Scots used by MacDiarmid and other modernist writers of the Scottish Renaissance movement.

8. Leonard's own father was an Irish immigrant from Dublin who worked on the railways for most of his life.

9. Leonard's presence on the Scottish poetry scene was first felt with the publication of *Six Glasgow Poems* (Glasgow: Midnight Publications, 1969). He has consistently looked to modern American poets, as well as British poets in the laboring-class tradition, for inspiration.

10. Muir was a central figure in the so-called "Scottish Renaissance," although his attitude to the Scots language led to a breach with MacDiarmid. Muir's family had moved to Glasgow in 1901, but within five years both his parents and two of his brothers died, creating in his mind a stark contrast between the pastoral world of his Orkney childhood and the harsh realities of modern urban capitalism. He published seven volumes of poetry and (with his wife Willa) important translations from the German of Franz Kafka and Hermann Broch. Between 1946 and 1949 he was director of the British Council in Prague and Rome, and in 1955 he was appointed Norton Professor of Poetry at Harvard. He died and was buried in Swaffham Prior, near Cambridge, England.

11. See also McGonigal 147. Morgan was a lecturer in the English Literature Department of Glasgow University from 1947 to 1980; he published numerous volumes of poetry and translations. In 2004 he was named as the first Scottish National Poet, "The Scots Makar."

12. Lockhart had spoken in remarkably similar terms of Scots language poetry as "written in the dialect of the lower classes . . . imply[ing] that they must be confined to a limited range of thought" (3: 329).

13. Coleridge's catachrestic description of Burns as a "shepherd" suggests a return to the traditional discourse of pastoral in relation to which even Mackenzie's "ploughman" looked like a critical innovation.

8
Hyper-Pindaric
The Greater Irregular Lyric from Cowley to Keston Sutherland

Simon Jarvis

The question of the relationship between poetry written in English now and that written in England at the beginning of the nineteenth century keeps opening up again, whenever "now" happens to be. Central to this question are those irregular grand lyrics which appear to come almost from nowhere— above all, Coleridge's "Dejection" and Wordsworth's "Ode [There was a time]." In the extent of their variation in line length, rhyme scheme, and meter, these poems revive and mutate a tradition which might well have been considered dead at their date of composition, that of the great irregular lyric, or "Pindaric," pioneered by Abraham Cowley, but then forcibly regularized by Congreve and most succeeding authors of English Pindarics. One thing which must have occurred to any reasonably well-informed reader of late modernist English poetry is the recurrent appearance in it, too, of a kind of hyper-excitable Pindaric. In poems such as John Wilkinson's "Harmolodics," J. H. Prynne's "Of Sanguine Fire," and Keston Sutherland's *Hot White Andy*, indentations vary widely, and different regimes of indentation are in place in different parts of the poems, although the degrees of indentation no longer, as they did in some eighteenth-century printed verse, contain a precise message about the metrical character of individual lines.[1]

In this essay I want to show why I think the connection to be, in the event, more than a superficial one. A full account of it would require discussion of many things and many poems which have had to be left out here but which, to go only so far as the middle of the nineteenth century, it is as well to signal in brief: an account of the place of the heroic line as underlying repertoire for the Pindaric, allowing a kind of home base from which a given poem can move away and to which it can come back (Dryden's funeral lament for Anne Killigrew); of the difference made by the idea of musical setting to the grand ode for music (Dryden's "Alexander's Feast"; Pope's 1713 *Ode for Musick*; Collins's "The Passions"; of the total transformation, not minor shift, in the compositional reality of this mode represented by the Congrevian or regularized Pindaric (especially Gray, "The Bard," and Coleridge's astonishing collision and fusion of Gray's and Collins's modes in his "Ode on the Departing Year"); the silent resuscitation of the Pindaric after 1800 in some of the greatest odes in the language (Wordsworth, "Ode [There was a time]"; Coleridge, "Dejection") and in minor works of great poets (Tennyson, "Ode to Memory").

If anything is to be said, not everything may be attempted. Here discussion is limited to two poems: *Hot White Andy*, one of the most recent, and Abraham Cowley's "The Resurrection," which has a good claim to be considered the first of English Pindarics. The discussion of these two widely separated terminuses prepares the ground for a future discussion of the great irregular "Romantic" ode, not as an inexplicable outburst of native woodnotes, but as a critical instance in that series of deaths and resurrections of the Pindaric which has characterized the grand English lyric ever since Cowley's reinvention. The great irregular "Romantic" odes are almost never considered from what one might have thought should have been the most elementary point of view, that of the ways in which they are put together, their rhyming patterns, and how these relate to the complex handling of rhythm and meter. It is as though their cloudy trophies should too rapidly be unwoven were they subjected to minute technical analysis of this kind. Yet, at the same time, these nuts and bolts constitute an essential condition, not only of the poems' versification, but also of their loftiest and most rarefied thoughts. No account of these technical elements and their importance can be undertaken, however, without a sense of their background in that long sequence of deaths and rebirths of the Pindaric of which Cowley stands at the origin. This essay, therefore, attempts at a minimum some of the groundwork necessary to a future appreciation of the "Romantic" irregular ode.

It aims also at a small contribution to literary theory. Recent commentary on "lyric" has come from a number of quarters. A group of articles in one of the profession's most visible journals offers reflections on the state of the field with respect to this term; in another part of the forest, two densely packed critical recensions of a recent British poem also get stuck into it.[2] "Lyric," unlike some other concepts, is not properly deployed emphatically. When the concept is deployed to propose an evaulation, that is, or to mingle evaluation and description, it usually, except in the case of certain quite carefully directed instances within individual authorships, becomes obfuscating.[3] One confusion which especially results is the idea that it would be in some sense necessary to take sides with or against "lyric," that lyric, for example, might be necessarily connected with some particular ethical or metaethical stance. This essay does not make any contribution to settling the controverted question of exactly what lyric is. It uses Culler's recent account as a working starting point and offers a rather sideways attempt partially to respond to Culler's invitation to "consider what the model of lyric as dramatic monologue misses: stress on the reconstruction of the dramatic situation deprives rhythm and sound patterning of any constitutive role (at best they reinforce or undercut meaning); it devalues intertextual relations, except when they can be assimilated to allusions made by the consciousness dramatized; and it ignores the characteristic extravagance of lyric, which frequently engages in speech acts without a known real-world counterpart."[4] Sideways, because rather than, as Culler desiderates, proposing an item in any new typology, I am instead returning to an old item in an old typology of lyric and trying to revive and extend it.

Strophe

The Pindaric, after its effective invention by Abraham Cowley, became in the public mind a synonym for uncontrolled license. Edward Young mocked the "beauteous strife" between the "cool writings, and Pindaric life" of certain moralists, where "Pindaric" is a synonym for "dissolute."[5] By the early eighteenth century Addison could apply it to gardening: "I think there are as many kinds of gardening as of poetry: your makers of parterres and flower-gardens, are epigrammatists and sonneteers in this art: contrivers of bowers and grottos, treillages and cascades, are romance writers: . . . As for myself, you will find, by the account which I have already given you, that my compositions in gardening are altogether after the Pindaric manner, and run into the beautiful wildness of nature, without affecting the nicer elegancies of art."[6] Addison's joke on himself, that he is a hopeless gardener, also contains the implication that Pindaric poets are simply poets who cannot write. Not being able to manage the nicer elegancies of art, they just get things down any old how. One risk taken by the Pindaric was that its freedom might become purely abstract, the freedom to include anything whatever. In an illuminating essay on the Pindaric, Joshua Scodel has suggested that the great licenses of the late-seventeenth-century Pindaric are best understood under the rubric of "diversion." "In his opening translation of *Olympian* 2," Scodel points out, "Cowley freely renders a Pindaric passage treating Theron of Acragas's chariot victory as a recompense for the violent sufferings of his mythical ancestry in order to suggest the need for Englishmen to forget the recent past: 'For the past sufferings of this noble Race / . . . Let *present joys* fill up their place, / And with *Oblivions silent stroke* deface / Of foregone Ills the very *trace*.'" Seen from this perspective, Cowley's is an "Art of Oblivion," and its freedoms would be diversionary, merely private.⁷

There is a kind of elective affinity between this view of Cowley's relationship to political freedom and the poems' vaunted metrical license. John Oldham's editor puts the contemporary version of this aspect of the case against Pindarics thus:

> We are acquainted with styles much bolder than the Pindarique both in technique and imagination. In their verse, Pindariques are free in so far as the lengths of stanza and of line, the disposition of the shorter and longer lines in the stanza, and the placing of the rhymes, are wholly at the discretion of the poet; the stanza need fall into no regular pattern, nor is one stanza to repeat the pattern of another. The metre, however, is consistently iambic. . . . Together with a dearth of verbal music, these over-worked conceits and hyperboles (often trite to begin with) afflict the genre, as it proliferates among imitators, with a mass of unnaturally inflated but incurably prosaic verse.⁸

Brooks thinks that whatever thrill Pindarics might once have provided is now gone. Even in freedom they have been superseded. The "much bolder styles of verse" must refer to "free" verse and its various hybrids and derivatives. Brooks does not consider the possibility that these much bolder styles of verse might be in any way connected to the Pindaric's earlier boldness, regarding them as simply disparate phenomena, even though the central complaint which Brooks rehearses—that the lesser Pindarics, at least, are "incurably prosaic"—also dogs free verse. But this characterization of Pindarics is descriptively misleading in one important respect. The meter is not consistently iambic, if by "consistently" we are to understand always and in every Pindaric. The exceptions are vital.

Consider what might be thought of as the inaugural English Pindaric, Abraham Cowley's poem "The Resurrection":

The Resurrection

1.

Not *Winds* to *Voyagers* at Sea,
Nor *Showers* to *Earth* more necessary be,
(*Heav'ens* vital *seed* cast on the *womb* of *Earth*
    To give the *fruitful Year* a *Birth*)

Then *Verse* to *Virtue*, which can do
The *Midwifes* Office, and the *Nurses* too;   5
It *feeds* it strongly, and it *cloathes* it gay,
    And when it dyes, with comely pride
Embalms it, and erects a *Pyramide*
      That never will decay
    Till *Heaven* it self shall melt away,   10
And nought behind it stay.

2.

Begin the *Song*, and strike the *Living Lyre*;
Lo how the *Years to come*, a numerous and well-fitted *Quire*,
All hand in hand do decently advance,
And to my *Song* with smooth and equal measures *dance*.   15
Whilst the *dance* lasts, how long so e're it be,
 My *Musicks* voyce shall bear it companie.
    Till all *gentle Notes* be drown'd
    In the *last Trumpets* dreadful sound.
That to the *Spheres* themselves shall *silence* bring,   20
    Untune the *Universal String*.
    Then all the wide extended *Sky*,
    And all th'*harmonious Worlds* on high,
    And *Virgils* sacred *work* shall dy.
And he himself shall see in one *Fire* shine   25
Rich *Natures* ancient *Troy*, though built by *Hands Divine*.

3.

    Whom *Thunders* dismal noise,
And all that *Prophets* and *Apostles* louder spake,
And all the *Creatures* plain *conspiring voyce*,
    Could not whilst they *liv'ed*, awake,   30
    This mightier sound shall make
      When *Dead* t'arise,
    And open *Tombs*, and open *Eyes*
To the long *Sluggards* of five thousand years.
This *mightier Sound* shall *make* its *Hearers Ears*.   35
Then shall the scatter'd *Atomes* crowding come
    Back to their *Ancient Home*,
    Some from *Birds*, from *Fishes* some,
    Some from *Earth*, and some from *Seas*,
    Some from *Beasts*, and some from *Trees*.   40

Some descend from *Clouds* on high,
Some from *Metals* upwards fly.
And where th'*attending Soul* naked, and shivering stands,
Meet, salute, and joyn their hands.
As disperst *Souldiers* at the *Trumpets* call,   45
Hast to their *Colours* all.
Unhappy most, like *Tortur'ed Men*,
Their *Joynts* new *set*, to be new *rackt* agen.
To *Mountains* they for *shelter* pray,
The Mountains shake, and run about no less *confus'd* then *They*.   50

4.

Stop, stop, my *Muse*, allay thy vig'rous heat,
Kindled at a *Hint* so Great.
Hold thy *Pindarique Pegasus* closely in,
Which does to *rage* begin,
And this steep *Hill* would gallop up with violent course,   55
'Tis an unruly, and a *hard-Mouth'd Horse*,
Fierce, and unbroken yet,
Impatient of the *Spur* or *Bit*.
Now *praunces* stately, and anon *flies* o're the place,
Disdains the *servile Law* of any settled *pace*,   60
Conscious and *proud* of his own *natural force*.
'Twill no *unskilful Touch* endure,
But flings *Writer* and *Reader* too that *sits* not *sure*.[9]

One consequence of the consensus about the inert irregularity of Pindarics
is that not much attention has been paid to what one might expect to look
for first: to the way in which an individual Pindaric is put together. If one
does something as simple as attempt to determine the rhyme scheme for this
poem, one already discovers important facts and difficulties:

1: a8 a10 b10 b8 c8 c10 d10 e8 (e)10 d6 d8 d6
2: a10 a14 b10 b12 c10 c10 d7 d8 e10 e8 f8 f8 f8 g10 g12
3: a6 b12 a10 b8 b6 c4 c8 d10 d10 e10 (e)6 e7 f7 f7 g7 g7 h12 h7 i10 i6 j8
   j10 k8 k14
4: a10 (a)6 b11 b6 c12 c10 d6 (d)8 e12 e12 c10 f8 f12

This is a mere schema rather than an analysis, so it glosses over certain important issues. Line lengths are given as a number (of syllables) but no fur-

ther metrico-rhythmic specification is attempted. Parentheses, here, indicate an approximate rhyme, varieties of which are thus not fully differentiated in this schema; more seriously, the schema does not register rhymes which operate across, rather than within, verse paragraphs (and this term itself is also unsatisfactory, so that one might prefer "sections": these groups are clearly not in any satisfactory sense "stanzas," and yet "paragraphs" implies a no more pertinent equable forward momentum). I want to return to the shortcomings of this schema, but note for now the strong prevalence of adjacent rhyming in Cowley's poem. The second verse section contains no cross-rhyming at all, and the third, and longest, hardly any. One effect of this is a metacommunicative signal. The continual use of adjacent rhyming, and the fact that these adjacent rhymes are very often couplets, can produce a sense that Cowley's Pindaric is in fact not certainly a form of lyric at all—that it is a strange kind of hybrid of a fantasy of irregular lyric, on the one hand, with something much more leisurely, the expository couplet poem, on the other. The hybridity of Cowleian Pindaric particularly shows up at those points where couplets turn into triplets, or occasionally quadruplets, or, quite exceptionally, quintuplets and sextuplets.[10] These moments can feel, depending on the circumstances, either like moments of inertia, at which the poet gets stuck, as it were, on an individual rhyme from which he cannot think how to escape, or, instead, like moments of reaffirmation.

Much depends on meter. Where the multiple adjacent recurrence of a rhyme coincides with a transient development of something like a regular beat, a sense of heightened rhythmicality can be produced. Where, however, the same rhyme trickles across three lines of different lengths, the effect is perhaps more likely to be one of a certain dwindling. Compare, for example, the final three lines of the first stanza with the triplet in the second stanza. At 8–11, the six-eight-six pattern of line length gives the triple rhyme an oddly dilatory feel and perhaps encourages us to hear it in relation to the suggestions about "melting away," decaying and nothing staying. At 22–24, by contrast, even though we are again dealing with an account of the end of everything, the effect produced by three consecutive rhymes is quite different, because the metrical conditions are different (three successive eights) and because syntax coincides with rather than interrupting these metrical units. The effect is almost triumphant, even though the poet is talking about the total destruction not only of the mere universe but also of the most imperishable works of classical civilization.

At this point I want to return to the question of the inadequacy of the schema sketched above. One problem which it drastically abridges is that of how long a rhyme stays a rhyme before it decays. The usual algebra of rhyme schemes performs adequately for brief lyrics but breaks down a little in the face of the Pindaric. We cannot say, in fact, when a line-terminal syllable might have expired as a possible provider of rhyme, since this question is not primarily one of time or space but of affective charge, of memory. Supposing a given line to be powerfully enough imprinted on our minds, then any sonic replay of its final syllable in a line-terminal position later in the poem might potentially be a rhyme with it, however far distant, because the concept of rhyme does not describe an inherent property of a textual object, but an aspect of the performance (silent or audible, scripted or recollected) and interpretation of poems.

This difficulty emerges as an aporia in the above schema. I recommence the algebra at the beginning of each verse section; otherwise it would trace rhyme effects that may not really be operative. Yet there are also difficulties with this, because no consistent rule can be established. Returning to 22–24, it could be argued that this triplet, together with this regularity, fixes in our minds its rhymes, so that we remember them when we come in the next stanza, to high/fly, which after all contains the same word in one case. English Pindarics in this way become studies in rhyme decay. How long does it take a rhyme to go out, to stop burning? This problem is also posed within verse sections, because one of the corollaries of the high prevalence of adjacent rhymes, and their conversions into triplets and quadruplets, is that cross-rhymes then take quite a long time to come back, to the extent that we may already have half-forgotten them. Take the rhyme of "course" (55), "Horse" (56), and "force" (61) in the final section. Two couplets intervene before "force," and one of them (59–60) has a consonance with our rhyme itself. I did not at first when preparing this analysis notice that "force" was in fact intended as a rhyme for "Horse." "Horse" is the second rhyme in its couplet. There is no necessary sense of expectation induced by it: we are not waiting for a rhyme to it, so we can miss it when it comes. The after-rhyme, "force," feels like an afterthought.

All this, I now want to suggest, needs to be understood primarily in relation to the irregular Pindaric's outstanding technical feature, underestimated by Brooks: its metrical instability.[11] The extreme variations in line length, even where iambicity is indeed maintained, have a more powerfully dislocating effect than is sometimes admitted. There is a tension between the typographical integrity of the line, its ungainsayable givenness as a printed unit, and its metrical friability. Derek Attridge comments in his *Rhythms of English Poetry* on the tendency of the fourteener to break down into an eight and a six, the components, that is, of ballad meter.[12] When fourteeners appear alongside lines of eight and six syllables, there is a good chance that to the ear they may break down into separate lines. Equally, where sixes and fours are next to tens, there is a chance that they may to the ear coalesce into larger lines. Because the line length is arbitrarily variable, that is, its alterations can produce a metrical instability which penetrates the entire composition, rather than being a merely superficial feature. This does not necessarily make it good or powerful in any way. The "prosaic" quality which Brooks detects is produced by metrical instability rather than metrical conformity.

And this metrical instability produced by line length is, despite what Brooks says about iambicity, also exacerbated by the fact that this poem is in a much more fundamental way polymetrical. A number of the lines in it are trochaic. They bear what Attridge calls a "falling" cadence (108–14, 129–32). This is most obviously the case in the passage of seven-syllable lines in the third stanza. These lines (38–42, 44) produce an entirely new prosodic note which has not at all been heard in the poem so far. The passage in question has a kind of incantatory music, because suddenly we have an extremely regular and extremely marked pattern of stresses reproduced in a number of successive couplets. This is then heightened further still by what Roger Fowler would call the "syntactic rhyming" of the lines themselves: not only the repeated anaphora of the word "some," but the entire syntactical structure of the line is in one case repeated.[13] Just how bizarre the metrico-rhythmic effects which Cowley can produce are, in fact, becomes clear right at the end of this passage (42–44). This sequence of five falling sevens suddenly gives way to a ragged rising twelve; yet immediately after this we go straight back to another falling seven.

This single interruption, devastating to the poem's metrico-rhythmic equilibrium and to the reader's sense of it, indicates that the metrical instability present in Cowley's Pindaric is much more than superficial. We should remember not to exaggerate the contrast between falling or rising rhythms, or between iambic and trochaic, if we want to call them that, because in many poems of this and later periods, rising eights and falling sevens could move along quite nicely together without any sense that the poem is polymetrical, without any sense, that is, that the underlying *meter* changes from one line to the next.[14] But this is why Cowley's variable line length is so important. It completely changes the meaning and effect of shifts from falling to rising rhythms. To shift from a falling seven to a rising eight need not produce the sense that anything much has changed, but in 42–43, the shift from a falling seven to a rising twelve produces, in fact, something much more like a sense that the machine is stalling or at least that the gears are grinding.

All this, I want to argue, has a much more than decorative or illustrative or thematic effect. It could be mistaken for expressive display but is not. What it means is that it is difficult to read the poem out without making a number of mistakes. It is easy to forget how much of the work a firmly established metrical set does *for* us in telling us how to read a poem. But determining a metrical set is something we have to do as we go along. We preread in this way; we take a guess based on a number of appearances, and pitch in. But in a polymetrical poem, we have continually to allow for the possibility that the entire metrical set, not merely the rhythmic realization of it, may be about to change, and in the Pindaric, of course, it can change at any point and for any length of time: the changes are not predictable, nor, in the absence of predictive typography, are we even warned about them.

It is certainly the case that this does not make for a "satisfying" rhythmic experience. It means, instead, that the poem is constantly threatened with a collapse into prose. Cowley's metaphor for this, of course, is the horse. It is especially impressive: a flying horse. All the more likelihood, then, that we might fall off it. What is needed, as usual, is a way of reconstructing, reimagining, and then reexperiencing the affects which were at stake in readings of these poems. Cowley's final line, which seems entirely deliberately to come off the horse, appears to suggest that the poem is a test of the reader's or performer's skill as well as the writer's. The pleasures of the Pindaric, that is, are in part masochistic, like those of an arcade racing-car game in which the challenge is to avoid crashing into the barrier. It is a well-established tradition in Christian apologetic deliberately to intensify the improbability of the resurrection of the flesh. The more improbable such an event is made to seem, the more miraculous God's ability to whistle each least atom and nerve out of those beds, bogs, and oceans in which they might have lain concealed and scattered, and back into the living individual.[15] This tradition always courts bathos, and Cowley's risible mountains, "confused" and running about looking for a safe place, are well within it. But Pindaric framing of this topos adds one further instrument and risk to this arsenal and venture, the instrument and risk of structural metrical instability.

"The Resurrection" is Janus-faced, looking back to sacred paradox and to a fantasy about Pindar, forward to the both exhilarating and compromised freedoms of free verse. Pindaric liberty is also and at the same time the moment of the invention of the possibility of bathos as a structural feature of the poem's metrico-rhythmic, melodic, and rhymological organization. The risk of prose is more deliberatively and consciously courted than at any previous point in English verse. The freedom to soar, the freedom to write about anything whatever, and the freedom to fall flat on one's face are to remain intimately related in the history of the Ode which follows on from Cowley.

Antistrophe

Keston Sutherland's new poem *Hot White Andy* has within a small circle of British readers and critics already generated a good deal of intelligent commentary.[16] One of the primary facts about this poem (and about this kind of poem) is its particular way of segmenting language into verse. This is at once one of the most superficial and one of the most deeply embedded features of this writing. One of the most superficial, not only because it is something which can be seen at a glance even by anyone who picks up the book and idly leafs through it for a few minutes before returning it to the table at the side of the poetry reading, but also because this fact of its being the first thing that meets the eye has long had a preponderant impact on what is done with verse. Verse is tendentially metacommunicative, in the sense that when the modes of segmentation and disposition of language in poetry cease to be a matter of shared resource and become instead a territory of contest among different parties in practitioners' poetics, verse segmentation and its detail tend to become a series of badges of party poetical affiliations. Yet "most deeply embedded," at the same time, because significant verse also fights this symbolicization of verse segmentation tooth and lung; seeks, by rendering its own cuts metacommunicatively illegible, to revive segmentation and the metrico-rhythmic signatures connected with it as a resource for poetic thinking. Thus, while it is imaginable that it could be correct (although I doubt it) to think of prosody as a merely surface effect from the standpoint of phonology, say, this characterization would be one-sided in the case of verse practice itself, where segmentation is at one and the same time the poetry's surface or its face and the site of its most stubborn and therefore deeply concealed resistance to symbolic thinking. This is just what makes of it both the most intimately effective aspect of poetry and at the same time something which it is almost impossible to make explicit without killing it stone dead.

I want to begin on *Hot White Andy*, though, with the same naively enumerating angle of approach which I tried with Cowley, jotting down the kind of elementary thing that anyone can see as soon as she opens the book and proceeding thence to the poem's interior wishes.

Sutherland's poem is quite clearly not one which could have been written by Cowley. Yet it ought to be clear that it is not one which could have been written without Cowley, either—that is, it could not have been written without Cowley's invention of the kind of ode employing the very extreme swerves of meter and rhythm and of line length represented by "The Resurrection." As we shall see, even though Sutherland's poem is by no means metrical, and even though it does not exploit the effects of line-terminal rhyme characteristic of Cowley's Pindarics, it has its own version of sublime or bathetic drastic transition from the substantially prosaic to the incantatorily lyrical, transitions which involve not only the sorts of disruption of syntax and topic which we have come to think of as belonging to so-called "free" verse, but which also draw on most of the repertoire of effects available to a poet like Cowley: rhyme, repetition, verbal instrumentation, contrasting line length, and so on. *Hot White Andy* is, I shall contend, not an abated but a sort of "hyper-" Pindaric. Effects made possible centuries ago by Cowley are taken as resources for bringing "free" verse to a point of visible crisis.

The poem is not metrical, but it is not merely unmetrical either. It is instead what one might call polyunmetrical. It is in three sections: *.A*, *.B*, and *.A*: TURBO. Not only tripartition but algebraic labeling recall strophe, antistrophe, and epode, certainly, but also a critique of positive negation, a refusal to allow two minuses to add up to a plus: there is no section *.C*.[17] Within each section there are markedly different sorts of blocks of text—mostly left-justified ones which then nevertheless break up into complex indentational patterns, rough shifts rightward of a tab; "lyric song-like structures, four of them each in five quatrain" (Prynne, "Keston Sutherland" 80); and, in *.A*: TURBO, passages of dramatic dialogue which are mostly in left-justified verse but can also become prose, in a smaller letter. There is a contrast, which Neil Pattison has explored, between what goes on in the first two kinds of text block. Nevertheless, the two are also cross-contaminated at every level (Pattison 84–94).

You pick it up and work out quite quickly what the main types of text are. The "first" thing one reads in this sense is the whole book, the prereading skim of orientation which proliferates hypotheses about what kind of thing this thing in front of us might be, and what kinds of sortings we might need to apply to its material. The next thing read, in those cases where reading continues, might be the beginning of the poem:

> Lavrov and the Stock Wizard levitate over to
> the blackened dogmatic catwalk and you eat them. Now swap
> *buy* for *eat*, then *fuck* for *buy*, then *ruminate* for *fuck*,
> phlegmophrenic, want to go to the windfarm,
> *Your* ·kids menu lips swinging in the Cathex-Wizz monoplex;   5
> *Your* ·face lifting triple its age in Wuhan die-cut peel lids;
> ng pick *Your* out the reregulated loner PAT to to screw white
> chocolate to the bone. The tension in an unsprung

r trap co
    → · The tension in an unsprung trap.   10
       ck QUANT unpruned wing: sdeigne of JOCK
       of how I together grateful anyway I was
       Its sacked glass, *Punto*
          → What is
be done on the sly is manic gargling, *to*   15
to blacken the air in hot manic recitative from a storm throat,
WLa-15 types *to* Tungsten electrodes Aaron Zhong,
feazing that throat into fire / under its
hot life the rope light thrashes in its suds, [is] *Your* chichi news noose
/ Dr. Unicef Cheng budget slasher movie hype on *Late Review*
                                                    20

I keep dreaming about you every single night last
night I you making love Stan, I didn't know him then
it hurts, and I disappear but the nights stick.

What is going on? Longer sentences than are ordinarily deployed by late
modernist verse are being subjected to a variety of interferences. These interferences do not generally work to produce wholly unworkable syntax, but
partially to deface it. The most obvious interference is the very fact of segmentation into verse itself. That segmentation works now violently ("to /
the," 1–2; "white / chocolate," 7–8; "*to* / to," 15–16), now rhetorically (5, 6,
10, 23). No numerical or metrical principle of segmentation is fully apparent, but there is a contrast between lines of very roughly similar lengths,
left-justified, and others which are tabbed inward to varying degrees. Even
the attempt to produce upper and lower syllable counts for these lines is
impeded, however, because in a number of lines there are clusters of letters
or phonemes which do not amount to a syllable: "ng" (7); "*r*" (9); "ck" (11);
"WLa" (17) In others there are symbols whose potential vocalic realization
is a matter of conjecture or improvisation for readers: notably "→" and "·".

From one point of view these obstacles to metrico-rhythmic analysis might
be thought of as a continuation of the Pindaric's initial venture at making
anything whatever part of the stuff it can work over. On the next page we
find the line "(*pw* symbolized by 3 gummy ribs: check http://lion.chadwyck
.com)." Even as I type this, my computer has helpfully turned the last part
of the line blue and underlined it, just in case I should want to deposit any
credits there right now, which, indeed, I could easily do, since I am now net-
worked: producing the feeling in me that I quite intensely do not want to
check this or care at this juncture what the "3 gummy ribs" might be. The

line's tumble into prose is a late descendant of "But flings *Writer* and *Reader* too, that *sits* not *sure.*"

With this recognition we might begin to detect some of the affective codings at work in all this interference. The verse slams over the barrier here, and a certain play-masochism (but masochism proper is play-masochism) on the reader's part is required to relish it. Yet this is not quite the force of "ng," "r," "ck," "WLa," "→," and "·." One kind of narrative might have these as ultraprosaic materials in whose case verse is showing that it can absorb, can work over, even these: a variant on the story of the autonomization of the work of art. Instead, the last two of these, at least, may be part of what is doing the working over. "→" is a marked underlining, as it were, of the tab which is imposed upon the lines which merely follow it. Like a kind of pointing equivalent of echolalia, it looks as though it might be mocking the portentousness of the tab itself. It snarls at the imaginary efficacity of shunting the text a few centimeters right—"like we could care less!" In doing so it forms a sort of reflex protest against the symbolicization of a prosodic code like indentation, that the indentation of a block of text in this fashion, for example, recalls the layout of much of J. H. Prynne's *The White Stones*, many of whose poems work with extended blocks of text at two or three depths of indentation. It is as though "→ " were a marker for a gesture on the poet's part, a hand movement trying to shove the text across the page against its will.

"·" is a slightly different case. It is a bullet point, of course, an item in the silent prosody of administrative reason, whose function is to set out a list without order, in which every item may be taken as being in principle of equal importance and as being granted equal prominence by being preceded by this bullet point. In this sense, the bullet point codifies total indefiniteness and obscurity as the essence of administrative clarity. In place of the potentially enormously delicate and elaborate learned rhythms of thinking represented by the sentence and the paragraph, these are something like anti-verbs, informing the viewer of them that what is required on his part is not ("difficult") comprehension but ("helpful") assent. We can begin to imagine a sort of prosodic value for "→," in that it connects visibly with an existing cue within a prosodic repertoire, indentation; "·," on the other hand, tempts performers positively to invent some little mouth or throat or tooth gesture, some click or gulp or clack, or perhaps some hand movement or some facial expression, which might put it into the poem. Verse demands, in proposing "·," that administrative reason speak up for itself, that its disappearing act be disbelieved.

These most obvious excrescences are a clue to what is happening at more deeply ramified levels of the verse. Even as the principle of segmentation becomes less evident than in obviously metrical verse, the fact of segmentation itself is more visibly insisted upon. Thus at 9–11, "co . . . ck" is severed not by a line break—this would be a bad joke—but by an intervening whole line, a tab, and a redundant tab sign. An attempt at a rhyme like a sticking plaster on a severed member then follows at the end of that very line, shouting to cover its dismay: "JOCK." The rhyme is ultrasubliminal because the severing of the word has destroyed the rhyme syllable. We have already said "coh" to ourselves by this time, so the rhyme can be put together only retrospectively, something which that part of any reader's mind which might be absorbed in such things is perhaps half-flapping at for the next few lines together. The line which interposes between "co" and "ck" has already been preordered at 8: but there, "unsprung" and "trap" are scissored not merely by a line break but by the mystifying and only partially rhythmizable character *r*.

The trap is sprung, as though the poem were, apotropaically, miming the pitiless devices the poet would like to escape. If poems are no longer thought to do anything at all to anyone, if this is widely understood as superstition, we nevertheless know all sorts and types of devices that can do all sorts of things to people, apparently of their own volition. Hence the poem's interest in inhabiting these devices in their own false first person: "I am adaptable for Binzel and Lincoln and Panasonic." Within the text itself, further "operator" functions, analogous with "→" and "·," are spelled out manually. Thus the instruction in 2–3, if followed literally, produces a further three lines which are not printed in the text but might nevertheless be considered to be part of it: "the blackened dogmatic catwalk and you buy them," "the blackened dogmatic catwalk and you fuck them," and "the blackened dogmatic catwalk and you ruminate them." The poem is trying to get a grip on something infinitely slippery—the total fungibility of everything with everything else in pansecuritized late capitalism, replace *x* with *y*—by the method of total immersion. The buried pun in "dogmatic catwalk" is the kind of thinking wrinkle which this poet everywhere salts his lines with: just as in Shelley, for example, wit's rubs and flips quite often detain that attention which the syntax and rhythm are at the same time irresistibly pressing forward.

Epode

The approach in this essay has deliberately attempted to count the small change. The large notes will not take care of themselves, but one or two suggestions may be ventured. The Pindaric starts as an invented tradition and then keeps getting reinvented, generally without the label. These connections do not, then, form that kind of tradition which would be a sort of unbroken relay race, what Wilkinson has memorably abhorred as "nightmare plangency, a tabernacle choir which absorbs every poet from Homer to Bruce Andrews."[18] They form instead a complex. On the one hand, they are a tradition of destroying and forgetting tradition in order to be free from it—that kind of anti- and pseudo-tradition which we have become accustomed to think of as "modernity." On the other hand, they deploy, mutilate, and grow traditions which are by no means constructs or simulacra but modes of largely inexplicit practical expertise and virtuosity in the particular handlings of given metrico-rhythmic repertoires such as the English heroic line. This complex is part of the forgotten prehistory of "free" verse. The finest late-twentieth-century English hyper-Pindarics—"Of Sanguine Fire,"[19] "Harmolodics,"[20] *Hot White Andy*—march into this area of damage not in order to dress in old clothes, to whatever gallant or ironic effect, but so as to push at the necessary entanglement between archaism and innovation in contemporary verse. *Hot White Andy* works out a determinate negation of that fantasy of abstract freedom which is improperly, but indelibly, associated with free verse. Diversion is itself diverted. It at the same time works voice further into print and print further into voice, subverting nothing but the needless assumption that literacy would mean the end of orality. Active inside whatever is still "active" now in "Romanticism" remain traditions and repertoires of verse thinking which long predate that retrospective classification—to such an extent that, it is suggested, late modernism's active recuperations of eighteenth- and seventeenth-century verse thinking are still more obscured, and no less essential, even than its relation to "Romanticism."

Notes

1. For one example, see Alexander Pope, *Ode for Musick* (London, 1713).

2. For the former, see the contributions to *Publications of the Modern Language Association of America* 123.1 (January 2008); for the latter, see Prynne 78–83; Neil Pattison 84–94. See also Ladkin 271–322.

3. de Silentio 1–123.

4. Culler 205. Especially valuable is Culler's refusal of that poetics of lyric which, conceiving of lyric merely as a subset of narrative, converts all lyric into a species of dramatic monologue: "Criticism and pedagogy, reacting against the Romantic notion of lyric as an expression of intense personal experience, have adopted the model of the dramatic monologue as the way to align poetry with the novel: the lyric is conceived as a fictional imitation of the act of a speaker,

and to interpret the lyric is to work out what sort of person is speaking, in what circumstances and with what attitude or, ideally, drama of attitudes . . . the New Criticism's insistence that interpretation focus on the words on the page, not on the author, which generated the assumption that the speaker of a lyric is not the poet but a persona" (201).

5. "O the just Contrast! O the beauteous strife! / 'Twixt their cool writings, and *Pindaric* life! / They write with Phlegm, but then they live with Fire; / *They* cheat the Lender, and their *works* the Buyer" (E. Young 7).

6. Joseph Addison, *The Spectator*, 6 Sept. 1712.

7. Scodel 186.

8. Brooks xxxvii–xxxviii.

9. Text: *The Poems of Abraham Cowley*, ed. A. R. Waller (Cambridge: Cambridge UP, 1905), 182–86.

10. For an example of a sextuplet, cf. "Brutus" in Cowley 195–97; lines 9–14.

11. The "reform" introduced by Congreve in *A Pindarique Ode* and thereafter widely imitated (in, for example, Gray's "The Bard"), in which the metrical and rhyme patterns of strophes and epodes may be freely devised, but in which each subsequent strophe and antistrophe must exactly reproduce the metrical and rhyme pattern of the first strophe, and each epode of the first epode, creates a completely different compositional mode and a completely different mode of verse thinking. Instead of working away from and back to repertoire, the poet is now pouring words into a highly elaborate mold. In this essay, only the irregular, and not the Congrevian, Pindaric is in question.

12. Attridge 87–89.

13. Fowler 184–99.

14. For an example, see the closing passage of Collins 46–52.

15. "But the Resurrection of the *Body* is discernible by no other light, but that of *Faith*, nor could be fixed by any lesse assurance, than an *Article* of the *Creed*. Where be all the splinters of that Bone, which a shot hath shivered and scattered in the Ayre? Where be all the Atoms of that flesh, which a *Corrasive* hath eat away, or a *Consumption* hath breath'd, and exhal'd away, from our arms, and other Limbs? . . . and still, still God knows in what *Cabinet* every *seed-Pearle* lies; and, *sibilat populum suum*, (as his Prophet speaks in another case), he whispers, he hisses, he beckens for the bodies of his Saints, and in the twinckling of an eye, that body that was scattered over all the elements, is sate down at the right hand of God, in a glorious resurrection" (Donne, "Sermon Preached" 98).

16. See, in addition to the sources mentioned above, Wilkinson; also Cooke 323–40.

17. Adorno, "Kritik der positiven Negation," *Negative Dialektik* 161–63.

18. John Wilkinson, "Off the Grid: Lyric and Politics in Andrea Brady's *Em-*

brace," *The Lyric Touch: Essays on the Poetry of Excess* (Great Wilbraham, UK: Salt Publishing, 2007), 131.

19. J. H. Prynne, "Of Sanguine Fire," *Poems* (Edinburgh: Agneau 2, 1982), 174–78.

20. John Wilkinson, "Harmolodics," *Parataxis: Modernism and Modern Writing* 1 (1991), 4–7.

9
Dysachrony

Temporalities and Their Discontents, in New and
Old Romanticisms

Judith Goldman

for Stacy Doris

Among other consequences of the death of the author, consider the following:

The text stands in our stead as though we were dead, has always already
entertained contexts that we, in *propria persona*, will never enter, grounded
only in the groundless inhumanity of writing. Dying in the distributed non-
instaurations of text as network (textile, "tissue of quotations"), the author
dies, too, in reading's multiplicity.

The pathos of this nostalgic textual paradigm becomes the more pro-
nounced, and perhaps the more impelling, when Life itself is at stake. For
the unrestful (now defunded) repositories of the many tons of nuclear waste
we gift to civilizations ten thousand years hence, the Environmental Protec-
tion Agency had tasked the Department of Energy with inventing warning
signage.[1] A reverse "Ozymandias": for the monument *will be here* (in this instance we may unfortunately use the future anterior without hesitation); it is
the title-claim that will be missing. A necessary-impossible ethical demand:
for not only must the toxins be identified, but the radically postdated Other
whom the message would serve must be envisioned. And it is only a strictly
unimaginable reader who should here be imagined.[2]

All writing is out of time . . . Yet here lies its endemic anachronism in ex-
tremis. In biopolitics.

$\sim$

One is reminded of the (fictional) *Essay on the Pericyclical Motions of the
Earth's Axis* by the astronomer Merrival, in Mary Shelley's *The Last Man*
(1826). A science fiction novel set in the twenty-first century, *The Last Man*
relates the story of human extinction through plague, yet Merrival, as described by narrator Lionel Verney, "was far too long sighted in his view of

humanity to heed the casualties of the day": "Merrival talked of the state of mankind six thousand years hence. He might with equal interest to us, have added a commentary, to describe the unknown and unimaginable lineaments of the creatures, who would then occupy the vacated dwelling of mankind" (M. Shelley 290). Here and elsewhere, the anachronistic Merrival provides one of several painfully ironic paradisiacal millenarian visions that appear in the book, allusions to the oversanguine political theory of Shelley's father, William Godwin, and husband, Percy Bysshe Shelley, on the perfectibility of humankind.[3] (Indeed, in the first edition of *An Enquiry Concerning Political Justice* [1793], Godwin asked rhetorically, "Why may not man one day be immortal?"[4]; in a displaced killing of the father['s science], Shelley kills off the human race.)

In the introduction to *The Last Man* Shelley fabulates the provenance of the novel: in 1818, she and a companion (her husband) discover the Cumaean Sybil's cavern in the Bay of Naples, where they find the Sybilline leaves inscribed in a number of ancient and—impossibly—*modern* languages; the ancient leaves contain prophecies of "events but lately passed," as well as, apparently, of those still to come (pictured in the novel). If *The Last Man* was a late arrival to the post–French Revolution "last man" genre, its "extremity . . . bears comparison with twentieth-century existentialist, absurdist, and nihilist reactions to two World Wars, the Holocaust, and the atomic bomb" (Lokke 116). Thus out of her time, Shelley's affective treatment of her material, no less her content, is futuristic. Yet her sensibility also reaches back to divine past, or, rather, original, affinities with the very first man, Adam. The epigraph to her novel cites another moment of prophecy, the dreadful vision of the diluvian future the angel Michael shows Adam when he leaves paradise—of, as Milton puts it, "The end of all thy offspring, end so sad, / Depopulation!" (11: 755–56). To which Adam responds, as Shelley quotes:

Let no man seek
Henceforth to be foretold what shall befall
Him or his children. (11: 770–72)[5]

Her family decimated—Fanny Imlay, three children, her husband, and, further back, her mother—it would seem Shelley had little ruth to spare this plea for ignorance, that is, for alpha and omega sundered.

〜

Anna Laetitia Barbauld's tour de force *Eighteen Hundred and Eleven* (1812), too, tells "the history of the future," projecting an epoch past imperial Britain's demise—when London has become a ruin to be visited by Americans of the next centuries.[6] As Emily Rohrbach notes, Barbauld's poem "renders the familiar present itself in historical perspective—that is, as a time as strange and remote as the past had come to be" (181), and this extraordinarily beautiful, ambitious poem becomes, perhaps, the more uncanny through the surety of its pentameter couplets as they sententiously dole out Fate.

Aggressively critical of the massive scale of death and suffering involved in the near-decade of the Napoleonic Wars (which followed the ten years of the French Revolutionary Wars) and written on the eve of the War of 1812, which was to become a major conflict, Barbauld met with the extreme ire of her male contemporary reviewers, for *Eighteen Hundred and Eleven* took the world historical fable of liberalism too far, pushing progress past the end of history to British decline. While, on one hand, the poem provokingly posits that America takes up Empire's mantle, what seems, on the other, even more subversive is its critique of militarized, imperial capitalism: though England proper has yet to be invaded, Barbauld writes, "Britain, know, / Thou who has shared the guilt must share the woe. / Ruin [. . .] is here" (lines 45–49); "Thy baseless wealth dissolves in air away" (line 53); "Yes, thou must droop; thy Midas dream is o'er" (line 61). Through her use of the present tense, the poet seamlessly joins this passage describing future doom to the passage on present-day events with which the poem begins:

> Still the loud death drum, thundering from afar,
> O'er the vext nations pours the storm of war:
> To the stern call still Britain bends her ear. (lines 1–3)

This rhetorization of grammar not only blurs time, lending a proleptic description the certainty of the contemporary moment but also (as the repetition of "still" in these opening lines indicates) creates a sense of a present in distended extension, with the ongoingness of the war.

Yet the poem does employ the future tense to describe how the accomplishments of British civilization will be remembered, in turn commenting on its own temporal divagations: "Where wanders Fancy down the lapse of years / Shedding o'er imaged woes untimely tears?" (lines 113–14). Openly acknowledging its anachronic itinerary, Barbauld refers with "the lapse of years" to *future* time (she might have written "*when* wanders Fancy" rather than "where"), going on to project Britain's return to "Night, Gothic, night . . ." (line 121), when "Time may tear the garland from her brow, / And Europe sit in dust, as Asia now" (lines 125–26). And while the poet suggests that a "Spirit" (line 215) or "Genius" (line 241) wanders haphazardly around the globe, choosing a favored nation for a momentary efflorescing of culture that

will inevitably pass away, she finally contradicts this logic of felicitous hap-
penstance to again condemn progress as maker of its own destruction:

> But fairest flowers expand but to decay;
> The worm is in thy core, thy glories pass away;
> Arts, arms and wealth destroy the fruits they bring. (lines 313–15)

~

Coleridge began his book *Sibylline Leaves: A Collection of Poems* (1817) with
putative anachronism, its lead poem one he often claimed written in his
childhood, though all known versions were written much later.[7] This poem
Coleridge titled upon publication, "TIME, Real and Imaginary, An Allegory,"
stating in his preface: "By imaginary Time, I meant the state of a school boy's
mind when on his return to school he projects his being in his day dreams,
and lives in his next holidays, six months hence: and this I contrasted with
real Time" (iii). And yet, not surprisingly, the allegory seems much more
complicated than that:

> Two lovely children run an endless race,
>   A sister and a brother!
>   This far outstript the other;
> Yet ever runs she with averted face,
> And looks and listens for the boy behind:
>   For he, alas! is blind!
> O'er rough and smooth, with even step he pass'd,
> And knows not whether he be first or last. (v)

Which child represents the temporality of the dreaming schoolboy, and
which "real Time"? The sister, with her redoubled vectors—forward and back—
could be the figure of one split in abstraction or distraction; just as likely is
the brother, lost to the world around him. Or can Coleridge mean that both
children together make up the daydreaming boy?

Perhaps more important here is our sense of Coleridge's untimely collaboration with Walter Benjamin, namely, his "Theses on the Philosophy of
History," where, in Thesis IX, he proposes Paul Klee's painting *Angelus Novus* as an allegorical figure contra the delusional fables of the world history
of modernization and, in the bad Marxism of the Social Democrats, of dialectical historical evolution. Reviling notions of progress and emancipatory
futurity, Benjamin posits the consequences of these ideologies as "one single
catastrophe." A figure for the violence and suffering erased by dominant nar-

ratives, the angel of history is witness to subaltern disaster; blown uncontrollably backward toward the future by the storm of so-called progress, it sees every document of civilization for its barbarity.

Benjamin's model of history and world historical action that would break from catastrophic logic is profoundly anticausal, antilinear—in short, anachronic. To view history as a chain of events—whether conceived as technological development or as the passing of cultural patrimony and political power from one set of victors to the next—is to incorporate an alienated temporality: as Benjamin writes in Thesis XIII, "The concept of the historical progress of mankind cannot be sundered from the concept of its progression through a homogeneous empty time." Benjamin, too, warns against the uses of tradition—even oppositional uses—as an instrumentalizing, reifying "conformism" (Thesis VI) that would illusorily link the present to history, a history as though *made for* a triumphal version of the present, denatured, eugenicized. Indeed, what must be done is "to make the continuum of history explode" (Thesis XV), *to stop time*: "A historical materialist cannot do without the notion of a present which is not a transition, but in which time stands still and has come to a stop" (Thesis XVI). Such a present is a "'time of the now' Jetzeit" that forms a constellation with a past moment by responding to the address of the dead as a force of contestation and antagonism, as resistance to continuity—creating an achronic filiation between "events . . . separated . . . by thousands of years" (Thesis A).[8]

We may see the sister in Coleridge's poem as Angelus Novus. But who or what is the boy who runs behind her? Could he be empty, homogeneous time—"O'er rough and smooth, with even step he pass'd"—or the time of the now, mind out of time—"he, alas! is blind! . . . knows not whether he be first or last"?

∾

One of Jalal Toufic's main theories of artistic creation is based entirely on anachronism: "untimely collaboration":

> Do artists and writers suffer unduly from an "anxiety of influence"? An artist cannot afford this reported anxiety of influence: he or she could not have created while having it, creation being an untimely collaboration.[9]

> Collaboration in the arts and literature is frequently the locus of the sort of paradoxes one encounters in time-travel situations. (115)

> Not being wedged in linear time, philosophical and literary creation is sometimes . . . a collaboration with past cinematic or literary or ar-

tistic works. Complementarily, any artistic or literary work is related
to the future. (35)[10]

∾

One of the more compelling images of *Eighteen Hundred and Eleven* is its
description of England as a metaruin:

> On spoils from every clime their eyes shall gaze,
> Egyptian granites and the Etruscan vase;
> And . . . midst fallen London, they survey
> The stone where Alexander's ashes lay. (lines 209–12)

Here Barbauld alludes to future American tourists viewing not simply
British remains, but the remains the Empire was plundering from past em-
pires (which include, most famously, the Elgin Marbles—much of the Par-
thenon's statuary, removed in a decade-long process by the Earl of Elgin,
completed in 1812). In collusion with its direct condemnation of the current
wars, the representation in *Eighteen Hundred and Eleven* of a ruin-culture-
to-come, William Keach writes, "rejects any prospect of restoration, elaborating instead a form of preservation- and propagation-in-ruin" (par. 14). (If
its remains will evoke past greatness, Britain nonetheless stays ruined.) Barbauld's futurism is also a way of bringing imperial ruination home, as Keach
suggests: "If the present ruins of imperialist war are still distant for Britons
not directly engaged in fighting, the future ruins the poem imagines pervade
the core of the metropole" (par. 12). Yet the efficacy of Barbauld's poem depends, too, on portraying the present home-effects of ruination supposedly
occurring at a distance:

> Oft o'er the daily page some soft-one bends
> To learn the fate of husband, brothers, friends,
> Or the spread map with anxious eye explores,
> Its dotted boundaries and penciled shores,
> Asks *where* the spot that wrecked her bliss is found,
> And learns its name but to detest the sound. (lines 33–38)[11]

∾

Forcefully amalgamating certain suspicions gathering amid the fallout of the
French Revolution, Thomas Malthus's *An Essay on the Principle of Population,
as it affects the Future Improvement of Society, with remarks on the Speculations of Mr. Godwin, M. Condorcet, and Other Writers* (1798) changed futurity (one hazards to say, forever). The essay appeared in the era of the

emergence of modern governmentality (*pace* Foucault, the governance of citizenry as population, one definition of biopolitics). Dealing with domains such as subsistence, reproduction, and public health, the disciplines of governance, medicine, and political economy could expect to regulate these phenomena in keeping with an ideology of progress. But Malthus, with a persuasive mathematical rhetoric that pitted the geometric rate of human growth against the arithmetic rate of food production, constructed a predicament of the human, as Jacques Khalip and David Collingwood put it, "shaped by a constitutive contradiction, a non-negotiable incoherence no administrative effort could finally extirpate."[12]

Malthus's theory of demographic pressure, with its classist pathologization of the procreation of the poor and its dispassionate treatment of banal deprivation and periodic massive catastrophe as necessary correctives to overpopulation, was indeed incorporated into governance (for instance, the antireform Poor Law Amendment Act of 1834). In fact, this bio-*cum*-necropolitik, far from simply accepting Malthus's story of catastrophe as a natural regulatory mechanism, harnessed it as an alibi and as *a productive force* for capitalism and imperialism, even as capitalist depredations recursively incurred disasters seemingly beyond its self-valorization.

~

The first edition of Malthus's *Essay* begins with an apologia on its timeliness. If new thought in natural philosophy and political science have effected an epoch, so has

> the French Revolution, which, like a blazing comet, seems destined either to inspire with fresh life and vigour, or to scorch up and destroy the shrinking inhabitants of the earth . . . [We are] touching on a period big with . . . changes . . . decisive of the future fate of mankind . . .
> . . . the great question is now at issue, whether man shall henceforth start forwards with accelerated velocity towards illimitable, and hitherto unconceived improvement; or be condemned to a perpetual oscillation between happiness and misery, and after every effort remain still at an immeasurable distance from the wished-for goal. (1–3)

We know how Malthus settled this question.

~

Nearly eleven years after the epochal date, the acceleration of the roll-out phase of neoliberalism instigated in the wake of 9/11 continues unabated: as though the towers came down yesterday, we live in a right-revoking state of exception, whose expedient but also real and traumatic referent, whether

explicit or implied, is that fateful event.[13] Living within this seemingly perpetual echo itself echoes the later British Romantic situation vis-à-vis the
French Revolution. "What is particularly striking," Maureen McLane observes, "is the continuing immediacy of the French Revolution: Shelley in
1817 wrote of the 'panic which, like an epidemic transport, seized upon all
classes of men during the excess consequent upon the French Revolution':
he invokes this panic as if it were recent news."[14]

And he was right to, in the sense that it was still *the* political point of reference for the British public. After all, in 1817, as we might note, history
seemed literally to be repeating itself: when the Prince Regent was stoned
on the way to Parliament, habeas corpus was suspended, the Gagging Acts
were reinstated, and there were major sedition trials (and imprisonments).
In 1792–94, there had been hugely sensational sedition and treason trials,
habeas corpus had been suspended in 1794, and the Gagging Acts were first
instated in 1795, which was also when George III was stoned on the way to
Parliament.

Not coincidentally, 1817 is also the year Percy Shelley wrote *The Revolt
of Islam*, an Orientalist romantic epic set in the fictional "Argolis," a representation of Greece under Turkish rule. As set out in his preface, Shelley's
purpose in this transposition was to replay the Revolution with a difference,
to set out its "beau ideal." What if there had been no Terror? No Tribunal?
No reinstatement of Empire? "When the last hope of trampled France had
failed / Like a brief dream of unremaining glory, / From visions of despair
I rose . . ." the first canto begins. The poem then unfolds a story of a blood-
less coup, in which Ottoman tyranny is overthrown through eloquence and
sympathy: a counterfactual future—what the Revolution might have been.
This subjunctive vision was, for Shelley, a way of reinvigorating a prospec-
tive orientation after the Revolution's failure had dampened futurity altogether (124).

Shelley had directly attacked Malthus in "A Philosophical View of Reform"
(1819), as well as in his prefaces to *Prometheus Unbound* (1820), and *The Revolt of Islam* (1817) (this latter noting a softening in Malthus's position on
"human improvement"). His emphasis on imagining, declared in the "Defence" as poetry's specific labor, "may be seen in part as a resistance or alternative to calculation," as "a commitment to a non-mathematizable future"
(McLane 114, 115). Above all, poets are conduits of anachronism: "Poets are
the hierophants of an unapprehended inspiration, the mirrors of the gigan-
tic shadows which futurity casts upon the present."

Yet *The Revolt of Islam* ends in disaster. The leaders are martyred. The ty-
rant is reinstalled.[15]

～

Toufic cites Kafka: "Art is a mirror, which goes 'fast,' like a watch—some-times."[16]

～

In his portrayal of the "complexity and density of historicist thought in Ro-mantic writing" in *England in 1819*, James Chandler points up the currency of the phrase "the Spirit of the Age," arguing that British Romantic culture was obsessed not only with contemporaneity—a preoccupation, on the En-glish scene, dating from the seventeenth-century pamphlet wars—but also with "comparative contemporaneities," or what Reinhart Koselleck has called "the contemporaneity of the noncontemporaneous."[17] Both are terms for "un-even development."[18]

Central examples for Chandler are Barbauld's *Eighteen Hundred and Eleven* and her later essay "The Uses of History." In that essay, drawing on Scottish Enlightenment philosophy of history, Barbauld goes beyond a simpler con-cept of relative uneven development to theorize chronology as the medium for developmental comparison. Her work is thus one locus of "the emergence of a new conception of anachronism" (Chandler 107): if "peoples of two dif-ferent historical moments [are seen] as belonging to the same state of civiliza-tion" (129), each nation's situation must then also be placed in terms of "the state of the world" as indexed to universal calendrical time. In its very title, *Eighteen Hundred and Eleven* makes evident the poet's cognizance that it mat-ters *when* in linear, chronological history a society has reached a particular stage, "whether a certain society reaches the commercial age, for example, in late antiquity, the Renaissance, or the eighteenth century or whether it has not yet reached it at all" (128). Her texts thus form part of the field of Ro-mantic culture in which "chronologies become better and better calibrated within the increasingly fine-tuned sense of time and timing of the bourgeois public sphere" (129).

～

The French Revolution surfaces in Benjamin's "Theses" as an anachronic event, a true moment of history, self-consciously fashioned against linear, chrono-metrical time: "History is the subject of a structure whose site is not homo-geneous, empty time, but time filled by the presence of the now [*Jetztzeit*]. Thus, to Robespierre ancient Rome was a past charged with the time of the now which he blasted out of the continuum of history" (Thesis XIV). The French Revolution, for Benjamin, thus instantiates a stoppage of time. As Giorgio Agamben puts it in *Infancy and History*: "True historical materi-alism does not pursue an empty mirage of continuous progress along infi-nite linear time, but is ready at any moment to stop time. . . . It is this time which is experienced in authentic revolutions, which . . . have always been lived as a halting of time and an interruption of chronology."[19]

Reinhart Koselleck, in *Futures Past*, creates quite a different, even inverted, description of Revolutionary time, making its "structural change in temporality" key to modern experience. In the period 1500–1800, Koselleck writes, "there occurs a temporalization of history, at the end of which there is a peculiar form of acceleration which characterizes modernity."[20] He, too, turns to Robespierre as a signal figure, specifically to note his urgency to speed time up: "On 10 May 1793 Robespierre, in his famous speech on the Revolutionary Constitution, proclaimed: 'The time has come to call upon each to realize his own destiny. The progress of human Reason has laid the basis of this great Revolution, and the particular day of hastening it has fallen to you'" (7).

The modern model of historical process or progress "opened up a future that transcended the hitherto predictable, natural space of time and experience" as it approached with increasing speed. The experience of the Revolution, Koselleck writes, "seemed to outstrip all previous experience" (33)—no contemporary analysis seemed timely enough to keep up. This "self-accelerating temporality" made the future unpredictable, as it "abbreviated the space of experiences, robbed them of their constancy and continually brought into play new, unknown factors" (17). Yet acceleration also transformed itself "into a concept of historical hope" (37).

Can self-accelerating time allow for a contretemps? It seems that whatever could be viewed as ahead of its time simply becomes a sign of time speeding up, while atavism is a priori ruled out, repressed.

～

Note Thomas Carlyle's deconstruction of acceleration in this passage from *The French Revolution: A History* (1837): "Here perhaps is the place to fix, a little more precisely, what these two words, French Revolution, shall mean. . . . All things are in revolution; in change from moment to moment, which becomes sensible from epoch to epoch: in this Time-World of ours there is properly nothing else but revolution and mutation, and even nothing else conceivable. Revolution, you answer, means speedier change. Whereupon one has still to ask: How speedy?" (154).

～

It is no small irony that in her *Letters Written during a Short Residence in Sweden, Norway and Denmark* (1796) Mary Wollstonecraft becomes subject to unsettling Malthusian visions, given that she was soon to wed William Godwin. This book of philosophical travel writing came out of Wollstonecraft's letters and journals during a 1795 journey when, after nearly three years in

France during the Jacobin takeover and the period of Revolutionary Terror, she had gone to Scandinavia to retrieve a ship and cargo coming from France that had been stolen from her American lover Gilbert Imlay, a blockade runner. As she approached the barren coast of Norway, Wollstonecraft perversely imagined a future in "a million or two of years" with the earth in a state of overpopulation even at its farthest corners.[21]

In an insightful reading of *Letters*, Scott Juengel observes that Wollstonecraft is beset by untimeliness, caught between a new Western understanding of deep geological time, which extended the planetary history indefinitely back before the advent of humanity, as well as forward past its extinction, and the accelerated time of the Revolution, "the political time of the 1790s" (par. 16). Subject to overlapping, incommensurable temporalities—a radical "elongation of time" versus compressed "immediate political chronologies," Wollstonecraft also experienced two disasters—through Jacobin totalitarianism, the loss of the Revolution's potential, and through her daymares of overpopulation, the sense of the inevitability of human catastrophe. Her haunting "by what was to have been the future" of the Revolution seemed to fuel her species-grief; both were cases of melancholia in and through prolepsis (par. 7).

Juengel notes that Wollstonecraft cannot properly be said to have experienced "Malthusian geometrical terror," since *Letters* was written three years prior to Malthus's *Essay* (par. 4). One might propose, however, Malthus's still-influential tract an untimely collaboration with the author of the *Vindications*.

$\sim$

Wollstonecraft's *Letters* reveals her continuing concerns with telling the time, knowing how to be on time, the dependence of the times on geographic situation. In the appendix, for instance, she speaks of "the benevolent reformer [being led] into a labyrinth of error, who aims at destroying prejudices quickly which only time can root out, as the public opinion becomes subject to reason."[22] Rooted in her firsthand experience of the hypertrophied historical agency of the Revolution, such convictions connecting the progress of "reason" to the timeliness of reform give way to a figure of national maturation as organic process, in which it is best not to intervene: "An ardent affection for the human race makes enthusiastic characters eager to produce alteration in laws and governments prematurely . . . [but] they must be the growth of each particular soil, and the gradual fruit of the ripening understanding of the nation, matured by time, not forced by an unnatural fermentation." Oddly enough, as Wollstonecraft continues, we find that this naturalized version of progress is nonetheless one of acceleration: "*And, to convince*

me that such a change is gaining ground with accelerating pace, the view I have
had of society during my northern journey would have been sufficient" (my
emphasis). Thus, a rising velocity of change is not in itself unnatural: we are
brought back to Carlyle: "Revolution, you answer, means speedier change.
Whereupon one has still to ask: How speedy?"

One object-lesson of untimely reform has been given in Letter XVIII,
"Copenhagen," where Wollstonecraft meditates specifically on Denmark as
throwback, the least progressed country she has ever seen, a state of affairs
that draws the late Queen Caroline Matilda into anachronistic relief. Matilda
had been imprisoned and deported for her affair with a lover, the king's doc-
tor, who, taking power during a period of the king's mental illness, enacted
many reforms against Danish custom. With unsurprising sympathy for the
queen, Wollstonecraft opines that her adultery would have been overlooked
if not for the reforming bent of the couple, as it is not for the affair, but "for
her very charities" that Matilda is still posthumously abused by the Danes.
Analyzing the queen's downfall, Wollstonecraft writes: "Disgusted with many
customs which pass for virtues . . . she probably ran into an error common
to innovators, in wishing to do immediately what can only be done by time"
(204). Yet it is only the drag of her atavistic context that installs her in an
untenable future-within-the-present. And this is not the last of the poor
queen's anachronisms: "the hapless Matilda was hurried into an untimely
grave" (206).

〜

Consider Stacy Doris's *Conference* (2001)—an avant-garde work that con-
sorts cross-culturally with an epic poem of the distant past. An untimely collaboration giving onto a future only through anachronic archaic entanglement, *Conference* appropriates or, rather, continues the twelfth-century Sufi
masterpiece *Conference of the Birds* (*Manteq at-Tair*), by the northern Persian poet Farid Ud-Din Attar. (Reciprocally, we might say [via Toufic] that
Attar had drawn on Doris's *Conference*.) Doris's Romantic, politicized time-
sensitivity rhymes with her Romantic concern with human catastrophe—
attending to those epochal events, as well as unending war and structural
violence, that hasten catastrophe and change the very texture of temporality.
Her Romantic dysachrony rhymes, too, with her simultaneous rigorous theo-
rization of and respect for alterity and attempted transcendence of it; with her
fascination with unicity and plurality, divinity and void, the metaphysics of
existence; with her investigations of love, melancholia, and transsubjectivity;
and, perhaps most especially, with her drive to make compelling poetic forms
out of and through these insights.

〜

Attar's 4,500-line *Conference of the Birds* is still revered and well known by present-day Iranians and other enthusiasts of Persian culture. It was written in modern Farsi, during a period of the strong, creative assertion of Persian language and culture after several centuries of the Arabization and Islamization (the Muslim conquest) of Iran. Like Rumi, Attar composed in the *mathnavi* form, a twenty-two-syllable line with internal rhyme considered a "medium par excellence for mystical instruction."[23]

A hagiographer of Sufi saints who was persecuted for heresy, Attar was interested in the more extreme, antinomian, ecstatic forms of Sufism, whose basic tenets include the ideas that "only God truly exists, all other things are an emanation of Him, or are His 'shadow'; . . . the soul is trapped in the cage of the body, but can, by looking inward, recognize its essential affinity with God; the awakened soul, guided by God's grace, can progress along a 'Way' which leads to annihilation in God."[24] For Attar, overwhelming, passionate love was the most important means of destroying the Self, as he so often depicts in the many parables in *Conference of the Birds* (19).

These stories are set within a larger allegory: Attar describes the stages of the arduous, lifelong Sufi path to union with God and provides instruction to followers through a narrative in which the birds of the world gather to seek a ruler, learning from the hoopoe, their sheikh, that their king is the Simorgh (a Persian mythological, phoenix-like flying creature) and that to find him requires a long, difficult, painful journey. Much of Attar's poem portrays the birds' excuses and questions as they are countered and answered by the hoopoe, who also explains the seven valleys through which they must pass: the Quest; Love; Insight into Mystery; Detachment; Unity; Bewilderment; and Poverty and Nothingness—the stages of the Sufi Way.

In riddle-like fashion, the allegorical narrative in Attar's *Conference of the Birds* also elaborates a pun: in Persian, *si morgh* also means thirty birds. In Attar, only thirty birds finish the journey to the Simorgh, and when finally admitted to his presence, they discover the Simorgh is a reflection of themselves:

> There in the Simorgh's radiant face they saw
> Themselves . . . and dared at last to comprehend
> They were the Simorgh and the journey's end . . .
> They ask . . .   how is it true
> That "we" is not distinguished here from "you"?
> And silently their shining Lord replies:
> "I am a mirror set before your eyes,
> And all who come before my splendour see

Themselves, their own unique reality;
You came as thirty birds and therefore saw
These selfsame thirty birds, not less not more." (219)

Doris weaves allusions to this generative, number-based wordplay throughout *Conference* by means of an ingenious device. The "Character Key" with
which the book begins codes each character-complex with a symbol; these
symbols are used in the poem to indicate who is speaking (1). As is likely
unknown to many Western readers, the glyphs used are the Eastern Arabic
numerals standing for the numbers 1–14.[25] These numerical traces of the cultures of origin of her major source texts connect with *Conference*'s investigation of the relation between multiplicity and unbounded unity in Sufi tradition. As she puts it late in the text: "Your being is extinguished. Why bother
with numbers?" (90).

The birds' mirroring of the Simorgh is also performed in Doris's text through
the inverted pair "bird" and "drab," which stand for existential states as elaborated in Sufi thought. Throughout *Conference*, Doris draws on the cosmology
in the masterwork of Sufi theologian-philosopher Ibn al-'Arabi, *al-Futuhat
al-Makkiyya* (The Meccan Openings). As 'Arabi elaborates, God is Real Being, a pure plenitude of self-revelation and self-awareness, who has created all
other things. These things are immutable, nonexistent entities that God may
choose to make cosmologically manifest or existent. Manifest entities are
God's self-disclosure yet occur in bounded, variegated forms that veil their
unity with God. The Sufi strives to see the cosmos and everything within it
as God's self-disclosure, recognizing their difference and identity with the
Divine, while she or he also reenacts divine manifestation at a lower level by
bringing out with the self the hidden attributes of God innate to humanity.[26]
In turn, Doris uses "drab" to designate undisclosed "existence"—the material
world of hidden divine immanence, while "bird" is the state (or process) of
unveiling. Conversely, the two can seem to trade places: "bird" can also be
nonexistence (or eternal, immaterial soul) versus "drab" as existence (body).
In keeping with Attar's imagery, Doris also continually figures the process of
(self-) disclosure and awareness as annihilation—death, but, at another level,
life: "dying to your life you wake into its dream, temporarily. And where you
emerge completely changed you see yourself then same as before" (7).

A further significant formal device in the text is the unpronounceable
diacritical mark ♭, the symbol in music for flatting a note (based on the letter *b*).[27] Doris uses this symbol to designate God—that is, Being or ♭-ing—
at once incomparable to "drab" and "bird" but also *literally* found, backward
and forward, in both. As we see in the "Invocation":

CHARACTER KEY FOR POSSIBLE SPEAKING
PARTS IN THE CONFERENCE

When the characters speak, these symbols are shown.

١ Belbel = the Baby-girl commandante Flea = Genocidal Logic = Crow = Angel = Luna = Ida Applebroog = Mohammed = US Military Pamphlet #94218 = Lolo Ferrari

٢ Tragedy = Comedy = Me = Jar = Folding-chair = Cockroach and Cloud = Emergency = Quail = Twin Moths = Praline = Pygmy from the Jungle = girl in the movie = my brother

٣ Attar

ح ♭

٥ Dad = Dad, all varieties, + all Yiddish folk songs

٦ Bird

٧ Drab

٨ My friend ≠, = Me

٩ Emily Dickinson = Muhyiddin Ibn 'Arabi = Kathy Acker

١٠ Mom = mom, all varieties

١١ Rabi'a al-Adawiyya = Martha Graham = Anselm Kiefer = Sappho

١٢ Men who love me = Men who do not love me

١٣ Women = Women

١٤ Pilot = Co-pilot

9.1. "Character Key," from Stacy Doris, *Conference.* Designer: Kevin Mount. Image used by generous permission of Potes and Poets Press (Peter Ganick).

First of all, ♭: . . . Since the air rests on nothing and everything is nothing, enthrones / more hidden than being a bird (in your body); hidden in the hidden / The different door to each breath . . . ♭ opens the path that lead[s] to ♭, which is nothing. (6–7; italics original)

It is these conundrums of identity-in-difference, life-in-death, nonexistence-in-existence, everything-in-nothing, and so forth that Doris, dervish, plays upon with such virtuosity:

♭ is not puffiness. If I say, "here, burn me" but I'm not ♭ I can't go up with the flames.

♭ isn't charity. It may be a mirror. If I thank you and you're not thanked, what have I done?

♭ may be no form of understanding. A bird speaks through somebody else, so in some way it's carnal, yet united. (8)

Because of the drab, if I hugely love ♭, ♭ is my drabness. ♭ was or becomes my drabness and drab's sense. If I become so drab, perhaps I am inanimate. Or bird. Or I want to die, since death destroys the drab space separating us. Does death end the between. (40)

The point to ♭ is the reunification or identification that makes the drab's being become the bird's being and vice-versa. This is what is meant when you hear talk of incarnationor infusionor ortransubstantiation transfusionor transmogrification through (92)

∿

Though not a familiar fact, Sufism dramatically converged with British Romanticism through the importance of Farsi to British imperial interests. Persian had been the language of science and culture, court life, and governance in the Mughal Empire in India from the sixteenth century and remained the administrative language there until 1834. Warren Hastings was governor general of Bengal from 1773 to 1784 (with his impeachment trial, the Crown took more direct control from the East India Company over British holdings in India). A student of Persian and Arabic literature, Hastings had made rule through knowledge of the language, customs, and laws of the subcontinent the core of his political ideology. The legendary Orientalist William Jones—a brilliant linguist and translator of many languages, including Farsi, Arabic, and Sanskrit—was a Supreme Court judge for the company from 1783 until his death in 1794. Jones had learned Farsi as a teen and in 1771 published *A Grammar of the Persian Language*, which went through many editions; his collected works appeared in 1799 and again in 1807.[28] From the last quarter of the eighteenth century through the first decade of the nineteenth, translations by Jones and others of especially Persian poetry flooded the British literary scene, as firsthand study of Persian, Arabic, Sanskrit, and Turkic also came to have pressing practical use. Thus, many great works of Persian literature, particularly the classics of Sufi poetry, were known to the educated British public at this time. Indeed, Persian poetry was used to lure students to learn the language and become civil servants in India.[29]

Yet works like Ferdausi's *Shahnama* (*The Book of Kings*) (the national epic of Iran) and those of the Sufi poets Hafiz, Sa'di, and Nezami were not so much translated, as John Yohannan stresses, as adapted and above all classicized, made to conform to eighteenth-century mores and aesthetics. At the same time, however, along with George Sale's 1734 translation of the Qur'an, which contained a well-known "Preliminary Discourse," and works like the letters of Lady Mary Wortley Montagu (1763) and Stephen Weston's *Moral Aphorisms in Arabic and a Persian Commentary in Verse* (1805), a sympathetic and somewhat demystified attitude toward Islam became available in British culture. Despite the heavy British acculturation of Oriental works, Jones and others extolled Persian and other Asian literatures as on par with the West's and urged writers to renovate British literature by mining these newly available exotic materials. Even more so than Jones's contemporaries, Romantic poets of the next generation capitalized on these colonial resources.

In *Romantic Imperialism*, refining Edward Said's insights regarding Orientalist power-knowledge, Saree Makdisi portrays the Romantic era in Britain as a time of transition between two main phases of imperialist representations of the East. This second imperial phase, beginning in the 1790s, constructed an image of the Orient according to a modernizing cultural logic, whereby the East was refigured as backward, undeveloped. A new transformative capitalism applied clock time to all cultural time and a paradigm of world historical evolution to every society's history.[30] Romantic literature, Makdisi writes, emerges alongside modernization, defining and, in ways, opposing it—becoming at times a site for upholding cultural and temporal difference.[31]

Byron's works, of course, obsessively construct locales and situations of the Orient. From boyhood, Byron had steeped himself in the literatures of Orientalism, from West's Sufi primers to Sale's Qur'an to Beckford's *Vathek*, while he also spent his grand tour in the Levant (in part to avoid traveling through the wars in Europe). The first two cantos of *Childe Harold's Pilgrimage* (1812), based on his own travels to Albania, Greece, and Turkey from 1809 to 1811, brought him immediate fame. The thoroughly exoticizing stanzas 55–66 of Canto II depict a meeting with Ali Pasha, a ruler in Tepellene, Albania, who "entertained Byron in the hopes . . . of fostering links with the English against the French."[32] Stanza 59 sets the scene: "Hark! from the mosque the nightly solemn sound, / the muezzin's call doth shake the minaret, / 'There is no god but God!—to prayer—lo! God is great!'" Ali is thought to have been a member of the Bektashi order of Sufism; perhaps not coincidentally, Byron alludes to Hafiz in stanza 62 when he describes Ali, only to note the leader's cruelty belies Hafiz's (supposed) truism, "Love conquers age."[33] The wildly popular "Turkish Tales" Byron published in 1813–14, too, contain numerous loan words (like "muezzin") that gave the works their aura of authenticity. *The Corsair*, which sold ten thousand copies its first day out, features in its second canto the protagonist Conrad, who penetrates the Sultan's palace disguised as a Sufi ascetic (lines 711–70). Byron had seen performances by whirling dervishes of the Mevlevi Sufi order in Athens and Constantinople, though it is unlikely they resembled the fight scene with the Corsairs that ensues once Conrad outs himself as a merely pretended dervish.

Byron's ambivalent attitude toward the mass culture of exoticism he had done much to feed is well known. As he famously self-satirized in his *Beppo* (1818): "Oh that I had the art of easy writing / . . . How quickly would I print (the world delighting) / A Grecian, Syrian, or Assyrian tale; / And sell you, / mix'd with western sentimentalism, / Some samples of the finest Orientalism" (stanza 51). Yet in *Childe Harold's Pilgrimage*, at least, as Makdisi argues, Byron presents the Orient as an autonomous place in "apposition" to Europe, a "discrete spatial-temporal sphere." If it is conscripted as an escape for the alienated (not to say scandalous) Briton, it is nonetheless a fully synchronous antimodern site from which to critique emergent modernity.[34]

〜

A Sufi-tinged temporality of synchronicity or achronicity is built into the very architecture of *Conference*, with its abundance of prologues, prefaces, invocations, and instructions. Time withdraws:

> Flight and love are pure before, with no possible after. Without any after, there is no during either. Because I can't last, because my nature is damage, I'm not so easily hurt. Because air is for a long time, it's the opposite. Unless the great part of me is air. Unless even water is, perhaps. Soul'soul. (46)

The ecstatic state of existence arrived at in joining with Being remains a "before" never congealing into an "after." This lack of "after" also upsets the

logic of "during"—the infinite is divested of time tout court. This elabora-
tion of achronicity also involves a rhetoric of paradox, the favorite Sufi trope.
"Because air is for a long time, it's the opposite": infinite temporal extension
really takes no time at all. This is the (non)space-time of universal mirroring: "Remember—don't think: reflect . . . subtracted from space, beyond time
and thinking" (66).

∾

The Way of the Sufi is experiential. Knowledge of God is empirical in the
specifically experiential sense of that term—a matter, for the Sufi, of spiritual
and imaginative empiricism. As a kind of performative translation, *Conference* is thus partly a formally uncontainable, exuberant record of attempts
at self-undoing towards this empirical knowledge of Being. It is also, partly,
an instruction manual: "Once there's an opening, there's absence. Departure. Open your mouth: you could fall through. The sky's an illusion and
I'm perhaps legion. Yes or no. *An opening is the nick of time*, maybe" (5; my
emphasis). How to nick time is what's at issue: "Opening—who knows what
it is? Let's say the flank of anything, or, in opening, you get this drab stuff-
ing, you yourself lining drabness, a part of its garment perhaps . . . In your
tender inside which you are, in the gaping instant, in the glimpse, keeping
count is so gone, it doesn't matter how we stumbled here, how stumped we
are" (5). The question of how to tear this hole (in time) is also the question
of how to die in life, to un-self, so as to join Being in this life, not the after-
life. *Conference*'s "Incidents and instructions" section interpolates conversations with a "friend" about taking this "jump" (18–20). Doris remarks: "I
do not want to die, no matter how pretty the grass is" (19). The friend says:
"'My faith has a lot to do with death. But my experience with these games
is there's a kind of giving up hope of ever holding onto any form, this being a person, as you sometimes call it" (19–20). Following the Way means
dying more and often. Yet isn't dying part of existence, rather than Being?,
Doris seems to ask. "But if drab is something already ravished by time, is
this a case of two rights making a wrong?" (21). The body is already subject
to mortality, so why make it die more?

∾

Conference is both a spiritual and a radically political text, in part because
Islam is always politicized in the Western context. Further, though the work
does not contain the Arabic word *jihad* ("struggle"), this concept informs
the work. A term with many meanings, "jihad" is most often used in the
Qur'an and in Sufi texts to refer to the self's arduous process of inward pu-
rification, even as today it also often signifies, East and West, martyrdom in
the defense of Islam, and military or armed conflict. "Directive," *Conference*'s

opening section, indeed metaphorizes Sufi spiritual self-annihilation, inner jihad, as "warfare." Enter Belbel, a leader figure who stands for the hoopoe in Attar's poem:

BELBEL's Argument
"Dear Living Things," began the Baby-girl commandante Flea, "I am your divine warfare personalized general, messenger of most invisibility. . . . However, I can't wage a whole war on my own. . . . Wash your hands of living and become an action figure.
We have a unity. Its name is ♭, and it dwells where tongues and imaginations drown. . . .
To enter what never stops, throw all you can away.
Count yourself out. (3)

∼

Conference makes ample use of paradox's cognitive violence as the mystic's indispensable tool for rending the veil of existence: "Looking, I look through her, and only then walk into her. She re-opens and each reopening reopens in a path of unenterings. I'm looking into where sight is not possible" (40). It is the breaching of death-in-life and life-in-death that the text most fully explores, brilliantly enfolding into itself many sources that explore this uncanny terrain.

Possibly the most brilliant of the text's interpolations is its use of Jean Genet's *The Screens (Les Paravents)*. Genet finished *The Screens* in 1961, at the height of the Algerian Revolution; while the play is "set in a nonspecified Arab land occupied by a nonspecified European colonial power," its characters stand for French colonists, the soldiers of the Foreign Legion, and Arab Algerians.[35] *The Screens* very potently evokes imperialist ruination—the blighting of Arab life through racism and subjugation, the hateful absurdity of colonial practices—as it constructs a live space in which revolution dismembers the institutions of the occupation as they also rot from the inside out. The play's sets are movable screens that reticulate the space of the stage into crossable zones of life and death; not only do many dead characters speak, but the living and dead also at times burst through the screens. *Conference* draws particularly on the eighth scene of *The Screens*, set in a cemetery; here the character of The Mother conscripts another character to be The Mouth of a new corpse so they can converse. In Doris's version (10–13), her own mother is The Mother, while she herself is The Mouth, conduit to the zone of the dead. The scene thus very precisely focuses on a literal opening between existence and nonexistence.

Conference further tropes Sufi jihad as disaster throughout its latter half, which contains fragments of scenes modeled on Greek tragedy (probably borrowing from Euripedes's *The Trojan Women*). The first depicts the aftermath of massive violence, a number of female characters described as coming "out from the tent, streaming blood" or "on the ground, smashed up" (49). They are linked to the ex-stasis of death-in-life and life-in-death: "We who are live are those who are dead"; "Me . . . a live tomb" (49). Doris later introduces a "Choral Song" called "*Wholesale genocide*": "Come: Neighbors kill neighbors / plumbers kill plumbers / doctors kill patients / teachers kill pupils. To each his own. / Don't mind the mess: / Corpses clean corpses" (61). This song recalls the earlier "PROLOGUE OF GENOCIDAL LOGIC": "GENO-CIDAL LOGIC: Everyone whose name begins with H go get everyone whose name begins with M" (20). The genocidal logic Doris invokes is Lyotard's paradox of the differend that besets the victim of genocide: "Either you are a victim of a wrong, or you are not. If you are not, you are deceived (or lying) in testifying that you are. If you are, since you can bear witness to this wrong, it is not a wrong, and you are deceived (or lying) in testifying that you are the victim of a wrong."[36] As Belbel later remarks: "If I go, I am or am not, and if I don't go, the same" (80). The differend is filiated with this catch-22-like logic, that also of God's paradoxical hidden self-revelation and the concomitance of life and death.

Yet another figure of jihad and of the surpassing of existence in life appears in *Conference's* adaptation of the documentary *When We Were Kings* (63–65). Here Doris commandeers Mohammed Ali's 1974 heavyweight championship boxing match with George Foreman in Zaire to metaphorize the Sufi struggle to unite with Being. In an almost supernaturally clever use of materials, Doris selects lines by Ali, renamed "♭ PUPPET (Mohammed)," and various commentators in the film to tell a story of Ali surviving his own death. Citing statements by Howard Cosell, Norman Mailer, and Drew Bundini Brown to the effect that Ali does not have a prayer against the God-like Foreman—"The time may have come to say goodbye to Mohammed"; "How you gonna beat God . . . Mister?" (63), Doris meanwhile mixes the cheers of the crowd, "*Ali, Bomboyeh, Ali, Bomboyeh*" (Ali, kill him!), with descriptions of gladiator blood sport in the Roman Colosseum. Ali's at times Islam-inflected braggadocio in turn very self-consciously positions him as a representative of his people: he transcends himself, larger than life, earning his Muslim name. The portrayal is amazingly prescient, for the boxer-poet has, in the last decade, strongly embraced a stream of Sufism.[37]

⌒

With his other vices, Byron had cultivated a taste for "the Fancy," the culture of bare-knuckle boxing that emerged in the eighteenth century and reached its climax in the Regency period. There was a close relation between poetry and pugilism in the Romantic era not only because Byron, John Keats, Thomas Moore, and other poets were crazy for the sport—an obsessed attendee of matches, Byron for years also took boxing lessons with trainer John Jackson at his gentleman's club—but also because they wrote about it. Moore, Byron's early biographer, composed a book of poetry on boxing as political allegory (1819), while J. H. Reynolds, in *The Fancy* (1820), published sonnets on the prizefighter Jack Randall, a book owned and admired by John Clare.[38]

Clare had been quite an enthusiast of "the Fancy" during his London days. Embattled in High Beech Asylum, he took on the identity of Randall as though frozen in time twenty years earlier, penning the notice "Jack Randalls Challange to All the World": "Jack Randall The Champion Of The Prize Ring Begs Leave To Inform The Sporting World That He Is Ready To Meet Any Customer In the Ring . . . All He Wishes Is To Meet with a Customer Who Has Pluck Enough To Come To The Scratch Jack Randall."[39] The challenge, which Clare signed as "Randall," appears in the same 1841 notebook in which he composed his untimely collaborations with Byron, writing his own versions of *Childe Harold* and *Don Juan* and signing his notes as "Byron." Clare indeed seems to have conflated Byron and Randall as he took on their personae, writing in one entry: "Boxer Byron / made of Iron."[40]

Visitors to Clare at both High Beech and Northampton Asylums recorded his remarks on his preparations for a prizefight. Spencer Hall remembers a conversation at Northampton in 1843, in which Clare stated: "'I'm getting tired of waiting here so long. . . . They won't let me go, however: for you see, they're feeding me up for a fight. . . . Oh poetry, ah, I know, I once had something to do with poetry . . . but it was no good. I wish, though, they could get a man with enough courage to fight me.'"[41]

~

It is in a late section of the text that *Conference*'s oscillation of jihad comes to a final crisis: here Doris inserts a verbatim excerpt in transliterated Arabic from the end of the black box transcript of EgyptAir Flight 990. This flight, carrying 217 people, crashed in October 1999, probably due to the purposeful actions of the copilot. In the section Doris excerpts, the copilot states eleven times, "*Twakaltu ala Allah*" (I rely on God), while the pilot asks what's happening and why the motors have been turned off, finally repeatedly commanding, "Pull with me" (cited in Arabic transliteration in Doris 81–82). Doris's use of these volatile materials is audacious: in a sense they are precisely suited to her project and yet incendiary in being framed as such. For this unsettled catastrophe remains split between Eastern and Western interpretations, in which the United States was/is seen as projecting onto the copilot an agenda of jihad that Muslim-world reporting denied was present, given the Egyptian analysis of the crash as mechanical failure. The documentary record obtruding into Doris's mystical tract is also turned to allegorical purpose as it figures the Sufi birds in flight on their journey.

∽

In keeping with many scholars' observations, François Hartog has influentially dubbed the "regime of historicity" or temporality of our current moment "presentism," arguing that the present has become "the focal point of the representation of time."[42] "Futurism has been destroyed under the horizon of presentism that replaced it," he writes. Historical time is suspended, even as the present itself is hollowed out, "a present already past before ever completely happening."[43] Presentism can turn in either temporal direction only out of self-referential expedience: it "has no horizon other than itself, daily creating the past and the future that, day after day, it needs" (14). Hartog sees presentism incipient at the end of the 1960s but singles out the fall of the Berlin Wall in 1989 as a pivotal event.[44]

Presentism, of course, had a euphoric tinge in "free market thought after the collapse of state communism in 1989," an event marking and enabling "the beginning of a market universe which is a perpetual present."[45] Yet many neoliberal apologists have had to acknowledge an end after the end of history—a further, seemingly radical break known as 9/11.[46] Though framed as a putative anomaly, 9/11 has never been outside of time, David Simpson observes. 9/11 not only reorganized time around itself but also functioned as an alibi, obviously, for pursuing "long-meditated military adventurisms and global realignments" (11). 9/11 has been used to license actions and narratives that are not "spontaneous" but have a "complex temporality," Jeff Derksen argues.[47] Changes in "the texture of everyday life" wreaked by globalism and neoliberalism "have been described as an epochal shift dramatically tacked to September 11"; instead, they belong to "a long social and economic project . . . finally brought into clear focus by the events and reactions to 9/11" (10). 9/11 and its effects are intensifications belonging to, rather than exceptional within, our neoliberal phase of history.

And yet, like the French Revolution, 9/11 was and remains "an emergency condition": because of what it continues to underwrite and authorize—functioning even now, in 2012, as an ever-persuasive figure for the engine of history.

∽

When Doris presented me with a copy of *Conference* late in 2001, she expressed a plaint regarding its front cover. Due to a printer's error, the reproduction of the quaint etching depicting birds, similar to past illustrations of Attar's poem, was lacking *the small airplane* supposed to appear at its top. (See figs. 9.2 and 9.3: the airplane is returned to the image in the book's second printing.) That is, through a sizing problem, the deliberate figure of anachronism got cut out.[48] Ironically, the missing emblem was compensated for on the book's title and colophon pages, both of which inaccurately state the year of publication as 2000.

Or was this antedating of the book inaccurate? For it serves to show that Doris's book is anachronistic on two main counts: as an untimely collaboration with Attar, and as an intellectually and aesthetically dazzling, poignant literary commentary, however proleptic, on 9/11 and the wars shortly following and extending to the present. Here, well and truly, is poet as "hierophant," her poem a mirror to future history.

A recording on PennSound gives us Doris performing *Conference* to a roomful of people at SUNY Buffalo just six weeks after the destruction of the twin towers and a week prior to the book's publication.[49] She chooses to end her reading with the transcription of the conversation in Arabic between copilot and pilot in the Flight 990 section. Doris is underscoring her clairvoyance, or rather performing her untimely sense of the gathering force that a particular kind of act of subaltern agency would assume in history.

This prescience or premonition is what she meant to communicate when she complained of her missing airplane.

~

In February of 2010, President Ahmedinejad announced the completion of a new satellite launch vehicle as part of the Iranian aerospace program. The rocket, which launches a satellite into orbit, is called the Simorgh. It is pictured on the back cover of *Conference*. Iran has plans to send the Simorgh into space in early 2013.[50]

~

Chapter 178 of Ibn al-'Arabi's *Futuhat* is a lengthy treatise on the divine Station of Love.[51] 'Arabi's thought on love is extrapolated in part from the Hidden Treasure *hadith* important to many Sufi works, in which God says, "I was a hidden treasure and I loved to be known, so I created the world that I might be known." The manifestation of the cosmos is thus an expression of God's love: "His love . . . brings the universe into existence moment by moment"; "God loves himself and in loving himself he brings the entities . . . from nonexistence into existence."[52] Yet God is hidden in His manifestation. Natural love is an expression in humanity of divine love, and it can reveal that any specific beloved is only the mediation of God's self-disclosure. In loving the lover loves the beloved freely and selfishly for his own sake, mirroring God's free gift of love.

Conference
STACY DORIS

9.2. Front cover, first printing, of Stacy Doris, *Conference*. Designer: Kevin Mount. Image used by generous permission of Potes and Poets Press (Peter Ganick).

9.3. Front cover, second printing, of Stacy Doris, *Conference*. Designer: Kevin Mount. Image used by generous permission of Potes and Poets Press (Peter Ganick).

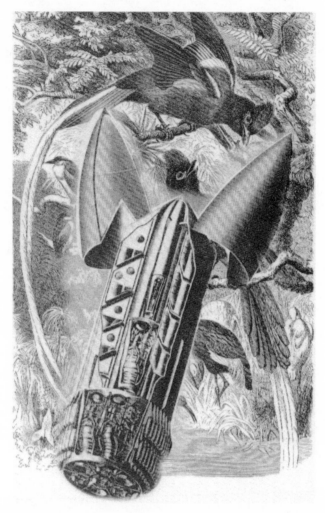

9.4. Back cover illustration (proposed anachronistic representation of Iran's satellite carrier rocket, Simorgh) of Stacy Doris,
Conference. Designer: Kevin Mount. Image used by generous
permission of Potes and Poets Press (Peter Ganick).

If Doris's previous book *Paramour* explored the history of Western poetic forms through the theme of love, *Conference* allows itself to be formally
deranged and undone by love and to think of love as the main agency of the
self's undoing into Being. Indeed, the entire book can be understood as a
working through of the complex theory of love as unbounding in 'Arabi's
theophany, as Doris's version of following the Sufi Way. The final section of

Conference, "End (Endless)," most especially articulates in parallel 'Arabi's Sufi concepts of the cosmos as the manifestation of God's love and of each created thing as the word of God and as partaking in His unifying breath. According to 'Arabi's thought, "In the eternal now, God speaks one word, and that is the command 'Be'! . . . God directs this word toward everything that he wants to bring into existence. . . . When he says 'Be!' [to things], they come to be articulated in his Breath. Their being belongs . . . to the divine Breath" (Chittick 59–60). Doris finally comes to equate love with death with ♭-ing with word with breath:

In the WORD there's a little "e" (echo?) of repetition which engenders a word as its own attribute—"the soul in the soul" etc. The soul'soul. A mirror. (88)

THE IDEA OF$^{\text{SEX}}_{\text{BREATHING}}$ IS CONF-USION. I'M FUCKING'S DARLING. I LOVE INVADING AND INVADING LOVES ME. (90)

The idea of$^{\text{FUCKING IS}}_{\text{LOVE IS}}$ conf-usion of bird and drab. The idea of$^{\text{KISSING IS}}_{\text{BREATH IS}}$ extinctions-in-contemplation. (90)

I never liked this WORD INHALE, IN "hole" but . . . I began to see it as flowing, grasping of form-in-from-of-breath-IN-breath or breathINformIN or ForMbreath. Please substitute then. Death¬*breath. (91)

When breath, mine, breathed out, becomes your existence, and vice-versa, that is called identification. Then I am whom I♭and whom I ♭ is I. (93)

〜

In Athenaeum Fragment 116, Friedrich Schlegel writes: "And [Romantic poetry] can also—more than any other form—hover at the midpoint between portrayed and portrayer, free of all real and ideal self-interest, on the wings of poetic reflection, and can raise that reflection again to a higher power, can multiply it in an endless succession of mirrors" (31–32).

There is no book I know that so well approximates raising "reflection again to a higher power" as does *Conference*—no book, thus, so *Romantic.* In *Conference,* Doris strives to capture a process of self-canceling into infinite Being that endlessly reprovokes itself. She puts a nominal stop to this dynamic, at least enough to enclose her book in its covers, by allowing God or ♭ to make an appearance at the very end, giving the mandates of the dialectic of unity and difference, always preserving the upper hand of pure ♭-ing. Yet her final words are: "I am beyond describing; undetermined." Following Sufi doctrine, the divine is unbounded in an absolute sense; it is not bound even by unboundedness. Similarly, Doris's sealing of the book is really a yet more radical undoing and opening.

∼

In keeping with his theory of untimely collaboration, Toufic writes: "The destruction of the future would be felt in the present by writers. . . . Long before the future is abolished (through a nuclear conflagration, ecological catastrophe, etc.), we will feel one of the main effects of such an absence: those close to the disaster in the future will to a large extent be unable to think properly since they receive from no one. . . . Long before this disaster happens we will no longer be able to think it; this disaster will be preceded by that other disaster: our inability to think the disaster."[53]

The end of human time—a future Disaster snuffing all futurity—will have its anachronic register only through its absence. Here there is no last man. The unichronicity into which this void seals the text becomes its own form of disaster.

Caught in infinite reflection rebounding between disaster and love, *Conference* postpones its sense of that postfuturity. Its engagement with Islam performs a premonitory labor of mourning—in the form of a disciplined overcoming of binaries, a becoming-Sufi, toward (perhaps) averted total destruction: "Dove all day mourning. Drab and bird in a continuum, then, not a contradiction" (71). *Insha'Allah.*

Notes

1. See the entry for "Yucca Mountain nuclear waste repository" in *Wikipedia*. See also the chapter "Hot Legacy" in Alan Weisman's *The World without Us*.

2. One wonders whether this accords with what Jalal Toufic notes in *(Vampires)*, contra Derrida: "According to Derrida: 'All writing . . . in order to be what it is, must be able to function in the radical absence of every empirically determined addressee in general [I disagree with Derrida on this point: there can be no writing that is not an untimely collaboration with a determined albeit unknown addressee]'" (359, note 208).

3. See Paley.

4. Godwin, *An Enquiry Concerning Political Justice and Its Influence on General Virtue and Happiness* (1793) 2: 862; cited in Ni 26.

5. My thanks to Bruce Jackson for drawing my attention to this epigraph.

6. Rohrbach 181.

7. My thanks to Jeffrey C. Robinson for this insight into Coleridge's oeuvre and manuscripts.

8. This interpretation borrows from Philippe Simay, "Tradition as Injunction," particularly 146–55.

9. Toufic, *Distracted* 38.

10. Untimely collaboration has its limits: "I would define epochs by whether this untimely collaboration is possible: what belongs to different epochs is what essentially cannot collaborate in an untimely manner. Despite the deep affinity an Iraqi poet or thinker may feel toward Gilgamesh, he will not have when writing on it the impression that he collaborated on its production" (Toufic, *Distracted* 41).

11. This point recalls Mary Favret's work on the mediated experience of violence in the Napoleonic Wars in *War at a Distance*.

12. Collingwood and Khalip, "Introduction" Para. 6.

13. The introduction of Jeff Derksen's *Annihilated Time* discusses Jamie Peck and Adam Tickell's model of the "rollback" and "rollout" phases of neoliberalism (20–21).

14. McLane 118.

15. Of course, the very last scene of *The Revolt of Islam* is not the burning at the stake, but the martyr's experience of postmortem paradise.

16. Gustave Janouch, *Conversations with Kafka* 143; cited in Toufic, *Distracted* 36.

17. Chandler 107.

18. As Chandler points out, in German Marxist historiography, the phenomenon is called "nonsynchronism" (*Ungleichzeitigkeit*).

19. Agamben, "Time and History" 105.

20. Koselleck 5.

21. Wollstonecraft, *Letters* 132.

22. The appendix in the original volume is not paginated.

23. Arberry xx.

24. Attar 11–12 (introduction by Darbandi and Davis).

25. The decision to create a character key came out of Doris's correspondence with Kevin Mount, the book's designer. My thanks to Mount for this information.

26. This discussion draws on William Chittick's introduction to his major book on 'Arabi, *The Self-Disclosure of God*, as well as Jaakko Hameen-Anttila's "The Immutable Entities and Time."

27. See Niecks.

28. For this information, see Schwab. (This is a brief excerpt from Schwab's important groundbreaking book of 1950 on Romanticism and Orientalism, *La Renaissance Orientale*.)

29. For this information, see the first half of Yohannan.

30. See *Romantic Imperialism*, chapter 5 and conclusions.

31. Yet the Orient appeared with many valences. In "Literature, National Iden-

tity, and Empire," Makdisi observes that the figure of the Oriental despot was integral to the early Romantic era discourse on the "Rights of Man"—for instance, in Mary Wollstonecraft (72).

32. Sharafuddin 225.

33. Blackstone's "Byron and Islam" seems to go overboard in suggesting that Ali actually invited Byron to become a Sufi initiate. His discussion, however, of the prevalence of Sufi allusions in Byron's work is persuasive.

34. Makdisi 123–33.

35. Finburgh 211.

36. Lyotard, *Differend* 5.

37. See Deborah Caldwell's 2005 interview with Ali's daughter Hana Yasmeen Ali.

38. See Strachan; also Bate 262–64. Byron alludes to his boxing escapades throughout his letters of roughly 1806–1814.

39. *John Clare By Himself* 266. In "John Clare: The Poetics and Politics of Taxonomy," Francesca Cuojati writes that Clare's taking on multiple identities was not simply a symptom of mental illness but a strategy combating psychiatric evaluation and confinement, a way of overwriting the identity forced on him through psychiatric taxonomy.

40. Bate writes about Clare's conflated obsessions with boxing and Byron in the chapter "Dr. Bottle-Imp and Boxer Byron." See also James McKusick, especially 232.

41. Hall 166.

42. Hartog, *Régimes D'Historicité: Présentisme et Expériences du Temps* 28; cited in (and translated by) Hannoum 458.

43. Hartog 14.

44. Many have concurred with Hartog.

45. I borrow this phrase from Jameson 63.

46. Simpson 4.

47. Derksen 59.

48. Again, my thanks to Kevin Mount for this information. Mount notes further that the cover illustrations he devised, in collaboration with Doris, comprise "bits from a book from the Wernher von Braun era of rocketry stiched to Newnes [Pictorial] Encyclopaedia engravings" ("Long lost reply," e-mail message to Judith Goldman).

49. The recording took place on 30 Oct. 2001.

50. See "Iranian Satellites Fajr, Nahid and Zafar to Be Launched on Schedule."

51. Hirtenstein 192.

52. Chittick, *Ibn 'Arabi* 50, 46.

53. Toufic, *Over-Sensitivity* note 114.

10

The Influence of Shelley on Twentieth- and Twenty-First-Century Avant-Garde Poetry

A Survey

Jeffrey C. Robinson

> Every great poet must inevitably innovate upon the example of his
> predecessors in the exact structure of his peculiar versification.
>
> P. B. Shelley, from "A Defence of Poetry"

The reputation of Percy Bysshe Shelley and his influence upon later poets have produced irreconcilable differences in understanding among poets and readers. At the Shelleyan poles stand on the one hand the Arnoldian Shelley, the ineffectual angel who becomes Palgrave's prime instance of a "poésie pure," a singer far above the world of social life; on the other hand is the radical political poet inspiring Chartists, Frankfurt School theorists, and the revolutionaries in Tiananmen Square. These two positions invite a third one that reconceives Shelleyan poetry in a way that takes account of both "lyric" and political radicalism.

In this essay I will show how some politically and poetically radical twentieth- and early-twenty-first-century poets found in Shelley a model for formal experimentation and playfulness in poetry that, together with an understanding of him as an example of an unpredictable personal and political life and who was sensational in his death, helped to form their own explicitly innovative poetry and poetics. I will begin with brief discussions of three major precursors to this radical understanding, Yeats and Eliot, who acknowledged some of what the radical poets called on but came to very different conclusions, and in a somewhat similar vein a poet of the next generation, W. H. Auden; then I will turn for the rest of the essay to some work of eight avant-garde poets.

By looking at how these poets engage with Shelley, I hope to indicate that there can be more than one line and model of influence. The paradigm of influence à la Harold Bloom as it affects twentieth-century poets' responses to the canonical Romantic poets has been beautifully articulated (in the primarily British line) by Michael O'Neill in *The All-Sustaining Air*. Shelley's presence figures in many of the poets discussed by O'Neill, particularly notable being Yeats, Eliot, Auden, Spender, Stevens, Heaney, Mahon, Muldoon, Hill, and Fisher. O'Neill argues that the later poets participate in a "strenuous tussle" (1) with their Romantic precursors and are consequently interested in a "dialectic" within the moderns themselves, courting and drawn to Shelley's (and more generally the Romantics') visionary and utopian excess but then correcting those tendencies as a function of modern social realities through a sense of a more imaginatively temperate function for poetry itself.

Some twentieth-century poets, however, have seen Shelley's influence as that which invites a recasting of his poems and his poetics (the principles upon which his poems are made) not in the mode of skepticism but in the mode of greater or more current realization of their visionary utopian possibilities.[1] For these poets Shelley is a poet of transformations, and, as the poet Michael Palmer has said, of "radical alterity" (204). The poets represented here—George Oppen, Robert Duncan, Robert Kelly, Gregory Corso, Barbara Guest, Susan Howe, Andrew Mossin, and Alan Halsey—bring to light, realize, and at times "liberate" the thematic and formally innovative elements of Shelley underlying the poetry, the poetics, and the man in his life and in his death. Indeed, in all cases, visionary transformation seems to demand an accompanying formal experiment. All of these poets, moreover, would assent to Barbara Guest's confession about Shelley as poetic guide for imaginations narrowed and stymied by dark times but wishing to break out of them: "I assume his stewardship through the cold and mist."[2]

The first modern poet strongly influenced by Shelley, and strongly influenced by Victorian views of him, was William Butler Yeats (1865–1939). Yeats as a young poet worshipped the Shelley of visionary utopias (*Laon and Cythna, Prometheus Unbound*) and the romantic alienated adventurer (*Alastor*) (Yeats, *Essays* 65–95; *Autobiography* 42). He went so far as to pronounce *Prometheus Unbound* one of the "sacred books" of the world. Further into his career, however, he saw Shelley as a poet weakened by his radical politics: "Shelley the political revolutionary expected a miracle, the Kingdom of God in the twinkling of an eye, like some Christian of the first century" (*Essays* 419).

Wanting not to deny the power of Shelley as a figure of visionary Romanticism, Yeats, in some of the poems of his middle and late periods, developed a more complex response to the Romantic poet, constructing a poetry of "dialogue," in which the positions within the poem itself, as Michael O'Neill argues, swing from a visionary idealism to a skepticism about the validity of such idealism. "Ego Dominus Tuus" and "A Dialogue of Self and Soul," moreover, may find their origins in a roughly similar poem of Shelley's: "Julian and Maddalo." Yeats, in other words, picks up on the Shelley that is skeptical of himself, not the utopian, feminist, transgressive, intensely lyrical, and formally experimental poet. Similarly, in the essay on *Prometheus Unbound*, Yeats accounts for a way to continue his admiration of that poem in terms of what he sees as Shelley's self-critique of that radicalism; Yeats calls it a "nightmare-ridden work," one that "forced him to balance the object of desire conceived as miraculous and superhuman, with nightmare" (*Essays* 420).

In reading Shelley this way, Yeats confirmed or perhaps helped to create his view of the strengths and weaknesses of the poetry of Romanticism as a whole. In this he both reinforces the late-nineteenth-century view of Shelley and sets the stage for what might be called the establishment High Modernist reading of both Shelley and Romanticism.

Yeats's view of this reading acknowledges the falling off from the visionary past and imagines the loss of the guiding presence of reason ("the worst are full of passionate intensity"). In "Coole and Ballylee, 1931" Yeats declares his youthful Romantic identifications and the subsequent changes to modern life that for any alert poet must put an end to Romanticism:

> We were the last romantics—chose for theme
> Traditional sanctity and loveliness;
> Whatever's written in what poets name
> The book of the people; whatever most can bless
> The mind of man or elevate a rhyme; . . .
>
> . . . But all is changed, that high horse riderless,
> Though mounted in that saddle Homer rode
> Where the swan drifts upon a darkening flood. (lines 41–48)

In Yeats's assertion that the modern horse of poetry is riderless, all energy and passion but no consciousness, "Romanticism," as appealing as it may be, becomes the word for that failure to acknowledge in art the "cold" reality of the present; it is a failure of mind and of ideas.

T. S. Eliot, to whom I now briefly turn, agreed with Yeats that Shelley's ideas were immature, but Eliot makes clear what is really at stake: he, and presumably Yeats, do not approve of the merging of poetry with ideas as part of a radical political program, particularly when "poetry" means, as is true of Shelley, intense lyricism. In an enormously influential pronouncement (from *The Use of Poetry and the Use of Criticism*), Eliot criticized Shelley precisely because the "adolescent" poet insisted upon his "ideas" and, more important, upon their merging with his poetry: "Shelley both had views about poetry and made use of poetry for expressing views. . . . I find his ideas repellent; and the difficulty of separating Shelley from his ideas and beliefs is still greater than with Wordsworth."[3]

But why should visionary and lyric art, except in the mode of skepticism and irony, have to exclude consciousness? Or, as the above-mentioned Michael Palmer asks, in a brilliant essay on Shelley that finds the position of Eliot a major roadblock to the former's proper estimation in the contemporary world: "And why must a poet be separable from his ideas? . . . Dante and Milton cleansed of ideas? . . . What is most striking . . . is [Eliot's] rage against Shelley's ideas. Which, one cannot but wonder, seemed to Eliot the worst: Shelley's feminism, his progressive egalitarianism, his ecotopic perspective, his idealism joined with an active interventionism . . . ?" (203). Eliot's demand that poetry remain separate from ideas applies only because of the radical, transformative nature of Shelley's ideas and the (correct) assumption that the intense emotional response elicited from Shelley's poetry would spill over into the enactment of the ideas in social life.

This perspective on Shelley and more generally the Romantics provided by Yeats and Eliot has appealed enormously to the subsequent "mainstream" tradition of poetry, from Auden and Spender in the 1930s, to the so-called confessional poets such as Lowell, Sexton, and Plath in the 1950s and 1960s, to more recent British poets such as Larkin and Hughes. W. H. Auden, for example, was one of the first and most articulate poets to pick up on this tradition and propel it forward to the present.

He once wrote that the Romantic poets and their nineteenth-century followers "turned away from the life of their time to the contemplation of their own emotions and the creation of imaginary worlds, Wordsworth to Nature, Keats and Mallarmé to a world of pure poetry, Shelley to a future Golden Age" (O'Neill, *The All-Sustaining Air*, 93). "Shelley," often a stand-in for Romantic sins, is one who characteristically puts the visionary at the center of the work, staking all on it, as if a poem were equivalent to its vision. To the High Moderns this often appeared as an act of naive exclusion of the "real" world, with all of its materiality and, at times, its tragedy and needed "correction." Thus Auden can tout in "Musee des Beaux Arts" (1940) Pieter

Brueghel's paintings of the Nativity and of the Fall of Icarus as properly representing those moments of vast cultural and social significance by placing them alongside quotidian moments (for example, the daily work of the ploughman).

Poets like Auden and his followers attend to form not so much with experiment as with the placing of a kind of pressure on, or resistance to, the (Romantic) "flow" of the line itself, an increase in its "density" (over a perceived vagueness and airiness in "the" nineteenth-century line), a packing together of consonant and stressed syllables. At other times these poets "correct" perceived Romantic escapism into excessive "poetic" diction by means of a more quotidian, "prosaic" one. The language of "Musee" resists figuration and "the poetic" yet, in straightforward declarative sentences, speaks with assured praise for Brueghel's vision:

> About suffering they were never wrong,
> The Old Masters; how well they understood
> Its human position; . . .

Continuing the prosaic account of the painting, Auden then lengthens the line from these pentameters (the Wordsworthian or "Romantic" line of subjective meditation) to a longer, freer one that actually includes the expanded world of daily, repetitive life:

> . . . how it takes place
> While someone is eating or opening a window or just walking dully
>   along; . . .

There is a significant difference, however, between Auden's formal attentiveness and that of the avant-garde: in "Musee des Beaux Arts" the transformation of vision does not really occur. By contrast to Brueghel's painting, in which the viewer is forced to see a ploughman and a falling Icarus simultaneously, to feel the stunning juxtaposition and thus revisit the entire cataclysmic mythological event in the presence of the quotidian, Auden's poem simply diminishes the significance of one part of the juxtaposition. "For [the ploughman] it was not an important failure." The reader is not asked to take in both events at once, as an act of imagination that alters the reality. Thus the form of the poem does not encourage a similar act of transformative imagination—for example, a rethinking of the Nativity—in terms of the quotidian.

It is precisely the merging of politically progressive ideas, experiments with form, and, as Robert Kaufman has called it, "song," that drives the poetry and the poetics of the poets whom I will consider in the rest of this essay. All of these poets would agree with Palmer about the necessary unity of Shelley's poetry with his politically progressive "ideas." But a poetry that is simply a conduit for ideas does not raise people's hackles; only when ideas are wedded to the *form* of the poem, when it is "song" and thus pleasurable aesthetically and apparently innocent of thought, does a poem stimulate an Eliot to find its ideas repellent. It follows that poets who practice in the wake of a Shelley demonstrate again and again a commitment to the transformation, or deformation, of poetic form as the way to activate those ideas through the destabilization of the very medium in which they are presented.

Leaving Yeats, Eliot, and Auden behind, I can now ask: What, then, in Shelley's life, poetry, and poetics might have appealed to and guided the radical poets of the twentieth and twenty-first centuries whom I shall be discussing? They perceived that Shelley was a poet who, in his work and in his life, rejected the prevalent (and still prevalent) notion that an ideal poem existed in order to unfold the inner life, the drama, of the speaking subject. In Shelley's own time poets and other readers identified William Wordsworth as the leading exponent of this understanding of poetic purpose. But Shelley argues (in "A Defence of Poetry") that love is, and poetry should be, a "going out of one's own nature." While a poet like Wordsworth might not have quarreled with this statement as such, he would not have embraced it in the way that Shelley's later, innovative interpreters in poetry have done.

They saw his life on the periphery of society, his exile, and his early death by drowning as standing for a life, a self, sacrificed to poetry and the political ideas embedded in it. This view of the poet seems to have had the emotional correlate for Shelley himself in a figure constantly pursued, at times violently, like the Actaeon described in *Adonais*, a self devoured or dismembered yet occasioning beautiful myth, an exiled person become a breathless "form."

These twentieth- and twenty-first-century poets consequently might have noted at least two characteristics in Shelley's work that follow from the extremism of a life sacrificed to poetry. First, his poems are replete with imagery and literary figures, the "poetry," so to speak, of poetry. Examples include the lyric songs embedded in *Prometheus Unbound*, many of which are imbued with a utopian orientation; or the paratactic figuration, the metaphor and metonymy, in poems like "To a Skylark" and *Epipsychidion*. This language often overwhelms the (classical) sense of figure as ornament to the narrative line or (Romantic) sense of personal monologue as the center of the work. Second, later poets, therefore, would see in Shelley not a poet as a figure of stability but rather one performing and participating in transgressions and transformations. He was fascinated with mythic or fabulous personages who take distinct pleasure in unsettling the known borders and the constitution of the familiar. In his long poem *The Witch of Atlas* he created a figure who causes grotesque changes to occur in people, the effect of which is not to destroy but to realign in a positive way their thinking about themselves, their goals, and their world. In this she is like Mercury (Hermes), the god of transformations, of playfully wicked transgressions, the crosser of thresholds. Shelley translated the great Homeric *Hymn to Mercury* at roughly the same time that he wrote *The Witch of Atlas*. Part of the drama of the Homeric Hymn involves a kind of conversion of the god Apollo to the ways of the thieving genius of Mercury: "poetry," Shelley argues, insists upon such transgressions and indiscretions.[4]

Indeed, what these twentieth- and twenty-first-century poets see in Shelley may be what I have argued elsewhere is essential to the most vital faculty of Romantic poetics, the "Fancy." To have figures like the Witch of Atlas and the god Mercury as presiding geniuses over one's poetry may indicate a preference in Shelley for that poetic habit of mind—playful, dispersive, image making, destabilizing, and often improvisational. In contrast to the Imagination, where the focus is reflective and synthetic (in Coleridge's famous phrase in his *Biographia Literaria*, concerned with the "reconciliation of opposite and discordant qualities"), the Fancy is perfectly content with the accumulation or juxtaposition of images from different domains of experience. The playfulness of the Fancy in Romantic and particularly Shelley's poetry permeates the radical side of the poetic spectrum, in part because it indicates a mind attuned to "reality" but liberated from its strictures.[5]

This in turn encouraged a poetry less committed to convention in form, syntax, and language itself; a more experimental poetry became possible, one in which the destabilizing of form, as well as a writing in the present, became essential for a poet trying to alter conventional modes and structures of thought. Interestingly, Shelley's own poetry does not immediately call attention to itself as formally radical (although a poem like *Epipsychidion* could be said to reverse the formal ratio of the account of the speaker and the density of figure). But later poets unquestionably associate Shelley's merging of "song" (form) and radical politics, which may turn out to be his greatest contribution to modern experimental poetry.

In the American Objectivist poet George Oppen's (1908–1984) reworking of Shelley's "Ozymandias," called in fact "Ozymandias," we can immediately discern that, generated by Shelley's poem, experiment with form goes hand in hand with critical analysis of the modern person in a world blanketed by the market economy:

> The five
> Senses gone
>
> To the one sense,
> The sense of prominence
>
> Produce an art
> *De luxe.*
>
> And down town
> The absurd stone trimming of the building tops
>
> Rectangular in dawn, the shopper's
> Thin morning monument. (59)

Oppen sustains Shelley's theme by updating it for the present: the fate of monomaniacal tyrannies is recast as the success of the world of high commercial capitalism, seen as the tyranny of "the sense of prominence" over the other five senses. Formally, and in keeping with the critique of the market economy, he revises the sonnet and the idea of the sonnet: with his spare, short lines, he visually projects the critique of tyranny as a critique of the "monumental" form of the sonnet. He further extends Shelley's emphasis on the pastness of Ozymandias ("I met a traveller from an antique land, / Who said . . .") and the failure of monuments and the tyranny associated with them to last. For the politically radical Shelley the spirit of Ozymandias comes forward into the life of the Regency decade moment. Oppen seems to begin right here in his own present—mid-twentieth-century New York City—where there has been no ruin, nothing "shattered." Thus both poets engage in an important "improvisational" feature available to poetry, that the focus is ultimately on the present: a poetry of participation. The poet does not meditate on or reflect on its subject as much as observe it.

Where lies the tyranny of the King of Kings?—in today's "down town" world of shops, in which the only identifiable person is one whose attention to the world through "the five / Senses" has vanished, through Ozymandias as the specter of capitalism, to be replaced by identity as acquisition. The new "monument" (the sinister last "remaining" word in the poem) is not an empire as such but a department store. The only line to equal Shelley's in length is a ten-syllable line mocking, for a post-Poundian poet, the stony monumental one.

One could read Shelley's sonnet as a critique of "the monumental" associated with the misuse of power in poetry as well as in society. If the sonnet is a "monumental" abstract form, even visually chunky, in the spirit of the poem it deserves to be "shattered" by a later poet: otherwise for Oppen characteristically shorter lines seem to indicate the vanishing of the monumental or the ephemeralizing of it. Conversely, these very short lines have, as they do in much of Oppen's work (or in the work of other poets also in the "objectivist" tradition such as Louis Zukofsky and Lorine Niedecker), the sense of new beginning, slight eruptions of the visionary imagination out of the oppressive Ozymandian silence. If you count spaces between lines, the vertical length of Oppen's poem comes to fourteen, the length of a sonnet, all of which is to say that the poem's social critique has a correlate in formal revision.

Oppen's poem, then, is an example of a poetic *deformation*,[6] in which an "essence" of the vision or life of a form is sought by a radical reworking of form: in this case, the sonnet's requisite number of lines are kept, but its horizontal vector, the ten-syllable line, is deformed. Deformation at once recalls the original while it acts as a critique that simultaneously releases the energies of the original. In this case Oppen is realizing, or translating, or deforming, Shelley's vision of tyranny and critique of monumentality into the twentieth century.

The principle of deformation works in the next example by the North American poet Robert Duncan (1919–1988), although here the poet intends to liberate a Shelleyan lyric from what he perceives as an outworn metrics. Simultaneously he proposes to release the erotic energies of Shelley's elegiac version of Ovidian myth by recasting Shelley/Ovid as a comedy of the fulfillment of love. Duncan took Shelley's Ovidian lyric "Arethusa" and made it new: "Shelley's ARETHUSA set to new measures." Using much of Shelley's language, imagery, and narrative, Duncan, from his point of view, updates and revivifies the Romantic's poem. Luckily, the motive for the revision has been recorded in Duncan's letter to Denise Levertov, in which he describes his experience of reading "Arethusa" out loud with his partner Jess: "Then we tried the Shelley aloud, but its onrushing regular stresses and rimes rang ludicrous in our ears, as if they did monkey imitations of themselves, having lost some secret of conformity—yet something in the poem haunted and asked to be renderd [*sic*]. It was a bet too, over coffee, and I set myself to keep the current, the stream-form of the original, and wherever I could to keep the original intact: the basic thing was to get a shifting pace and pattern to it—to have pools, eddies, and fast and slow onrushes etc." (Duncan and Levertov 288).

Duncan's "Shelley's Arethusa" "deforms" the original in the sense that, while Shelley's actual words are maintained, they are loosened from their archaic syntax and grammar ("Alpheus bold" becoming "bold Alpheus"); and while the poem's overall vertical movement is maintained, its characteristic triplet—two dimeters followed and closed by a trimeter—is loosened. Shelley's words then become "winged," floating, sliding. Duncan's version of Arethusa before Alpheus's chase catches, I think, the mobility in the words that Duncan wants to restore:

> As if still asleep, she goes, glides or
> Lingers in deep pools. (lines 11–12)

Duncan's initial seemingly skeptical response to the Romantic's "Arethusa" leads him not to a skepticism about Shelley's project but to an effort to realize the intention of the original and what "haunted" him about it. The letter goes on to recount beautifully the impulse to bring more life to the original than Shelley's had, to refresh the rhythm and the images, to allow a "labor in love of form." As Levertov's reply indicates, Duncan's version is like an "inspired translation . . . one that didn't try to copy the original slavishly but to give it new life by imitating the spirit of it" (Duncan and Levertov 291).

Duncan realizes Shelley's work in part by recasting the earlier poet's account of Ovid's mythic version of Alpheus, the River God, and the nymph Arethusa: Alpheus attempts to rape Arethusa, but the god of the Ocean saves her by transforming both of them into the river itself, where they live eternally together. Here is the final section of Shelley's poem:

> And now from their fountains
> In Enna's mountains,
> Down one vale where the morning basks,
> Like friends once parted
> Grown single-hearted,
> They ply their watery tasks.
> At sunrise they leap
> From their cradles steep
> In the cave of the shelving hill;
> At noontide they flow
> Through the woods below

And the meadows of asphodel;
And at night they sleep
In the rocking deep
Beneath the Ortygian shore;—
Like spirits that lie
In the azure sky
When they love but live no more.

And here is Duncan's rewriting:

When now from Enna's mountains they spring,
    Afresh in her innocence
Arethusa to Alpheus gladly comes.
Into one morning two hearts awake,
at sunrise leap from sleep's caves to return
    to the vale where they meet,
drawn by yearning from night into day.

Down into the noontide flow,
    into the full of life winding again, they find
their way thru the woods
    and the meadows of asphodel below.
Wedded, one deep current leading,
    they follow to dream
in the rocking deep at the Ortygian shore.

    Spirits drawn upward,
    they are divided
into the azure from which the rain falls,
    life from life,
seeking their way to love once more. (Duncan *Roots and Branches*
    78–83)

Even though Duncan describes his complaint with Shelley on the level
of prosody and idiom, his reworking starts with the revision of Shelley's account of the Ovidian myth itself, which operates in an economy of scarcity: if
the human is absorbed into the natural, its human attributes—difference and
identity, "life" itself—vanish. They lose their maturity and become "cradled"
in the nature that receives them. There is an elegiac side to Ovid and the
Romantic's version of him. But Duncan presents their transformation in an
economy of abundance. Not only love but "life" comes "from life," and re-

newal of love, not its pastness, becomes the principle upon which the poem ends. One feels this in Duncan's rewriting of individual lines, both in the content and in the greater expansiveness of the lines themselves (compared to the shorter ones in "Arethusa"), including a new density of sound in alliteration and assonance: "Down into the noontide flow, / into the full of life winding again" (lines 75–76). Ezra Pound's discussions of the need in modern poetry to increase vowel lengths that had been foreshortened by the domination of "meter" in the nineteenth century seems behind Duncan's rewriting of the prosody of Shelley. By seeking to liberate the sounds of poetry to match the onrush of the violent energies of desire and escape along with the suddenness of transformation, Duncan catches not only something fundamental that is latent in Shelley but something that "haunted" both Duncan in his reading of "Arethusa" and Levertov in her return to the Romantic poem.

Strikingly, a number of twentieth-century poets writing with Shelley's ideological and formal revisionism in view seek to liberate in a contemporary idiom what I referred to above as the playful poetics of the Fancy. His late poems to Jane Williams have somewhat surprisingly spurred interest where one might not expect it, among some of the "Beat" poets, past and present, and also in Frank O'Hara, who wrote a short group of lyrics to the artist and friend, Jane Freilicher: "A Terrestrial Cuckoo," "Jane Awake," "A Mexican Guitar," and "Chez Jane," all in *Meditations in an Emergency* (24–29). In his version of "Jane poems," O'Hara recasts Shelley's playfully imaginative but also utopian and deeply felt love poems into a postsurrealist playfulness; he picks up and extends the casualness of Shelley's exchange (unusual in Romantic poetry) with his interlocutor. Formally he carries Shelley's poetics of the fancy (e.g., short-lined rhymed couplets in long, unending streams, whimsical myth making) into a poetry of comic juxtapositions of language and image.

At times Shelley's "Jane poems" seem like short-line riffs on his massive poem of passion-love *Epipsychidion*. Although Shelley referred to one of them as an "ariette," they contain much passion and intensity, much utopian idealizing and erotic longing; it is in this context that their playfulness must be considered: "A spirit interfused around / A thrilling silent life." O'Hara pushes the fancy-fulness further, in the way of a postsurrealist New York poet. In "With a Guitar: To Jane" Shelley gives her a gift of the guitar with a poem that ventriloquizes Shakespeare's Ariel and then creates a "myth" of the guitar's creation. O'Hara extends this kind of creativity to a playfully erotic juxtaposition of images, indeed an updating of that Shelleyan density of image, but also to dancing a fandango to the strains of a "Mexican Guitar":

Our shouting knocked over a couple of palm trees
and the gaping sky seemed to reel at our mistakes,
such purple flashing insteps and careers!
which bit with lavish envy the northern soldiers.

In each of the exhibits given to this point, a poet does not simply respond to but intervenes formally and thematically in or with reference to a poem of Shelley's. The North American poet Robert Kelly, in his recasting of Shelley's *Mont Blanc* in a thirty-eight-page blank version meditation with the same title, makes the formal part of the intervention apparent from his prefatory comment to the poem:[7] "Inscribed in the spaces of Shelley's 'Mont Blanc.'" Not only asked to realize that Kelly's lines are massive intercalations between Shelley's, the reader also learns to think of the poem (both poems) spatially and comparatively: Shelley's poem appears at the back of the book for easy reference. This allows one to see easily how Kelly is "deforming" it, including what he might mean by "spaces." Moreover, both front and back end-pages have copies of a detailed early map of the Mont Blanc region of France, with the rivers Arve and Drance figuring centrally. Not on the map but right near the beginning of the poem, reference is made to the Hudson River near where Kelly lives in the United States, where he has been teaching at Bard College and has become an extremely prolific and heavily anthologized poet over the past half century. Kelly's poem encourages one to look at Shelley's spatially as well, as a geography of mind. The "spaces" in Shelley belong to that geography; thus it is Kelly's intention to fill them with his own language and thinking by following out Shelley's implications or to take them along new pathways. The inscriptions in (his) *Mont Blanc* are the formal equivalent of his thematic, in this case philosophical, recasting of Shelley's meditation on the sublime.

The speaker in Shelley's poem worries the connection between a power outside the self and the mind of persons, a version of the sublime in which access to that power may "repeal / Large codes of fraud and woe"(lines 80–81). How, the poem continually asks amid the speaker's overwhelming solitude in the presence of Mont Blanc, can one write about forces that are fundamentally other, the sources of which are far vaster than any human faculty can imagine and yet which could have enormous power for the human mind? The emphasis ultimately falls on a capacity of the "awful power," not to tyrannize but to free up that mind in its imaginings, a liberation that involves full acknowledgment of the mystery of the other.

Kelly recasts the drama of mind, in the sublime, in terms of the presence of the other as his beloved; indeed this is the biggest "space" in Shelley's text that Kelly fills: he turns the solitary meditation into an address to the beloved who is at once present and to be discovered. The poem moves back and forth from the Hudson River of home to the River Drance; the journey celebrates her presence and their fulfillment while it journeys far to discover the same thing, a *via negativa*. Charlotte, wife of the poet, moves back and forth between a figure of the quotidian, a comfort on the social scale, and a lover on the scale of, say (at least in imagination), Emilia Viviani or perhaps Jane Williams. The world swings from present-day New York State to the world-in-exile of Shelley and Byron (the cover of the book pictures the castle of Chillon). Similarly, he says of language that it is the "network of its pasts." Kelly, in other words, works precisely among the different registers of being found in the great epics—social, historical, mythic—and like Shelley asks, how does one define "the human" in relation to outsized and mysterious embodiments of reality? In terms of the address to the beloved the poem becomes an intense and extensive exploration of love.

But why Shelley in the first place? In an amusing comment in the poem, Kelly declares: "there is nothing north of Boston," presumably a reference to the title of an early book of Robert Frost and thus a swipe at one whom Kelly would deem (in Robert von Hallberg's term) a "poet of accommodation."[8] The journey of discovery therefore must go farther afield than a quick car trip from New York State along the Massachusetts Turnpike to Frost's northern New England countryside. Moreover, Frost's poetics of containment will not suffice for the exploration of essential mysteries of love and power ("Visit the hidden"). This exploration includes in its purview the failures of modern societies to care for the inner as well as public lives of its members: he therefore must journey back to the radical Romantic Shelley.

The life and in some cases the death of the radical Romantic Shelley also fascinated twentieth- and twenty-first-century poets, sometimes as a biographical fact but always as a precise locus for what gives his visionary poetry its authenticity. This Shelley tragically but heroically "sails" from the life of the social person into poetry—a "world" of rhythm, song, and image. In the late nineteenth century the poet Algernon Charles Swinburne, a great promoter of Shelley, wrote: "He alone was the perfect singing-god; his thoughts, words, deeds, all sang together. . . . Shelley was born a son and soldier of light, an archangel winged and weapon'd for angel's work."[9]

Eventually an account of a poet-as-person resonates to a way of thinking about his or her poetics. In the 1950s through the 1970s the Beat poets revered the figure of Shelley as a boy-man of poetic energies, a precursor to the politically and poetically radical enthusiasms they themselves

needed, at least in principle, in order to counter the perceived repressive-
ness of post-McCarthy North America. The Jack Kerouac School of Disem-
bodied Poetics, founded by Allen Ginsberg and Anne Waldman in 1975 and
continuing to this day, championed this understanding of Shelley particularly in its first twenty-five years. And no one (other than perhaps Ginsberg
himself and Diane di Prima) was more vociferous on the subject of Shelley
than Gregory Corso, whose letters are full of praise of and identification
with Shelley. "If I heed all my Catholic upbringing then surely Shelley is in
Hell. I once asked a priest, 'Do you really think beautiful Shelley is in hell?'
And he said, 'He left his wife didn't he? Married another didn't he? Was an
Atheist, wasn't he? Then surely his soul rests in hell.' But I said, 'Look at his
poems, he loved God!'"(Corso, *Accidental Autobiography* 117). Corso wrote
a poem of sheer hero worship, titled "I held a Shelley manuscript (written in
Houghton Library, Harvard)," that openly rejects the kind of self-conscious
distancing and criticism seen in Yeats's later poems and in his accounts of
Shelley in the *Autobiography* and the essay on *Prometheus Unbound*: "I would
have taken the page / breathing in the crime!" (22). Corso's (and more generally the Beats') Shelley is authentic precisely because he is the *senex puer*
who thrives at the peripheries of the consciousness of "middle age," or that
of the social person. Corso describes himself, playfully, à la Shelley as "A
poetman / become an olding messenger boy / O silver tongue of spiritus!"
("Sunrise").

Such poems are less self-deprecating than they are defining of a quality
to be preserved or reconstituted in the present. "On Gregory Being Double
the Age of Shelley" acts as a challenge to a poet who has long lived past the
age at which "authentic" poets like Keats and Shelley died; as such we should
contrast the idea of this poem with Wordsworth's "Resolution and Independence," in which the middle age of the speaker requires, in relation to the
wunderkinder Chatterton and Burns, a new poetics: How do you write poetry and survive? The result has been the mainstream tradition of lyric that
privileges the poem of the drama of the (surviving) lyric subject. But for
Corso (2 Jan. 1961) it is different: "If Shelley gave me anything, it was a kind
of nobility, an effort at plagiarizing the Gods as it were. . . . He's a pure angel-
man" (Corso, *Accidental Autobiography* 273–74). That is, how do I survive
and still be "angel-man," still plagiarize the gods and not worry too much
about craft, the curse of the nonvisionary but resolute and independent ego?

Very similar to Shelley here, Corso's poet as "angel-man," with the an-
ticipation of a destabilized identity, at times leads him to promote as ideal
poet the god of transformations and thresholds, Hermes or Mercury, just as

Shelley (and Keats) did. A favorite epithet (to be found in Shelley's "Defence") is "herald"; a book of Corso's is called *Herald of the Autochthonic Spirit*. The herald, or "messenger," is Hermes, "the orphan god," alone in these late days but crucial, as he was for the poet of *Homer's Hymn to Mercury* and *The Witch of Atlas*, for an artist wishing emphatically to awaken the consciousness of citizens.

If Shelley's life, which merges the person with the poet, commands Corso's attention, Shelley's haunting death by drowning helps other poets characterize the essence of Shelley's contribution to poetry. In the accounts of his death begun by contemporaries including Mary Shelley, Leigh Hunt, and Edward Trelawney poetry is intimately entwined with death: depending on the account, Shelley is washed ashore holding the latest book of Keats, the plays of Aeschylus, or the plays of Sophocles in his hand or in his pocket, while remnants of water-soaked Shelley manuscripts also belong to the constellation. The poets with whom I will conclude this discussion associate the merging of life, death by drowning, and work with a poetry that gains its hold over us as social beings because it locates itself beyond or outside the social, and goes deeper into origins than a poetry of the drama of the lyric subject typically does. Moreover, their preoccupation with drafts from Shelley points to an interest in Shelley as a poet of process or event rather than of finished artifact (writing a monumental poetry of recollection and pastness). These poets also associate the "draft" with an open-form poetry of their own.

A beautiful poem by Barbara Guest, alluded to previously, "Shelley in the Navy-colored Chair," which begins "I sit so close to him [Shelley]," directly brings the drowned person into conjunction with a transformed, living language. She observes: "He breathes into the alphabet I found upon my chair" and continues

> . . . he failed to ride the unswept sea, and like
> a nautilus drowned in heavy seas, windswept
> like the alphabet he enriched. . . .
> To add more stanzas to this alphabet
> is the view Shelley takes.

To be transformative with our language requires a poetry that comes from the sources of life, the sea of his drowning, implicitly a place where language has not distinguished itself from the person uttering or writing it. This is the implication of a moment in Susan Howe's preface to her book of (often lyric) essays *The Birth Mark*; writing about the use of manuscripts (Dickinson's,

Hölderlin's, and Shelley's) for the understanding of poets' engagement with them, she discusses one that "was pulled from the wreck of the *'Don Juan'*— which the poet had hoped to christen *Ariel*." She focuses on the text at the moment of Shelley's death, the text dredged from the sea itself and "heavily damaged by water, mildew, and restoration," which is to say that the "product" cannot be separated from its physical history and the body of its author. Since they are drafts, the text cannot be separated from the process of its making. Moreover, Howe picks as specimens passages that themselves blur the boundary between the artifact and the person producing it: (1) "A Poet is as- nightin gale who sits < > dar kness & sings to cheer its own so li tude w ith s w eet sounds" ("Defence"). (2) "He is a portion of the loveliness which once he made more lovely" (*Adonais*).

Thus when Andrew Mossin in his fascinating long, open-form poem *Drafts for Shelley* says that it represents his effort to "find 'Shelley,'"[10] he alludes to the feverish activity that occurred in 1822 to find or recover the body of the drowned poet. But here it stands for an extreme way of writing that at once recovers a "complete" and immediate version of the earlier poet through and for the sake of an expanded version of the later one: drafts from Shelley (reproduced occasionally in Mossin's text) become drafts for him. In both cases drafts signify process, which in turn revives the person in the text. The "find"ing of the poet, his or her recovery, becomes itself a construction of a poetry very much his own but unabashedly "derivative," in which he, in the spirit of Howe's editing, "often ventriloquized the repetitions, crossouts, and rewordings that score the pages of his notebook and contribute to their physical and graphemic beauty." "I sought to erase and fracture the language of Shelley's 'original,' thereby arriving at a poem whose language remained Shelley's yet whose form was my own" (n. pag.). It is not difficult to see this as a poetic reclamation of the Actaeon-like dismemberments with which Shelley himself identifies and of the drowned body ravaged by water and the creatures feeding on it. The "Shelley" reclaimed by poetry is not by any means solely the biographical and social person, not simply the Shelleyan ego against which he and his Cockney companions protested, but attracts to himself like seaweed to the drowned body the "portion of that loveliness" that is his own poetry as well as all of the elements of the mythic and historical collective in which he has participated.

Mossin moves this process forward into his own life in a manner that recalls Kelly's shifting of Shelleyan solitude to the context of unalloyed love. Much of *Drafts for Shelley* was written during the two years marked by the births of his two daughters; in an effort to record that intense experience, what he describes as a trance, he would sit "with the blue Bodelian note-books on my lap and transcribe myself into Shelley/Shelley into myself."

Finding Shelley means finding and collecting fragments of Shelley's poetry and presenting them as such: a constellation of fragments (Mossin writes in open-form fragments) that create a strangely new, unpremeditated and un-anticipated, yet strangely familiar, Shelleyan, whole. Looked at in terms of the politics of literary history, such a poetic project as Mossin's refuses a sen-timentalized or idealized version of Shelley and his poetry. This, I believe, is the main point of the extraordinary book-length poem by the British poet Alan Halsey, *The Text of Shelley's Death*. Halsey exploits the fact that there are many accounts of Shelley's death, some eyewitness and some retrospec-tive and secondhand; but no one account fully agrees with other accounts, and often the facts from one telling contradict those of another: "the text of Shelley's death is an embodiment of contradiction" (61). Memoirists and literary historians have attempted to resolve the differences or insist on one authentic one, but Halsey takes a different approach: he presents all the vari-ants, often in the spirit of a variorum edition. In other words, he wants the text of Shelley's death to honor, even celebrate, the contradictions. In con-trast to almost all of the accounts of Shelley's death, which dwell in the spirit of pastness and the tone of elegiac loss, this one actually radiates the feeling of recovery.

By accepting the impossibility of knowing irrefutably "what happened," Halsey's construction works against an idealization of the poet that began with his death and that led directly to the Arnoldian Shelley of ineffectu-ality and to a certain chasteness under the guise of "maturity" that one still sometime encounters in versions of this poet. "The boat disappeared into thick haze" (9). This line concludes a brief, three-quarter-page opening re-telling ("Everybody knows the text of Shelley's death"). The book that follows lays out many details that produce a thick haze, not to be suffered but to be embraced as the way to finding Shelley. It assumes the disfiguring, the frag-mentation, and the dismemberment of body and work as the starting point. Halsey's characterization of Shelley picked from the shards of his language and the surrounding narratives belongs to a quotidian, erotic, often self-absorbed world but also one drenched in sounds, rhythms, and figuration.

The closing "Index" accumulates a lake or bay (the Bay of Spezia in which Shelley drowned) of poetic language. The alphabetical presentation of im-age phrases, replete with the ambiguous or multivalent nature of images, leads to a metamorphic flowing of one image into another: reading it like a poem, one becomes aware of sound, of intense alliterative transmutations.

The *topicality* that one usually associates with an index becomes all signifier and movement. There are no page numbers, nothing to look up; thus the language here is not referential. Each letter of the alphabet, separated by a vertical space from the preceding and succeeding ones, becomes a "poem," the letter a rule for the poem to follow, giving it a shape, but also open for any number of specific entries. It reads like an open-form or aleatory version of a Shelley poem (a bit like Duncan's "Shelley's ARETHUSA" and Kelly's *Mont Blanc*). Here, for example, is the beginning of "t":

Tempering the cold and radiant air
That band of sister-spirits
That planet-crested Shape
That strange boat like the moon's shade
That thinnest boat
The boat of my desire. . . . (78)

The text of Shelley's death absorbs and transforms the poet-as-ego into a much larger and more poetic version of self, linked to mythological figures of his own referencing (like Prometheus or Mercury) and to poetic language. In his last paragraph Halsey says: "At moments the text reads as a sailing into metaphor into the unavoidable image of Shelley's own sea of metonymy and symbol: if this is an illusion it is one borne out by the outsider-tellers' reliance on a Shelleyan vocabulary" (81). Halsey has given us a twentieth- and twenty-first-century Shelley of radical transformations, a Shelley whose poetic calling sacrifices normal life for a total world of images. Perhaps she had Shelley in mind when Laura Riding wrote: "Appearances do not deceive if there are enough of them" (19).

"The romantic kind of poetry is still becoming; indeed, its peculiar essence is that it is always becoming and that it can never be completed" (Rothenberg and Robinson 901).[11] The poets considered in this essay seem to understand Friedrich Schlegel's aphorism instinctively, in a conclusively different response from that of Yeats described earlier, in which modernism and its sequelae are a falling off from Romanticism and even its predecessors.[12] That Shelley, as quintessential Romantic poet, became a lightning rod for their continued acts of becoming and renewing tells us precisely how he "flowed in" to their own thinking and making. As we have seen, part of the becoming these poets have participated in assumes the truth of Ezra Pound's dictum: "All ages are contemporaneous in the mind" (Rothenberg and Rothenberg 41).[13] That is, Shelley seems to have inspired an immediacy or presentness in their making of poems. To the degree that "Shelley" belongs to the past, he must not remain in the recollection of a modern poet but must be brought forward into "now": his perceptions, his prosody and form, his politics, and finally the collective dimensions of his person must be "found" now. Clearly not many poets of the past have evoked such an urgency for renewal:

Scatter, as from an unextinguished heart
Ashes and sparks, my words among mankind!
Be through my lips to unawakened Earth

The trumpet of a prophecy![14]

Notes

I wish to thank Elizabeth Robertson for her help with the construction of this essay.

1. See McGann, *The Poetics of Sensibility* for an articulation of such distinctions in the interpretation of Romantic and modern poetry and poetics.

2. From "Shelley in the Navy-colored Chair."

3. T. S. Eliot, from *The Use of Poetry and the Use of Criticism*, 1933; quoted in Palmer 202.

4. In an unpublished dissertation on the importance of the figure of Hermes or Mercury in Shelley's work and thought, Lisa Fishman has argued that (like the Witch of Atlas) Shelley as Mercury juxtaposes the contradictory and apparently unrelated.

5. See my book *Unfettering Poetry: The Fancy in British Romanticism*.

6. See Jerome McGann and Lisa Samuels, "Deformance and Interpretation," ed. Jerome McGann, *Radiant Textuality* (New York: Palgrave, 2001).

7. Kelly.

8. *Culture and Value*, taken up in Charles Bernstein's "Artifice of Absorption" (from *A Poetics*) and then in Palmer 203.

9. In her late novel *The Waves*, Virginia Woolf, as Jane Goldman has told me, quotes from Shelley's poems many times, often in the mode of what might be called visionary naturalness.

10. Mossin, *Drafts for Shelley*. This and subsequent quotations come from an unpublished draft of an introduction to the book.

11. Friedrich Schlegel, from "Athenaeum Fragment #116." Quoted in Rothenberg and Robinson.

12. See Yeats again, "Three Movements" (from *The Winding Stair and Other*

Poems (1933), reprinted in *The Collected Poems of W. B. Yeats*, ed. Richard J. Finneran (New York: Simon & Schuster Inc, 1996), 240.

> Shakespearean fish swam the sea, far away from land;
> Romantic fish swam in nets coming to the hand;
> What are all those fish that lie gasping on the strand?

13. Quoted, without reference, in Rothenberg and Rothenberg.
14. From Shelley's "Ode to the West Wind."

II

The Dialectic of Romantic and Postromantic Ethopoetics (after Certain Hispano-American Visual Poetries)

Heriberto Yépez
translated by Jen Hofer

I. Neruda's "Walking Around" and Its Visual Transcreation by Lorca

I will remark on a series of twentieth-century avant-garde poems written by Hispano-American poets that revise and dismantle the conventional Romantic notion of the stable lyric subject, as it appears in the topos of "the walk," by considering that subject in a visual medium. Very roughly, one can speak here of a revision of "Romantic" into "postromantic," but one can also argue that the "Romantic" already contains within itself the capacity for its own revisions and self-critique. Although his work is typically categorized as modernist, Pablo Neruda's classic poem "Walking Around," which is part of the second section of *Residencia en la tierra* (*Residence on Earth*) (1925–1931), will serve here as a late instance of Romanticism. I will then demonstrate how visual poems by Federico García Lorca and Nicanor Parra brilliantly enact critiques and expansions of Neruda's poem. Finally, and although it does not refer back directly to the subject as walker, I will read Juan Luis Martínez's *Pequeña cosmogonía práctica* as a further extension into the present of what might be called the Romantic/postromantic dialectic.

I will ground this discussion in a Latin American definition of the Romantic and in my own use of the term "ethopoetics." The definition of the Romantic that will serve as a starting point belongs to the Cuban poet and thinker José Lezama Lima and was published in *La expresión americana* in 1957, a very influential work in the field of Latin American poetics. According to Lezama, history can be understood as a succession of "imagos," which he defines as "image in participation with history" ("la imagen participando de la historia"). Lezama's poetic morphology sees a "humanity divided by eras that correspond to their potential to create images" (59).

Each one of these "imaginary eras" is embodied in a specific "metaphoric subject." One of these "metaphoric subjects," whose image both determines and is determined by history, is the Romantic subject, creator of and participant in a particular type of imagination. "That metaphoric subject acts to produce a metamorphosis toward the new vision" (53).

What I am calling an *ethopoetics* includes both a modification of the historical form of writing and a modification of the historic form of subject, a rewriting of text and self. This correlation between the production of new forms of writing and the production of new forms of subjectivity is present in the poems that I will analyze, and wherever poetry is understood to constitute a way of reconfiguring "world." In the ethopoetic realm, a change in the subject's way of seeing—by force of poetry-making—results in a change in the structure of subjectivity. Thus, ethopoetics refers to how the subject changes itself through poetry-making. According to Lezama, one of these "metaphoric subjects" that transform reality and its own being through image-production is the Romantic individual in the Americas, defined as the "romantic exiled [desterrado] . . . forced to wander through the first scenario of an American in rebellion" (111).

Lezama's Romantic "metaphoric subject" is marked by pilgrimage and persecution. Lezama gives several examples of Romantic subjects (Frey Servando, Simón Rodríguez, and Francisco Miranda) who embody the "romantic exile" and the "Weltbürger," who, often fugitive, wander as a way to reconstruct a world. In Lezama's definition, Romanticism is not a literary style or school, nor is it just a cultural period; it is an "imaginary era" historically situated in real time and space but also posed as a retrospective construction wherein, again, through elaborating a series of images, a poetic subject creates a new *mode of perception* that changes itself, the world, and the past. Walking has long contributed to the poetic representation of the privileged lyric subject, a speaker or narrator describing or embodying the state of simultaneous resistance to the activities of the world around it and yet paradoxically vulnerable to them, at times and famously, in the cases of Wordsworth, Whitman, and Baudelaire, vulnerable as well to epiphanic conversion moments. These moments can occur in either the country or the city and are much less often available to female than to male subjects, for whom walking allows an at least temporary transcendence of class position and political disposition. The prominence of the walking subject, nearly archetypal in power, is typically so great that a reader can consider it as a victory of the human subject over inimical forces. Yet in Neruda's famous example, the walking lyric subject begins to critique the "Romantic" stereotype from within the structure of the walking topos itself.

The poem's renowned first line, "Sucede que me canso de ser hombre" ("It just so happens that I'm tired of being a man"),[1] first of all imparts a sense of the casual or the accidental ("Sucede"), as if to disarm the expectation of stable subjectivity. The line should, however, be read not just as an exhaustion with being human, but also, literally, as an exhaustion with being male. It is important to remember that one aspect of the Romantic is derived from peripheral patriarchies[2] and the imbalance produced by the repression of the culturally feminine (in both sexes). Additionally, Romantic values or forms tend to function as psychocultural performances of the attempt to reincorporate the "feminine," the attempt to escape from the consensual performance of gender. At the same time, we can read this moment as a neopatriarchal attempt to appropriate supposedly feminine archetypes and stereotypes. Neruda's sensibility produces a strange dialectic between traditional "feminine" imagery and the search for an alternate masculinity.

In "Walking Around" the images allude to figures of rebirth typically associated with the feminine: "como un cisne de fieltro / navegando en un agua de origen y ceniza" ("like a felt swan / that steers across a sea of origins and ashes") where the water—in the form of sob, dampness, or rain—calls forth the underground presence of a regenerative order and a presumed return to the origin ("Sólo quiero un descanso de piedras o de lana"; "I only want a little rest from stones and wool"):

No quiero seguir siendo raíz en las tinieblas,
vacilante, extendido, tiritando de sueño,
hacia abajo, en las tripas mojadas de la tierra,
absorbiendo y pensando, comiendo cada día.

I don't want to keep on being a root in the darkness,
irresolute, pulled from all sides, till a dream leaves me shaking,
dragged down through the seeping bowels of the earth,
absorbing and thinking, stuffed with food every day.

The subsequent stanzas of the poem consist of variations on the theme of the poetic subject's rejection of conventional identity. Though one aspect of this rejection makes reference to the "natural" order, another is directed toward the working world:

Por eso el día lunes arde como el petróleo
cuando me ve llegar con mi cara de cárcel,
y aúlla en su transcurso como una rueda herida,
y de pasos de sangre caliente hacia la noche.

So the day called Monday started burning like oil
when it sees me pull in with my face of a jailhouse,
and it howls on its way like a wounded wheel,
and leaves tracks of hot blood in the direction of night.

The poetic subject projects onto "Monday" his own feeling of being sick
and tired of his job:

Y me empuja a ciertos rincones, a ciertas casas húmedas,
a hospitales donde los huesos salen por la ventana,
a ciertas zapaterías con olor a vinagre,
a calles espantosas como grietas.

And it shoves me into certain dark corners, into certain moist houses,
into hospitals where the bones sail through the windows,
into certain shoemakers' shops with their odor of vinegar,
into streets full of terrible holes.

Monday is chosen, obviously, because it represents the beginning of the work-week, but also because it is the day of the moon, the cosmic body of alternative consciousness and poetic desire; this allows us to perceive an extremely marked ambivalence around differing conceptions. The walker feels oppressed by the civilizing-working world throughout the poem. In order to *decom-press* that identity, on the one hand he *ex-presses* it—that is, he causes the pressure of Monday to *emerge*, and demonstrates its oppressiveness but also its contrary lure for the wanderer. He at once liberates himself from it and exhibits it, embodies it, exposing it to view. On the other hand, the walker also declares that the working-civilizing-patriarchal order is the force that produces within him desires whose objects ("certain corners," "certain houses," "hospitals where the bones sail through the windows," "shoemakers' shops with their odor of vinegar," "streets full of terrible holes") have a sexual, corporeal, damp, secret resonance, in which the apertures (windows or holes) and the darkly sensual become simultaneously repulsive and attractive: magnetic.

The title of the original poem appears in English precisely in order to highlight the foreignness of the walker's compound identity. At the same time, it is likely a wink to Baudelaire's—also originally titled in English—"Anywhere Out of the World," where Baudelaire's poetic subject wanders in an imaginary restless space—"This life is a hospital where every patient is possessed with the desire to change beds"—and with which "Walking Around" shares both imagery and sensation. Further, the title inadvertently reflects the rejection of the structures of linear-civilizing-habitual time in favor of wandering ("just walking around"). Simultaneously, it reflects the paradox of the vicious circle the poem represents in general: the walker wanders (*walks*) in order to escape the straight line, but as he does so he ends up going in circles (*around*).

In any case, what one could call the politics of "Walking Around" lies in a perceiver-walker who finds a tension between the magical or transcendent (represented by the moon) and the quotidian or social (represented by the workweek). We can thus see the poetic subject's crisis carried out within a Romantic framework.

That crisis reappears in a little-known transcreation of "Walking Around"—a visual version that Neruda and Federico García Lorca created in Buenos Aires in 1934, as part of a book of which there is only one copy—"made in honor of Doña Sara Tornú de Rojas Paz"—titled *Paloma por dentro o la mano de vidrio: Interrogatorio en varias estrofas* (*DOVE WITHIN, or THE GLASS HAND: Interrogation in a Few Stanzas*), consisting of titles of Neruda poems with drawings by García Lorca.[3]

Although Lorca's visual works are defined as "illustrations," they are actually visual reinventions, reinterpretations of Neruda's pieces. Through one of these we can gather information about Lorca's reading of "Walking Around."

Lorca's piece traces the perceptual journey of "Walking Around." The drawing is composed of two parts. The upper part consists of a black circle resembling an eye, out of which emerge four lines in the form of rays or branches, at the ends of which there are lips; these seem to be feminine, harking back to the rhetoric of femininity in Neruda's poem. Farther down the page we have three sets of lips joined by irregular lines, rivers, or ropes. This movement from eye to lips can be read as describing a movement from a distant, ocular perception into a proximate, erotized verbal description alluding to many of the at times abject images in "Walking Around."

The division between the upper and lower sections of the drawing is not especially marked. On the contrary, at first glance it produces the appearance of unity due to the continuity of the mouths (seven in total). If we thus read the piece as making a unified gesture, the circular black spot (or eye) can be understood as a center or source, out of which four arms emerge directly. This spot is then the "cause" of the lower structure, which seems to be foregrounded. In this case, the visual poem describes a poetic subject who constructs his poetry through a process of first "seeing" and then "saying."

However, if we read the poem not as a unified image, but instead as constructed of two distinct parts (upper and lower), we can argue that Lorca

Walking around

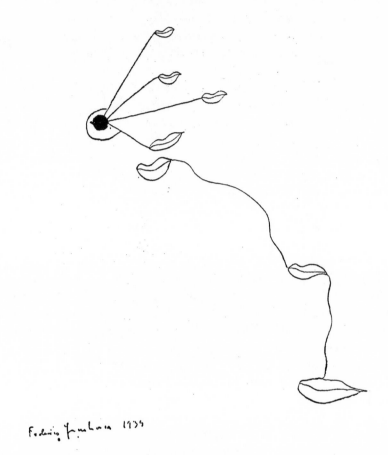

11.1. Pablo Neruda. *Obras completas.* Vol. 2.

displays a shift in poetic strategy, a shift from "Romantic" to "postromantic." In this second case, we have to notice that the bottom half of the drawing lacks an ocular center. Instead it presents only lips, connected by irregular lines. Furthermore, it is possible to read these lips as instead closed eyes, which might press us to consider that Lorca is rejecting the ocular center as a source for poetry and is instead insisting that poems must now originate from language itself, language simply interacting with other language in a nonlinear fashion.

Thus, this visual version of "Walking Around" combines distinct ways of conceiving the function of the poetic subject as a perceiver-describer. This

11.2. Pablo Neruda. *Obras completas.* Vol. 2.

is a zone where two ethopoetics intersect, where a Romantic ethopoetics (the imaginary construction of a subject possessing a dissensual Vision that nonetheless arises from the Origin) engages in an exchange with a post-romantic ethopoetics (the imaginary construction of a subject arising from a paratactic, acentric discourse). The acephalic subtext of Lorca-Neruda's "Walking Around," incidentally, is underlined in the last visual poem in *Paloma por dentro o la mano de vidrio*, in which two severed (and bloody) heads, named as García Lorca's and Neruda's, float atop a table and are observed by a cyclops-moon. On one of the corners of the table there is a sort of bouquet that bears resemblance to the upper subsystem of "Walking Around."

In his transcreation, Lorca highlighted the ethopoetic nature of the Nerudian enterprise by revealing what was always in play: a severe mutation—a decapitation—of one model of poetic subject, a transformation of the ethopoetic order in culture-literature inside (and moving toward the outside) of the Hispano-American avant-garde. As he decapitates both himself and Neruda, Lorca apparently judges that they occupy the same space in the history of imagination. The drawing envisions a transformation that these two poets can only anticipate, which then becomes manifest in later poets.

II. Postromantic Visual Critique of the "Romantic" Subject: Nicanor Parra and Juan Luis Martínez

In precise contrast to Neruda's dwelling in a Romantic poetics of self, Nicanor Parra, starting in the middle of the twentieth century, constructed his project of "antipoetry." This project was also a critique of Vicente Huidobro, and of Chilean and Western poetics generally, as they are linked to the Romantic model in which the poet is considered as having extra-ordinary perception. Parra's antipoet is a profane and even ridiculous figure, with no Romantic aura.

If we want to locate a work of Parra's that clearly delineates his contraposition with the Romantic model, we might take his visual poem "Poeta Lírico Pithecantropos Erectus" ("Lyric Poet Pithecantropos Erectus") from his book *Artefactos* (Parra 317).

Here we have a comic appropriation of a cartoon depicting a simian vagabond—with perhaps a racist undertone, a parodic transformation of Neruda's walker, or the lyric poet in general. The textual element names the lyric poet as an ancestor of the contemporary "antipoet," humorously signaling the irrelevance of this lyric poet in contemporary life. The poet, no longer extraordinary, instead emerges from the languages of popular culture (comics) and normalized science and technology.

Furthermore, the drawing implies that the figure of the poet evolves, and within that process there is a natural dynamic (referenced by the quadruped) and a social dynamic (referenced by the ripped clothing). This beggar-beast suggests a link between the poet and the savage or primitive, and at the same time situates the poet in a context of social deterioration—Latin America and capitalism in general—such that poetry belongs to a decrepit ideology whose former prestige has been worn out (literally, frayed).

While one can understand "Poeta Lírico Pithecantropos Erectus" as a rep-

POETA LIRICO
PITHECANTROPOS
ERECTUS

11.3. Nicanor Parra. *Obras completas & Algo †* (1935–1972).

resentation of the Nerudian walker in his true state of ridiculous defenseless-
ness, this de-Romanticized poet, despite having detached himself from total
identification with the Romantic model, still preserves a significant portion
of his features. That vestigial Romanticism grants him an ambiguity; he is
at the same time Romantic and postromantic. From the start, this walking
hominid recalls the Origin and the Beginning, categories that are eminently
Romantic. Like the Nerudian walker in "Walking Around," Parra's vagabond
alludes at once to a loss of direction and an exploration of new territory in
which old identities are useless: both poems, however, signal a *way out*.

We will now follow this dialectic between Romantic and postromantic
constructions of the subject in Chilean poetry into one of the central visual
poems of Latin American experimentalism: Juan Luis Martínez's "Pequeña
cosmogonía práctica" ("Small practical cosmogony"), found in *La nueva
novela* (*The New Novel*), constructed between 1968 and 1975 and published

in 1977. (Martínez originally planned to use the title of this poem as the title of his book.) Still more radically than with the works previously discussed, Martínez's poem, with its verbal-visual and linear-spatial oscillations, presents a challenging, ambiguous poetics of Romantic and postromantic divergences and realignments (Martínez 33).

There are a number of ways that Juan Luis Martínez codified his apparent separation from Romantic poetics. His *bookworks*—to borrow Ulises Carrión's concept—like *La nueva novela* or *La poesía chilena* (*Chilean Poetry*)—carry a rupture in their very structure. Even the prosaic speaking style of antipoetry turns out to be still too poetic and at moments is substituted by pop visual images, with no trace of the visionary or even of originality.

The cover and title page contain two author names: ~~Juan Luis Martínez~~ and ~~Juan de Dios Martínez~~; this doubleness suggests a kind of indecision—found in the work itself—and finally enacts the crossing out of any capitalist propriety over the work. How else does "Pequeña cosmogonía práctica"—a title that plays with Raymond Queneau's *Petite cosmogonie portative*—extend the questioning of a Romantic ethopoetics?

Martínez's piece begins with enthusiastic and parodic instructions that would seem once again to take up an Edenic-Romantic poetics (that is, a coherent, comic vision of I-Thou relations in which all is possible).

"Solución 1" ("Solution 1") corresponds to a psychoanalytic schema, or narrative—synthesized in Freud's "Mourning and Melancholia"—in which the human being loses a beloved person and enters into a psychic crisis from which she or he can escape (enacting complete mourning) or fail (melancholia) in the attempt. Martínez approaches this Freudian concept in a way that allows for more than one possible reading.

According to Freud, after the loss of the beloved other, the subject who does not successfully detach from the other experiences not only the desire to recuperate that love, but also an "identification of the I with the lost object," as Martínez writes in his poem (appropriating Freud's idea and phrasing). Such a mourner might even take the image of the beloved as her or his own. Thus the phrase "IN MEMORIAM" might allude to the death of the subject—after a suicide, we might say. But we also might read this ending in the opposite way: "identification of the I with the lost object" as a return of libidinal energy, now no longer directed toward the beloved but rather toward the self (a solution that involves a narcissistic turn). In this second case, only the other dies.

"Solución 2 (La Nueva Novela)" ("Solution 2 [The New Novel]") might seem to confirm this second solution, taking into account its ending (the destruction of the portrait). However, this would establish that "Solución 1"

PEQUEÑA COSMOGONIA PRACTICA

Construya un mundo coherente a partir de NADA, sabiendo que:
YO — TU y que TODO es POSIBLE.

(HAGA UN DIBUJO).

SOLUCION 1.

PERDIDA DEL OBJETO LIBIDINOSO

**DESEO DEL YO DE RECUPERAR
EL OBJETO PERDIDO**

**IDENTIFICACION DEL YO
CON EL OBJETO PERDIDO**

IN MEMORIAM
✚

SOLUCION 2.
(LA NUEVA NOVELA):

11.4. ~~Martínez, Juan Luis~~ and ~~Juan de Dios Martínez~~. *La nueva novela*.

and "Solución 2" are two variations of the same thing, and not two different, alternate solutions.

Before deciding whether "Solución 1" is simply the verbal description of "Solución 2" (which is primarily visual), and conversely "2" an "illustration" of "1," it is necessary to note that the subtitle of "Solución 2" is "(La Nueva Novela)," which would seem to imply that it is different in nature from "Solución 1." (And it should be noted that the parentheses suggest the germinal nature of this New Novel—that is, "New" Identity.)

In "Solución 2" four frames unfold; these might be read in two ways. The first would be from left to right and from top to bottom. The second would be from top to bottom and left to right.

If we read from left to right, in the first frame we see a humanoid figure with a prominent (phallic) nose and an egg-shaped skull carefully examining a portrait. We can immediately surmise that the figure in the portrait is a woman, though this reading is not substantiated by anything other than cultural suppositions, since the figure in the portrait itself has relatively short hair and there is no outstanding feminine feature; this is significant for the poem's general ambiguity.

In this reading, the second frame appears on the upper right, where the man looks out at us and holds a pistol to his right temple—incidentally, with his left hand placed directly on his genital area, as a possible unconscious allusion to the narcissistic-masturbatory-sexual-fantasy nature of his impulse.

If we continue this line of reading, then, the third frame is the one in the lower left corner, where the figure of the man once again looks at the portrait, now presumably reconsidering, as he has withdrawn the pistol from his temple.

If we take the other route in our reading, then the order of these three initial frames shifts in the following way: the first frame of the man observing the portrait is followed by the lower left frame, where he has opened his legs and raised the weapon to the level of his knee, leaning his left elbow on the table to consider suicide, the prelude to which would appear in the upper right frame.

The order of "Solución 2" is not irrelevant; it does not just add polyvalence to the poem but also shifts the placement of the key (meta)discursive moment (the lower left frame) in which the man examines the portrait with the pistol facing the floor. In the first reading, this moment of contemplation takes place in the third frame; in the second reading, this reconsideration takes place in the second frame.

The implications for Martínez's postromantic poetics are remarkable. If the shot against the portrait is preceded immediately by meditation, then Martínez is emphasizing a postromantic metadiscursiveness as guiding the subject's actions. If instead, the shooting of the portrait is immediately preceded by the subject holding the gun to his own head, then Martínez is emphasizing a Romantic impulsivity or passion. In this ludic version, the choice to preserve one's life depends primarily on a basic desire to survive as a poetic subject at the risk of disappearance. This is not so much a conceptual decision as a psychological and psychic one. Or even a cynical one.

What is in play here in these dialectical readings is the extent to which Romantic elements—desperation, disillusion, passion, impulsivity—intervene in the antirealist ethos of postmodernist postromantic experimentalism.

In both readings, however, the eventual shooting of the portrait still suggests a rejection, on the conceptual level, of the identification of representation ("the portrait") with reality. In the "Nueva Novela" the poetic subject not only no longer identifies language (alone) with reality, but he also destroys the means of realistic representation ("the portrait") associated with this premise.

"Pequeña cosmogonía práctica" in this way summarizes the poetics of *La nueva novela* and of more than one variety of experimentalism, still with reference to Romanticism, on the American continent during the seventies. (And this occurs in Chile in the repressive context of the neoliberal dictatorship of Pinochet, which terminated Salvador Allende's leftist project. *La nueva novela*, incidentally, is an experimental book with a political position and a coded but very effective critique; in order to escape censorship, the work employs code.) The last frame does more than signal the destruction of the portrait—whether due to a metadiscursive-postromantic decision or a passionate-Romantic one, according to the order in which we choose to read. If we examine the image, the explosion also generates a kind of microcosmos that originates with the *small bang* of the gunshot. In this way, "Pequeña cosmogonía práctica" acquires a new meaning, one that references the fact that it is the violent Romantic impulse that continues to propel changes in modes of Western poetic representation.

Here we have the reason that "Solución 2" is titled "La nueva novela." That is, while it is a neologistic, innovative project, it still belongs to the era of the "novel," the modern era, centered on the *drama of the individual*, the adventure of the dissensual person whose theater of struggle continues to be the singular body. And yet this "negative work" (to use Tzara's words) still rests on Romantic premises: a violent attack against representation, and even the poet as a "small god" (to use the renowned line from Huidobro's "Arte poética"). This demiurge initiates a new world, developed out of a drastic re-active act, a product of the debacle of a relationship with an internal world shaken by the instability of the external one.[4]

It is crucial to investigate further whether poems like "Solución 1" and "Solución 2" are divergent (the first as a Romantic solution; the second, a postromantic one) or whether they are two ways—one verbal and the other visual—of positing one single solution, the destruction of old modes of representation. And yet this poem also suggests the reiteration of the persistent centrality of the Romantic *I* or the lyric *I* in the Chilean experimental project. And, in its broader reading, "Pequeña cosmogonía" synthesizes what we have found in the preceding visual poems: a mechanism for the intersection of both ethopoetics. Is there, in other words, a "solution" beyond Martínez's "synthesis"?

This poem by Martínez registers our ambivalence in relation to the Romantic, and, indeed, in some form or another it still enacts a Romantic dialectic—or a dialectic in the face of the Romantic—which guides the historical development of Western poetry in this era. "Pequeña cosmogonía"—which corresponds to the model of the poet as a small god—is a "practical" cosmogony most probably because Romantic ideology is already vanishing (it is a cosmo(a)gony) but continues to be in operation, as part of a consensual and dissensual poetic praxis. Romantic textual production techniques (the mixing of genres, linguistic flows, wild use of palimpsest, parataxis, shock, collage, chance, subconscious, etc.) continue to reign within supposedly postromantic poetics. The poet as a practical small god.

Here, as in all of these contexts of the Romantic that we have examined, the postromantic appears, in fact, as Romanticism's complement or its condition, rather than its successor. And perhaps the elements that have been called "Romantic" were a strategy for the negation of what we call today the "postromantic," and today's "postromantic" is a strategy for the negation of "Romantic" elements that continue to be operative in writing and culture.

If we want to speak of succession, then, the succession of one—the Romantic—would implicate the succession of the other—the postromantic. It might be that succession is merely an illusion of substitution or alternation produced by this costructure.

Notes

1. All quotes in English from "Walking Around" are from the translation by Jerome Rothenberg in *The Oxford Book of Latin American Poetry*, ed. Cecilia Vicuña and Ernesto Livon-Grosman. (Trans. note)

2. By "peripheral patriarchies" I intend to point to the fact that there is not just one single patriarchy, but rather various patriarchies (in conflict among themselves), and some of those are peripheral, subordinate to others. In this way, for example, a Mexican macho is subordinate to a white macho; or a literary patriarchy might be peripheral to another patriarchy within a particular culture.

3. This series of visual poems is included in the second volume of Neruda's 1968 complete works, in a section without page numbers near the end of the volume.

4. Nor is it chance that Martínez's project should have tutelary figures like Rimbaud and Marx as its "Eternal Return."

12

The Sublime Is Now Again

Julie Carr

> But the chaos of surfaces compels us towards new states of happiness.
> Lisa Robertson, *Occasional Work and 7 Walks*
> *from the Office for Soft Architecture*

As we encounter it in textbooks, on *Wikipedia*, in introductions to anthologies, the Victorian period is often, and in many senses justly, described as dedicated to gradual, developmental social progress. Pax Britannica, the Reform Acts of 1832 and 1867, advances in labor and marriage laws, the development of liberal political philosophy, science's steady move on religion—all of this is achingly familiar to any student of the nineteenth century and shades the period in our popular imagination in tones of brown and gray (until, of course, we arrive at Oscar Wilde's green carnation).

And yet, numerous studies from Jerome Hamilton Buckley's seminal book *The Triumph of Time* (1966) forward have revealed that the latter half of the nineteenth century, in tension with this sense of gradually advancing progress, experienced an "apocalyptic mood," a mood encouraged by rapid developments in physics, geology, biology, and by growing religious doubt. Buckley traces scientific transformations especially but also discusses Britain's diminishment of economic and military power during the latter half of the century, concluding that from the 1850s on, "a deep malaise recurred throughout the whole period till at last among intellectuals it became a principal element in the modern temper" (71). Contemporary critics have followed (Alison Sulloway, Philip Drew, Patricia M. Ball, and Owen Chadwick), describing from various angles the period's fears and fascinations in the face of sudden transformations and losses.[1]

In addition to scientifically and theologically motivated anxieties, historians and critics have shown that the period is marked by an increasing sense of imminent and catastrophic political transformation. Mark Francis and John Morrow, among many others, describe the reemergence and development of socialist thought in Britain during the 1880s and 1890s (293–307). Isobel Armstrong remarks that Victorian poets "exist[ed] with the constant possibility of mass political upheaval and fundamental change in the structure of society" (Armstrong, *Victorian Poetry* 3). And more recently, Stephanie Kuduk Weiner writes, "Between 1866 and 1874, as a result of the success of Continental democratic movements and the growth of republican sentiment in Britain, the proverbial republican sunrise seemed imminent" (255).

If we therefore accept that at least from the 1860s on, the period produces not so much placid attitudes of tempered optimism, but real apocalyptic fears and messianic hopes, how do these ruptural, as opposed to gradualist, models of temporality find their place in poetry? How do some of the nation's most innovative poets reveal their own fascination with ruptural models of temporality and the sudden transformations that they imply? I would like to suggest that the decorative intricacy—the attention to the surface play of language, by which I mean its sounds, textures, and visual effects—in much of the poetry of this late Victorian period, while often deliberately employed to provoke intense affectivity, also and importantly serves to evoke this ruptural sense of time. Thus, the very basic features of all poetry—alliteration, assonance, orthographic and grammatical complexity and play—are intensified in this poetry to such a degree that they do not merely support the work's cognitive meaning, but instead create an alternate experience, one of temporal rupture.

Dante Gabriel Rossetti, William Morris, and Gerard Manley Hopkins all provide examples of what I have called elsewhere "surface tension" in poetry, in which such an intensification of the sonic, visual, and syntactic play of the words and phonemes draws the reader's attention as much to the sensations that poetic language creates as to the cognitions it might provoke. All also provide examples of artists dedicated to (as opposed to nervous about) ruptural transformation, though the transformations they imagined belong to differing realms of experience—the psychological, the political, and the spiritual, respectively. Indeed, the complex surface, in all three cases, is offered as a means toward, not just a representation of, such ruptural or sudden transformations (though again, this functions differently for each poet). Later in this essay I hope to show how this works in just one of these poets, Dante Gabriel Rossetti.

What also ties these late Victorian poets together is what has been called their (belated) Romanticism, which, as others such as Jerome McGann and Antony Harrison have argued, can also be read as a preemptive postmodernism. That they share with some British Romantics (Blake, early Wordsworth, Shelley) an interest in transformation—both political and personal—is evident, as both groups confronted revolution as a real presence, even if not at home. What seems as intriguing is how their "Romanticism" can be located in their indebtedness to John Keats, less for any sense of "rupture" in his work than for how he enlivens language's ornamental qualities, its sensations—of mouth and ear and eye.

Keats was the most beloved poet of the Pre-Raphaelite Brotherhood; drawn not only to his enthrallment with sensation, but also to his medievalism, and the struggle in his work between the ideal and the real, the "PRB," and Tennyson before them, turned to Keats as an important, even necessary, predecessor. Pre-Raphaelite painter Holman Hunt's first exhibited painting at the Academy was *The Eve of St. Agnes*, taken from Keats's poem of that name. John Millais's first painting that bore the PRB insignia was of a scene from Keats's "Isabella" (Thompson 51). The convergence of the original Pre-Raphaelites—including Rossetti, Hunt, and Millais—occurred at least in part because of their joint enthusiasm for Keats. Some critics maintain that it was in fact Keats's interest in Italian art before the time of Raphael that inspired Rossetti to come up with the term "Pre-Raphaelite" (Ford 108). William Morris concludes his utopian novel *News from Nowhere* with a direct reference to the last line of "Ode to a Nightingale" (Meier 96).

"Keats the sweet-maker, the sweet-taker, is too conspicuous, childish, appetitive, excessive," writes Susan Wolfson, discussing Keats's negative reception in his time. "Not just a poet, Keats was also a language" (259, 244). The language of desire no doubt, but Keats's work also brings us to the desires of language, to the ongoing restlessness that (especially poetic) language's indeterminacies generate. Indeed, the reasons for Keats's appeal to the later Victorian poets (and certainly the reason Matthew Arnold rails against the Keatsian School in his famous Preface of 1853) has as much to do with the intense sound-play, the frequent puns, the packed meters of his poems, with their "surface tension," as with the mad pursuit of ongoing desire that the poems thematize. Or, perhaps Keats's appeal has everything to do with the *relationship* between surface play and such "sweet unrest."[2] Romanticism, or the Romanticism that these late Victorian poets admired and emulated, is a poetics of intense surface play and disruptive desire.

But in considering further how Victorian poets can be thought of not only as belatedly Romantic but also as protopostmodern, I would like to turn briefly to a more contemporary source, to one of the essays that has helped us define "the Romantic" in ways productive, rather than reductive—active, rather than static—an essay that not only considers Romanticism to be an activity, rather than a period, but that also ties the advent of Romanticism directly to the development of the postmodern, and that is Jean-François Lyotard's "The Sublime and the Avant-Garde" (1984). In making explicit the kinship between Romanticism and postmodernism, the essay makes a case for the importance of the aesthetic *surface* in both aesthetic movements.

The essay is well known, so I will not rehearse all of its arguments here, but I would like to draw attention to one key point. Lyotard begins with Barnett Newman as a way to consider "the sublime." Newman's stark vertical forms might seem an odd choice—a far cry from Snowdon, that "emblem of a mind / That feeds upon infinity" (*Prelude* 1850, bk. 14, 70–71). But then not. Pointing to Newman's 1948 essay "The Sublime Is Now," Lyotard explores what "now-ness" might have to do with the surface textures of Newman's paintings ("the 'it-happens' is the paint," writes Lyotard), and what such "now-ness" might have to do with the with term "sublime," so important to Romanticism, to Newman, and to Lyotard (Lyotard, *The Inhuman* 93).

Tracing Newman's version of the sublime to Burke's (as opposed to Kant's) theory, Lyotard argues that what Newman is after, what he means by "sublime," *is* the aesthetic representation of this "now-ness." Thus Newman's title, "The Sublime Is Now" takes "is" as a verb of equivalence and "now" as an abstract concept, rather than a specific moment in time (May of 1948, for example). Aesthetic objects, writes Lyotard, that work to represent this feeling of "now-ness" create in their viewers what he calls an "ontological dislocation," a disturbing but exhilarating sense that the self is unknowable to itself. In trying to "present the fact" of the "unpresentable" *now*, the work of art offers the viewer a dismantling but ultimately transforming experience, more disruptive, but also more productive than the comforting experience of "beauty" (Lyotard, *The Inhuman* 101). "What kind of time was Newman concerned with, what 'now' did he have in mind?" asks Lyotard. Not the "fleeting" present, he argues, but instead a "now-ness" that "is a stranger to consciousness and cannot be constituted by it." This sense of now, says Lyotard, "is what dismantles consciousness, what deposes consciousness, it is what consciousness cannot formulate, and even what consciousness forgets in order to constitute itself" (90).[3]

I want to be sure to underline that for Lyotard the apprehension of "now-ness" is a transformative experience; when time's ongoing flow is ruptured by a perceived sense of "now," made accessible through an aesthetic surface, the experience for the viewer (or reader) is shocking. An art of surfaces—or a poetics that focuses on the surface of the text—explains Lyotard, can more readily approach this shocking and dismantling experience of "now" because of how it moves away from a mimetic relationship to moments and toward the text (or painting) as a moment in its own right. "Free from the verisimilitudes of figuration," verbal or visual works that veer closer to abstraction, that draw our attention to the presence of their materials and that combine these materials in new and shocking ways, remind us of the "(something) *happening*" in the work itself (rather than in some prior experience or some "beautiful" thing that the work seeks to represent) (100).

Lyotard thus provides us with a way of thinking about Romanticism's fascination with the moment (Wordsworth's "spots in time," Keats's bursting grape and suspended kiss) in connection with the mid-twentieth-century turn from figurative painting. He allows us to consider both aesthetic movements as attempts to represent the experience of "presence." And he allows us to see that this experience must be understood not as a relaxing acceptance of what is, but instead as a shocking break out of an ordinary and habitually sensed chronological time.

As we begin to think of this "now" as a tear in the fabric of ordinary time, some readers might feel very much in the vicinity of Benjaminian "now-time," might be reminded of his chiseled notion that every moment in time might be the "strait gate . . . through which the Messiah might enter" (Benjamin, *Theses* 264). Benjaminian messianism has played a formative role in some contemporary avant-garde writing, providing contemporary poets and critics seeking redemptive value in poems that engage present moments through an embrace of sensation and surface with workable aphorisms. It might seem harder, however, to tie such notions to the poems of the Victorian era, poems that have been thought of more for their historical obsessions, their narrative mode, or their devotional content than for their interest in ruptural time or the sudden transformations that encounters with ruptured time might engender.

And yet, where these ideas find their cousins in Victorian poetics is well summarized by Jerome Bump in his discussion of Victorian "Radicals," who, he argues, "thought they could reach their [political/visionary/aesthetic] goals by . . . break[ing] through linear time into a cyclical, reactualizable time and/ or into an eternal presence" (27). Included in Bump's group of "Radicals" are Hopkins and the Pre-Raphaelites. Bump reads Hopkins's poetry as offering a "radical" notion of the Eucharist (or more broadly, God's presence) in which "we are not suddenly brought into the world of the eternal present, but reminded that we *are* already there" (38).[4] "In a flash, at a trumpet crash, / I am all at once what Christ is, 'since he was what I am, and / This Jack, joke, poor potsherd,' patch, matchwood, immortal diamond, / Is immortal diamond" writes Hopkins, reproducing the ruptural moment of divine presence as a hard-won revelation. Indeed, one could say that this revelation is in fact created by Hopkins's twenty-two-line poem ("That Nature is a Heraclitean Fire and of the comfort of the Resurrection") with its dense sonic resonances and repetitions, its almost impenetrable wall of sound. Only such an intensification of sensation, it seems, can deliver us, in Christian terms, to the eschatological arrival, or in secular terms, to the sublimely shattering apprehension of "now."

Again, Lyotard argues that the painting allows access to this transformative experience of "now-ness" when (because of abstraction) the work becomes an example of "something happening" in the moment. But how does this work in poetry? Language can never be purely abstract, must always (or almost always) serve some mimetic function, no matter how slight. But while some poems, if read only as descriptive language events, might seem to simply describe moments, when read also for their surface play, and especially when that play is intensified, can become moments, become the "something" that is "happening" ("The poem should not mean / but be.") In this way, a poem of ornate surfaces can be read as an instance of "now-ness," comparable to the rupture of ordinary temporality and the corresponding "ontological dislocation" that Lyotard finds in gazing on Newman's abstract canvases. I would like to turn now to one key Victorian poet, famous for his ornate surfaces, who ties an intensified experience of now-ness to the transformative possibilities of such "ontological dislocation," and that is Dante Rossetti. We will look at two poems.

Silent Noon

Your hands lie open in the long fresh grass,—
The finger-points look through like rosy blooms:
Your eyes smile peace. The pasture gleams and glooms
'Neath billowing skies that scatter and amass.
All round our nest, far as the eye can pass,
Are golden kingcup-fields with silver edge
Where the cow-parsley skirts the hawthorn-hedge.
'Tis visible silence, still as the hour-glass.

Deep in the sun-searched growths the dragon-fly
Hangs like a blue thread loosened from the sky:—
So this wing'd hour is dropt to us from above.
Oh! clasp we to our hearts, for deathless dower,
This close-companioned inarticulate hour
When twofold silence was the song of love. (136)

The stilling of time, this breaking of time's flow, is announced most obviously near the poem's conclusion when the hour spent lying in the grass becomes a "deathless dower" granted to the lovers in their mutual silence (lines 12, 11). But this sense of suspended time is offered too by the title, in which "noon" seems to quiver in its palindromic balance. The beloved's fingertips poking up through the grass are given an object-like status, as if they no longer belong to a temporal body. And yet, much of the language of the poem connotes motion, not stasis: the fingertips are "rosy blooms," the pasture "gleams and glooms" (and "gloom" here probably takes its much older meaning, which is "to glow" rather than to frown or sulk), skies "scatter and amass." While we might pick up feelings of immobility from the odd simile "'Tis visible silence, still as the hour-glass" (which in fact can be still only when the hour is complete, or when, perhaps like the lover, it is lying on its side), such stillness is undercut by the crucial metaphor in line 12. There the hour is compared to a dragonfly, a creature that can appear to hover in stillness, but only because of its intense agitation.

And thus, it seems that the "now" of the poem is importantly not a cessation. Rather, intensified feeling creates the sense of suspension, even as time inevitably, perhaps thankfully, moves on. So what kind of time is this? If not the end of time (because death*less*), it is certainly not ordinary time either; what is a wing'd hour that "drops" rather than flies? What is a deathless dower? If time does not stop but instead has the appearance of stopping, what does such an experience of ruptured time offer the poem's lovers? Does Lyotard's "ontological displacement" occur here?

To help us think about these questions, I would like to look at another of Rossetti's poems, the considerably more surface-y—which is to say more dense with sound play, visual rhyme, and complex, resistant syntax—"The Monochord":

> Is it this sky's vast vault or ocean's sound
> That is Life's self and draws my life from me,
> And by instinct ineffable decree
> Holds my breath quailing on the bitter bound?
> Nay, is it Life or Death, thus thunder-crown'd,
> That 'mid the tide of all emergency
> Now notes my separate wave, and to what sea
> Its difficult eddies labour in the ground?
>
> Oh! what is this that knows the road I came,
> The flame turned cloud, the cloud returned to flame,
> The lifted shifted steeps and all the way? -
> That draws round me at last this wind-warm space,
> And in regenerate rapture turns my face
> Upon the devious coverts of dismay? (162)

The speaker is preceded by a threatening force that draws him forward only to draw life from him. This force might be of air or ocean, of "Life" or "Death" (time or no-time). The speaker's breath is held, is *being* held by this terrible and "ineffable" power. This prevailing force, like the God of Exodus to which it is compared, is both threatening and liberating. The use of the word "bound" in line 4 to suggest, most literally, the liminal space between earth and sea (or metaphorically, between life and death) has, if read as a verb, other and opposing meanings: the breath is both constrained and ready, determined. Thus, as in "Noon," in this octet we have a scene that positions the speaker *between* stillness and motion, between life and death, or, we could say, between time and its end.[5]

I would like to focus our attention now on a single sound: the "Oh" that marks the poem's turn. This sigh, this exhale, frees the bound breath of line 4. This "Oh" that stands at the Volta of "The Monochord" introduces another kind of circle, a "wind-warm space," like a mouth, wound by sound, by breath (our wind)—an embrace that does not constrain, but moves the subject outward, like a birth.

If we can therefore read this poem as figuring the transforming rebirth of the subject, let us see what precedes this "Oh." What makes such transformation possible? Turning to lines 6–8, we find, fittingly enough, that just before the "Oh" of the subject's emergence is a "difficult labor" (8). The breath quails only until the poem turns, and in the gap between octet and sestet, in this turn that is also a silence, the artist is rapturously reborn, even (like the Israelites everywhere here alluded to) liberated. This "tide of all emergency"— this rising tide that threatens to subsume the subject—holds within it the emergence of autonomy, just as the Red Sea holds within its "wind-warmed space" the emergence of a liberated people.

Thus the temporality of the poem, the "Now" that "notes my separate wave" (7), is the now of voice, the moment of expression felt in the mouth as breath (or poem). That breath, that song, becomes in this poem a transformative force. But it is important to note how the poem's surface functions as an instance of this "difficult labor" through which the subject can be rapturously reborn. There is the obvious use of alliteration (vast vault, bitter bound, now notes, wind warm, regenerate rapture), of rhyme and near rhyme—but there are many other more subtle uses of consonants and assonance, such as the opening stuttering "is it this"; the pairing of "life/self"; the trio "death, thus, thunder"; the reach from "ineffable" to "difficult," from "vast" to "last"; and the near repetitions of "turned/returned/turns." As in Hopkins's "That Nature Is a Heraclitean Fire," the experience of sudden rebirth or rupture (or perhaps rupture as rapture) occurs through the "difficult labor" of the densely packed textual surface. While these surfaces are not, like a Newman painting, purely abstract, their reliance on sound-play and visual rhyme presses them in that direction, toward what Walter Pater called "the condition of music."

To return now to "Noon," we can see a similar process at work. The subject's access to "now," to the "deathless dower" of the moment, allows him a transformation that, while not as dramatic as the rebirthing in "The Monochord," is nonetheless significant as an instance of "ontological dislocation." For the dropping into "now-ness" that the poem enacts leads the speaker to temporarily but importantly transcend the boundaries of his own subjectivity. This happens in line 12, which, perhaps not coincidentally, also begins with an "Oh!": "Oh! clasp we to our hearts, for deathless dower." The "ontological dislocation" of the poem is here, when the addressed "you" becomes a "we," when the distinction between the two lovers is momentarily blurred—they are mutually clasping, mutually clasped. The syntax here is inverted, for in fact the object of this clasping is not the lovers themselves, but the hour. And yet, the function of the enjambment (and syntactical complexity is an aspect of what I am calling "surface") allows us to think (with Rossetti, I believe) that in this moment "we" have become at once subject and object. In the "Oh" of now, the "I" of the poem (to return to Keats) is "not myself." Thus, once again, surface play is directly tied to a rupture in time, which leads in turn to "ontological displacement."

But in "Noon" the "now" of the moment does not shimmer for long—in the final couplet Rossetti returns us to ordinary time, and he does so by employing the past tense, reminding us that the poem is not, or is no longer, a "now." "This close-companioned inarticulate hour / When twofold silence was the song of love" reads the couplet. The sonnet's form, the poem's end, demands the end of the moment, the end of now, and so the unjoining of the lovers—the reestablishing of subjective stability.

I hope I have begun to indicate that a late Victorian poet like Rossetti (or, if I had more space, Morris, Christina Rossetti, Hopkins) is necessary to us now in part because he demonstrates many of what have become our strongest beliefs about what poetry *should* do: that it should deeply engage a specific moment; that it should recognize the materiality, or surface, of language; and most importantly, that it should suggest violent or sudden rupture in order to imply that some transformation, whether on the level of the personal, or, as in the case of William Morris, the political, is yet possible. Of course personal or psychic transformations, such as those imagined by Rossetti, are not one and the same with political transformations; some would say a focus on the personal necessarily eclipses the pressing need for social or political change (and some would say the opposite). What remains for us, the inheritors of Romanticism (in which I am including these late Victorian poets), is a desire for art to indicate some hope, even in the face of what might feel like art's total capitulation to the market, even, or especially, in the face of the disasters—economic, ecological, political—that our century continues to deliver. Let me turn finally, then, to one contemporary poet whom I read as similarly and strikingly conjuring the transformative possibilities of ruptural time embedded within a textual field irradiated by surface tension, and that is the Canadian poet Lisa Robertson.[6]

Robertson is one of the key figures in what we could call "post-language" experimental poetry (though such labels are purely a matter of convenience).[7] Her work, from the 1997 *Debbie: An Epic*, to the 2001 volume *The Weather*, the 2003 essay collection *Occasional Works and 7 Walks from the Office for Soft Architecture*, and the more recent *R's Boat* (2010), has consistently concerned itself with the materiality of language; the ornamental and often semantically resistant phrase, sentence, or page; and the redemptive potential of "now-ness." I will begin by turning to her 2009 volume, *Lisa Robertson's Magenta Soul Whip*, in which she extends her densely surfaced poetics to directly embrace images of transformation.

In *Magenta Soul Whip* Robertson is rather explicit about how poetry might, through its engagement with sensual, textual, and surface detail, invoke a break in time, a movement into the no-time (or "now-time")—which she calls Utopia. "My idea of Utopia," Robertson says in an interview, "is not that it's an elsewhere, a situated elsewhere to strive towards or that is contained only within an imaginative projection, but that Utopia could be considered more almost in phenomenological terms as a *sensed present*. What I think I mean is that . . . political transformation has to be situated in what we are already in the midst of experiencing" (Carr). The term "Utopia," then, which occurs frequently in Robertson's work, is meant to suggest not some future time of redeemed social life, but instead an intensification of "now," a transformation that becomes possible when "now-ness" is deeply, as she says, "sensed."

In the second section of the poem "A Hotel," we find the following: "I'm speaking of the pure sexual curves / Of Utopia, the rotation / Of its shadows against the blundering / In civitas" (*Magenta Soul Whip* 19; lines 11–14). Utopia, then, casts its erotically charged shadow across the present as if it is simply an "other life" sliding across this one. And yet, the "Big problem of poetry" (line 18), as she puts it a few lines later, is *how* to evoke this redeemed time, how to gesture toward redemption while immersing oneself in the here-and-now sensations of the text. "On this very beautiful surface / Where I want to live / I play with my friends" (lines 21–23). But this admission of pleasure is not a rejection of political agency or urgency; quite the opposite: "I believe my critique of devastation / Began with delight. Now what surprises me / Are the folds of political desire / Their fragile nobility, Sundays of / Rain" (lines 29–33).

Critique begins and ends not with analysis, not with suffering, but with pleasure, the pleasures of the social, the pleasures of the poem, the pleasures of the body in the present. Thus the poem, as a surface dedicated to pleasure ("Some think only of pleasure in their projects / I am one of those people / . . . I'll solicit nothing / But ornament" [lines 42–43, 59–60], Robertson asserts later in the poem), is itself a form of critique. And yet, the tension between engaging in such pleasures, and the "political desire" for a redeemed social space presses against this poem, forcing it into the mode of a defense. Perhaps this hint of self-implication provides the "whip" of *Magenta Soul Whip*. And yet, again and again in Robertson's work, sensation itself, ornament, pleasure, bodily experience, are offered as the means toward an intensified experience of "now," and such an experience, as she argues in poems, interviews, and essays, is itself the redeemed or "utopian" moment.

The long poem "Utopia," which appears in *R's Boat*, is specifically concerned with the relationship between present-time sensation and utopian renewal. "I wanted to study the ground, the soft ruins of paper and the rusting things," Robertson writes, "I discovered a tenuous utopia made from steel, wooden chairs, glass, stone, metal bed frames, tapestry, bones, prosthetic legs, hair, shirt cuffs, nylon, plaster figurines, perfume bottles and keys" (51), suggesting that poetry, in its propensity to name, to gather, to engage language as thing, is a kind of scavenger hunt performed by the poet in the present and on the ground. Or it suggests that utopia is precisely this act of gathering, studying, observing, this act of engaging with one's sensations: "Women," she writes, "from a settlement called Utopia focus on the intricate life that exists there." And then later, "What we are proposing already exists." A page later Robertson asks, "Which is a surface? / What is the concept of transformation?" (52–53), offering quite directly the guiding questions of this essay.

The poem presents time, the marking of time, as one of its central preoccupations. All but one of its eighteen stanzas open with a reference to a date or season: "In the Spring of 1979"; "The season called November"; "At about midnight in Autumn"; "At about four in the morning, that first day"; "It is late October"; and so on. And yet, no chronology organizes these references; rather, time seems to be collapsing into itself. Further, even as the months and seasons might want to pull us into past or future, the paratactic (and present-tense) mode of Robertson's sentences bring us into present-time experience again and again. "Pollen smears the windows. / The blackberry vines are Persian. / The boulder smells faintly of warm sugar" (62). These sensual present-time descriptions remind us too of the pleasures of surface: the smear on a windowpane, the scent on the surface of a stone. "The day shows a licked surface," and earlier, "The face moves across the human": the face here, like the shadows of Utopia in "A Hotel," becomes a surface that holds the potential for what I can only call redemption.

Once again I am reminded of Benjaminian now-time. Stéphane Mosès writes, sounding much like Robertson here, that for Benjamin, "utopia [is] a function of the experience of the present" (125). He goes on:

> For Benjamin and Scholem . . . Utopia, which can no longer be thought of as belief in the necessary advent of the ideal at the mythical end of history, reemerges—through the category of Redemption—as the modality of its possible advent at each moment in time. In this model of random time, open at any moment to the unpredictable eruption of the new, the imminent realization of the ideal becomes conceivable again, as one of the possibilities offered by the unfathomable complexity of historical processes.
>
> . . .
>
> The idea of "now-time" . . . that idea inspired by Jewish messianism, proposes a model of history that, after the collapse of the ideologies of progress, gives a new chance for hope by locating utopia in the heart of the present. (12–13, 14)

"What we are proposing," writes Robertson in "Utopia," "already exists."

Despite how the paratactic mode of the poem seems to defer resolution, as the poem moves on we do find Robertson's "Utopia" beginning to take form. As she puts it, "Quietly, a shape becomes noticeable" (66). A fantastical version of the self (dog's legs and a fish tail) drifts by a train window, "girls chat in trees about the mystical value of happiness," other girls pick fruit. (64). Quite closely echoing an important Rossettian moment, as we will see below, Robertson comes as near as she will to defining her notion of "Utopia" with the line "Everything is visible, barely disguised," possibly referencing the "unveiling" at the etymological root of apocalypse. The poem concludes on an image of a decaying reading chair, suggesting first that any vision of redemption must include some idea of decay or destruction, and second that utopian hopes and the practice of reading, the practice, one could say, of poetry, are deeply entwined.

Whether we share in this belief has to do, I think, with how we feel when reading these poems, with how we feel about the relationship between affect and transformation (political or otherwise). Robertson (like Rossetti, Hopkins, and Keats before her) presents affect—pleasure, lament—as the poem's primary territory, and her model of aesthetic agency relies on the poem's capacity to generate such affects at the level of its surface. "But the chaos of surface compels us towards new states of happiness."

For those who want to divide transformative content from the complexly patterned or even ornamental surface pleasures of a text, or who want to divide such content from subjective desire, this model of poetic agency will not seem viable. But for those—like Robertson, like the radical poets of the late Victorian period—who sense that ruptural change, transformations of all kinds, *must* be emblazoned with desire, such a model will be the only vital option.

By way of comparison and conclusion, I would like to turn finally back to Rossetti, to his famous sonnet "Heart's Hope" (129). The often quoted lines "Thy soul I know not from thy body, not / Thee from myself, neither our love from God," taken out of context (as they often are), seem to express a conventional deification of love and a conventional (Victorian) fantasy of the fusion of lovers. However, as we read through the poem, we find that rather than simply reinscribing such familiar tropes, Rossetti is advancing a theory of language and time, or, more specifically, a theory of poetry's ability to break through ordinary time into an endless, and endlessly redemptive, temporality.

Heart's Hope

By what word's power, the key of paths untrod,
Shall I the difficult deeps of Love explore,
Till parted waves of Song yield up the shore
Even as that sea which Israel crossed dryshod?
Lady, I fain would tell how evermore
Thy soul I know not from thy body, not
Thee from myself, neither our love from God.

Yea, in God's name, and Love's, and thine, would I
Draw from one loving heart such evidence
As to all hearts all things shall signify;
Tender as dawn's first hill-fire, and intense
As instantaneous penetrating sense,
In Spring's birth-hour, of other Springs gone by.

Much more directly than in other poems (such as "The Monochord"), Rossetti employs the crossing of the Red Sea as a metaphor for rebirth or renewal. He calls on poetry as the enabling force that would allow such a crossing. The "word's power," once discovered, becomes a key that "unlocks" the untrod path, the waters of "song" part to allow a crossing. But what is on the other side of this journey? The promised land is described here not in terms of freedom or sovereignty, but as the space (or time) in which "to all hearts all things shall signify," in which, for each individual, the world becomes entirely legible. (Now recall Lisa Robertson's line from "Utopia," "Everything is visible, barely disguised.") A focus on language's agency runs throughout Rossetti's poem: not only does "word's power" provide the key, also, the speaker would "tell" the truths he hopes to discover; he draws his evidence in the "name" of God, himself, and his love.

Language, or poetry, is imagined as carrying us into such utopian (because radically shared and absolutely legible) space, our time outside of time, for importantly, as Rossetti concludes this sonnet, he shifts from the dominant spatial metaphor (crossing) to a temporal one. Moving associatively, rather than causally, from line 11 to lines 12 and 13, Rossetti aligns the sudden legibility of the world with the "instantaneous penetrating sense" of endless time within the now, of all springs within this one.

Crucial to my reading is the surface effects of lines 12 and 13. Just when Rossetti wants to introduce the notion of timelessness, he creates a moment of intense textual density. "Intense," "instantaneous," "penetrating," and "sense" create an echoing rally of assonance and consonance until the line becomes an example of what Catherine Gallagher calls a "little knot of impacted, concentrated, dense language," which consequently seems to "thwart forward movement" (247). Thus Rossetti does not simply describe but attempts to enact this ruptural moment of timelessness that is at once a moment of absolute interconnectedness. The sonic density of language becomes an example of such "thwarted" movement, and, at the same time, the words themselves in their anagrammatical relations perform their own radical blending of selves, or, to return to Lyotard, they create a moment of "ontological dislocation." This instantaneous penetration not only of "sense" but of time itself can be understood in Benjaminian terms as an example of the "strait gate" of every moment "through which the Messiah might enter," for what is the Messiah but a messenger of love? Yet if "Heart's Hope" is a love poem, the love it depicts pushes far beyond the amatory themes Rossetti is known for. Rather, the poem imagines itself as producing a break in historical time and an entry into a radically utopian intersubjective space, one thoroughly legible to all.

Notes

Some sections of this essay were previously published in *Surface Tension: Ruptural Time and the Poetics of Desire in Late Victorian Poetry* (Dalkey Archive, 2013).

1. Alison Sulloway develops Buckley's claim for the "apocalyptic mood" of the sixties and seventies; Philip Drew analyzes some of the anxieties produced in Victorian thought by the second law of thermodynamics; Patricia M. Ball discusses the influence of scientific developments on Coleridge, Ruskin, and Hopkins; and Owen Chadwick discusses the prevalence and effects of religious doubt in the period.

2. Indeed, if periodization has anything to do with reception, then Keats is, in at least one limited sense, a Victorian poet. It was in the Victorian period that Keats's poetry, as George Ford puts it, "came into its own" (2). There were no reprints of Keats's work until 1840, and the first biography of Keats was published in 1848. Ford's important study, *Keats and the Victorians*, makes clear that the Victorian poets and Keats hold each other in mutual debt: while the former owe much of their art to Keats's influence, he owes much of his fame to theirs.

Matthew Arnold's 1853 preface to *Poems*, in setting out to describe and prescribe the function of poetry at the present time, rails against "the Keatsian School" precisely because of what Arnold deems contemporary poets' overindulgence in affect and sensation, including the surface sensations of language itself. Such work, Arnold argues, can serve no useful social function because it is *too* enamored of surfaces—too fascinated by momentary and sudden expressions of beauty, which fail to add up to any determinate meaning.

For Arnold, the problem stretches beyond aesthetics and into ethics and politics; his anxiety rises from the ways such work overinvests in specifically the non-productive affect of unresolved desire (which Arnold sees as a symptom or sign of "anarchy")—an emotional territory we cannot *not* associate with Keats. As such, Arnold does a lot of work for us in helping reveal the relationship between complex textual surfaces and ruptural or sudden transformation. For Arnold in 1853, Keats, or "the Keatsian School," represents destabilizations at the level of language *and* affect, destabilizations that constitute, finally, a social threat for how they indicate or adhere to ruptural change (precisely the kinds of transformations Arnold hoped to help England avoid).

3. "Here then is an account of the sublime feeling: a very big, very powerful object threatens to deprive the soul of any 'it happens,' strikes it with astonishment. . . . The soul is thus dumb, immobilized, as good as dead. Art, by distancing this menace, procures a pleasure of relief, of delight. Thanks to art, the soul is returned to the agitated zone between life and death, and this agitation is its

health and its life. For Burke, the sublime was no longer a matter of elevation . . . , but a matter of intensification" (100).

4. Bump locates the sources for Hopkins's ontology in the discourse of religious thinkers who influenced him during his days at Oxford, especially Edward Bouverie Pusey.

5. The distinction that Agamben draws between messianic and apocalyptic (or eschatological) time is useful here. Messianic time, Agamben writes, is "not the end of time, but the . . . time that remains between time and its end," whereas apocalyptic time is indeed the "end of time" (*The Time That Remains* 62–64).

6. In an interview from 2005, Robertson writes, "I work through the ear . . . for me a line has to have a presence . . . this sound structure I go for at first intuitively, then tweak by making small moves and shifts and adjustments so there is no sonic flattening within the line. It has to, for me, have this sort of knobby quality, or a torsion or a jaggedness or a swoony kind of movement from syllable to syllable, although now I seem to be exploring flatness as a sound quality." In this it seems to me Robertson is describing the process of creating poetry of surface tension, poetry driven primarily by complex sonic (or visual) relationships between words. See Fierle-Hedrick 49–50.

7. As Robertson states in an interview: "I don't see L=A=N=G=U=A=G=E as a camp. So I can't be associated with it. Mine is a different nationality, a different generation, a different politics. I feel more conditioned by the FLQ than by the language poets. I read many of their works and sometimes drink with some of them, but for me, as for those poets themselves I think, poetry is not bound by movements, periodicities and canons. Poetry is a continuity fueled by political passion" (Queyras, n. pag.).

13
Beyond Romanticism

Jacques Darras

Strangely enough, the manner in which around 1800 the Young German poets in Jena developed the art of "romanticizing," as Friedrich Schlegel would say, did not draw proper attention among French scholars until philosophers Jean-Luc Nancy and Philippe Lacoue-Labarthe published their excellent book *L'Absolu littéraire* (*The literary absolute*) in 1978. We are not yet out of Romanticism, they declared. The idealization of art and more especially literature developed by the Young Germans in Jena cannot be dissociated from Kant's philosophical revolution. By freeing the aesthetic subject from the rules of classical taste, Kant connected it directly with the Infinite. As a consequence, the transcendental Idea could be aroused by sublime representations.

Within that natural conception of Heaven, poetry was called on to federate all the arts. Although it later lost that function it still had to do with the *"autodépassement du langage, l'autodépassement du sens"* (self-surmounting of language, self-surmounting of meaning) (Lacoue-Labarthe). Poetry indeed would resist as long as an irrepressible impulse to sing and use rhythm would be felt at the core of language, in harmony with popular feelings. Romanticism, our philosophers daringly asserted, in view of the contemporary context, can never dissociate poetry from community: "I would like to say that there probably lies what we find so problematic and so difficult to grasp in the notion of common people and what we find so estranging in the basically communal quality of language as such." We were thus clearly reminded that Romanticism is a federator of all the ruptures, negations, and rejections that it originally helped legitimize.

If one reads the original *Philosophical Fragments* composed by Friedrich Schlegel, founder along with his brother August of the magazine *Athenaeum*, one notices that the French philosophers have managed to make them sound consistent in a manner totally different from their original abruptness. Two points stand out. One is that "the novel" is thought to be the essence of *Romanticism*. Or, as said in Fragment 252, "the keystone [of Romanticism] would be a philosophy of the novel," a point all too easily neglected by poets, though Walter Benjamin made it the pivotal aspect of his thesis *Begriff der Kunstkritik in der Deutschen Romantik*, in which he changes *novel* into *prose* and bluntly asserts that "Prose is the idea of Poetry" (94). Schlegel's thought may not have been as basically simple as that, for it takes poetry to be more comprehensive and accepts all kinds of forms and genres, on the basis of universality. The second point Schlegel emphasized, long before Victor Hugo, is the "republicanity" of poetry. "Poetry is republican speech: a speech with its own law and end unto itself, and in which all the parts are free citizens and have the right to vote" (Fragment 65). What an extraordinary prophecy! Only partially realized by symbolism, one might argue, though rather calling on a not yet existing type of Poetry, hinted at by Goethe's dramas.

Could that mean that the Romantic program has not yet even begun? Who among modern poets may be said to have adhered to the following recommendations according to which a truly universal Romantic poetry should "mix and fuse poetry and prose, inspiration and criticism, the poetry of art and the poetry of nature; and make poetry lively and sociable, and life and society poetical; poeticize wit and fill and saturate the forms of art with every kind of good, solid matter for instruction, and animate them with the pulsations of humour" (Fragment 116)? And yet the most vital tenet of Romanticism proposed in the same Fragment is the concept of "becoming." Here is what Schlegel says: "Other kinds of poetry are finished and are now capable of being fully analyzed. The romantic kind of poetry is still in the state of becoming: that, in fact, is its real essence: that it should forever be becoming and never be perfected. It can be exhausted by no theory and only a divinatory criticism would dare try to characterize its ideal. It alone is infinite, just as it alone is free; and it recognizes as its first commandment that the will of the poet can tolerate no law above itself. The romantic kind of poetry is the only one that is more than a kind, that is, as it were, poetry itself: for in a certain sense all poetry is or should be romantic" (Fragment 116).

Could Romanticism be considered as a declaration of war against France about the principle of Universality? Or a plot hatched by brilliant German minds sharpened by contact with the Revolution taking place in France at the time? The French have been confronted by such restless desire for change and novelty in both politics and literature ever since that some poets wonder whether we have not missed the point of those Jena years. In an essay published in 1995, "Habiter en poète" (Inhabiting as a poet), poet and philosopher Jean-Claude Pinson shows remarkable insight into the subject. His conclusions, unfortunately, revert to the same old ruts and routes: "Getting out of romanticism might well be impossible. Breaking away from its clichés, and even its metaphysical basis, is possible and highly desirable, but there will never be an end to the questions it asks from poetry and literature." Let us inhabit the earth as poets, Pinson concludes, echoing Heidegger's own echo of Schlegel's Fragment 116. Does it mean we, in France, should implement that program by calling on a Frenchified variant of Romanticism, to be developed in the twilight of Jaccottet's or Bonnefoy's poetry?

Don't the Germans themselves urge that we help them get rid of that much too heavy burden—Romanticism? Is there anything left to achieve in Germany through the "self-surmounting" (*autodépassement*) of language? Hasn't Paul Celan once and for all achieved such a goal through his deadly surmounting climbs? This should now be regarded without any complacency and lead us to examine Schlegel's program, wondering how a Republican poetry can be detached from memory or history. Romantic poetry, Schlegel says, must draw on myths. "The kernel, the center of poetry, is to be found in mythology and the mysteries of antiquity. Satiate the feeling of life with the idea of infinity, and you will understand both the ancients and poetry" ("Ideas," Fragment 85). Denial of history was never better expressed. And thus it came to pass, in conformity with Schlegel's dictum "No poetry, no reality" (Fragment 350), that Germania, land of myths, language, and philology would eventually become the land where paths lead nowhere but to a grim Grimm's tale with ogres—real because first imagined. Such confusion brought between ideal and history could not but end in dreadful ambiguity. The Romantics came to consider both the literary and the political legitimate as long as they were incarnated through nations, which prompted Nietzsche to try desperately to curb the philosophy of "becoming" under an ever-returning Apollonian rule. Politics, he hoped, would thus be barred from being ruled by the aesthetics of absolute desire, with all its dire consequences.

When Schlegel says, "The romantic kind of poetry is still in the state of becoming; that, in fact, is its real essence: that it should forever be becoming and never be perfected" (Fragment 116), does that not mean that the political "becoming" of Germany should be built on a messianic basis, aiming toward a mythical future? "The only thing one can criticize about the model of Germany, which a few great patriotic authors have constructed, is its incorrect placement. It doesn't lie behind, but before us" (Fragment 38). That the two-hundred-year-old Nation model should still be with us today, in spite of all the disasters we have suffered, shows that instead of opting out of Romanticism, we Europeans have never been closer to it. What does a Romantic nation dream of? The answer was given by the Jena Romantics themselves: myths and legends, an insatiable desire for future. One cannot help admiring the extraordinary foresight of their program. Whether it corresponded to an accurate analysis of the postrevolutionary world and a transfer of exclusive sovereignty from politics to art, is not really the matter. What actually matters is that we begin to take that program seriously, literally as it were, the better to go beyond it. Like Hegel's science, the kind of poetry Schlegel wanted to achieve was scientific and divine, in short all-encompassing. And yet, if the Romantic spirit undeniably inspired all modern poetic movements, especially in the twentieth century, in the form of incompleteness, dilatoriness, and repetitive infinity, very few encyclopedic epics of the kind Schlegel originally hoped for have concretely been attempted.

Why not push Romanticism to its very end, then? Why not contest it with poems surmounting it and criticizing it for what it really is, an unbearable dictator? How could one expect it to block the future in the name of infinite becoming? The most ambitious part of the program is precisely the one least put into practice. When Nancy makes a modest plea in favor of "little songs" to show that the common people's presence is felt at the bottom of language, he may be in conformity with Schlegel on poetry: "It embraces everything that is purely poetic, from the greatest systems of art, containing within themselves still further systems, to the sigh, the kiss that the poetizing child breathes forth in artless song" (Fragment 116). And yet, such Romanticism of the poor, if one may call it so, lacks ambition by comparison with other requirements expressed in the same program. Romantic poetry calls first and foremost for erudition in every field, scientific as well as philosophical, and for a good command of several techniques. If one wants to bring contestation within Romanticism one has to do it on its own terms. The only way to criticize it effectively will be to have it turn back to its beginnings and reflect upon some painful points concerning European political and religious history, of which Novalis alone in the whole Romantic bunch seems to have been conscious.

That is precisely the type of work I have attempted with *Van Eyck et les rivières* (Van Eyck and the rivers), a book I have no problem calling "Romantic." Not only is it advertised as *roman* (novel)—mentioned as such on the front cover—but it offers a mix of genres, "prose and poetry, inspiration and criticism, poetry of art and poetry of nature" (Fragment 116) in conformity with Schlegel's criteria. As to the action proper, it takes place almost exclusively on and about the borders between French- and German-speaking countries: Germany, Flanders, Switzerland, the Low Countries,

Brussels, Wallonia, and France. My narrator's research concerns a famous painting, Jan van Eyck's *Holy Lamb*, on display in Ghent's St. Bavo's Church. His amorous as well as poetical and mystical quest leads him to travel with great geographical precision through landscapes rarely dealt with by French writers. At the crossroads of land and river routes where traffic in religion, politics, and economy has been going on from the Middle Ages down to our times, he comes to understand and unravel a certain enigma. At this stage I should insist on the inchoative nature of his quest, its incompleteness, shall we ironically say. Does that make for Romanticism? I might have chosen to write a classical biography of Jan van Eyck by picking up threads that historian Johan Huizinga left hanging in his *The Waning of the Middle Ages*, but my goal was to give access to a fragmentary totality (like those bits of Flemish tapestry recovered from Charles the Bold's army, nowadays exhibited in The Historical Museum of Bern). I very much wanted the reader to do the linking and sewing up together of various scenes and recompose as best he or she could, following my method, the full-scale tapestry.

Here the Romantic tool is being used against itself, as it were. Although contradiction is at the core of the novel's machinery, as in Hegel's philosophy, nothing can "aufhebung" it (surmount it), no way opens up that would lead to a constantly renewed infinity. Everywhere time gaps separate men from each other, preventing their escape into sublimity. Two antagonistic versions of time are actually at war, poetry versus prose. Their confrontation ends up with neither carrying the day, nor is there surmounting or self-surmounting of any sort. National histories are magnificent perspectives in Italian style. But what about the "present continuous" we love to call "anarchic" or "disorderly," that the French language is so plainly deprived of, contrary to English? In this novel, I have chosen to express that present through the short syncopated rhythm of poetry. For me that rhythm best expresses individual protest against the laws of historical order, while drawing attention to the fact that the Infinity of desire rests upon the very frontiers it transgresses. In other words, the Absolute can be conceived of only as an exacerbation of ineffaceable limits. Witness those territories that we Europeans have inherited through interminable conflicts and that, imperfect totalities though they are, still give legitimacy to our respective nations, today, in the name of Romanticism.

Let us now suppose we in Europe wanted once and for all to dissolve those frontiers, get rid of mythical nations legitimized by "Romanticism"—linguistic roots, primitive folklore, and so on—and come up with a new organization. That could happen only through bringing communities together. As such it would have to go through a collectively rational decision. It would then have to impose new territorial definitions, new maps, and new frontiers on the ground. Would that be enough? Would the nonrational part in us—the "Romantic" part—be totally happy? Certainly not. We would want an invisible link to bind us in a much tighter, corporeal way. A feeling we have inherited from Romanticism. Undeniably the Romantics were the first to open up the formerly unexplored field of dreams at the bottom of human societies. We would therefore agree that some kind of space ought to be preserved for the mythical side of our lives. This is where my fascination with van Eyck's painting came into play. His Holy Prairie I saw and still see today as the vision of an ideal center with peripheral groups of men—the one hundred and forty thousand elect of John's Book of Revelations—revolving around it. Still more fascinating: on the grass of the Picard hill seen against a background of Flemish cities where they progress, they suddenly stop at a distance from the central figure, the Lamb, to pray and admire. They will not get closer.

The Center, van Eyck says, whether it is an object of religion or not—there lies the universality of his message—no human can ever inhabit. And yet, beyond all sorts of fragmented conceptions of the Universe, there has to be a Center. In order to hold, that Center has to keep us at a distance. And we, conforming to Yeats's famous line, must hold on to it for it to hold. Which entails that no change of frontiers on the ground can be attempted without its countermark in the world of imagination. Such is exactly what has been awaiting postromantic Europe, as I tried to show in Van Eyck and the rivers, and such is more generally what awaits humankind as a whole in times to come. Let us not doze off into border inertia; let us not passively accept the myth of national totalities. Let us rather actively work on exiting from Romanticism altogether. We should aim at the infinite, but tangentially as it were, rebounding on the curvature of light in order to change planets. For us the symphonic fusion of brass and wood that was so devoutly loved by the Niebelungen of the Romantic Land will give way to the clarity explored by van Eyck's Holy Lamb or more recently by Stockhausen in his modern polyphonic cantatas calling into play human voices in constant dialogue.

14

Accident over N

Lines of Flight in the Philosophical Notebooks of Novalis

Andrew Joron

Against infinity, saying something is the same as saying nothing. In mathematical terms, n divided by infinity equals zero. Caught between zero and infinity, the world and its saying can have only an accidental, arbitrary value. This, however, is the condition of freedom.

The German Romantic poet Novalis wrote: "We seek everywhere for the unconditioned [*Unbedingte*], but always find only things [*Dinge*]."[1] For many German thinkers at the cusp of Romanticism, freedom was derived from the *unconditioned*, a level of being—also known as the Absolute—that preceded and surpassed any condition whatsoever. However, as Novalis's ironic wordplay implies, if the "unconditioned" is nowhere to be found, then the cause of freedom is defeated: it becomes an Un-thing. Novalis—who died at twenty-eight of tuberculosis, but whose philosophical thought in many ways outpaced that of his contemporaries—saw that freedom, if it existed at all, must be manifested not in the nowhere of the Absolute, but in the now-here of the conditions of things. For Novalis—a lover of reversals—freedom itself was a limit-condition, a condition of being stretched to the breaking point between zero and infinity: an accident within substance, a crooked line across a coordinate system. Indeed, one of his philosophical notes refers to a "crooked line" as a "victory of free nature over the Rule."[2]

Throughout the philosophical notes of Novalis, the Romantic attempt to overcome the Kantian dualism between inner freedom and outer necessity was raised to a higher power or, in his words, "logarythmized." In his "systemless system," the contradictions of conditionality danced together, following a jazzy, nonlinear rhythm more akin to Monk's "Rhythm-a-ning" than the stiff, two-step waltz of the Hegelian dialectic. "The true philosophical system," Novalis wrote, "must be freedom and infinity, or to express it more strikingly, systemlessness, brought into a system" (*NS* 2:289). What resulted was not a form of resolution, but a state of suspension: Being as a suspense story whose outcome is an infinite Becoming.

N: "The world must be romanticized. In this way its original meaning will be rediscovered. Romanticization is nothing but a qualitative potentialization, an operation by which the lower self becomes identified with a better self. Just as we ourselves are such a series of qualitative potentials. This operation is still completely unknown. I romanticize inasmuch as I give the common an elevated meaning, the ordinary a mysterious aura, the known the value of the unknown, the finite an infinite appearance. Conversely the same operation holds for the higher, unknown, mystical, infinite—which, by means of this linkage, will be logarythmized. It goes by a familiar name: romantic philosophy. *Lingua romana*. Alternating elevation and abasement" (*NS* 2:545).

One of the key words in this passage is "alternating," as in a reversal of polarity. Romanticization operated by turning a thing inside out, then outside in—so as to potentialize, to *participate* in the way that the world flowed into and out of itself. To participate in this activity of alternation was to be inspired by the life-breath of the Universe. Novalis had learned from Kant and Fichte that the mind participated in constructing the world, but the young poet refused to sequester this active principle in the mind alone, seeking its operation in nature as well. Mind and nature were, in his mind, alternating flows of the same ineffable *Fluidum*.

The philosophical notebooks of Novalis—representing the poet's engagement with not only philosophy but the latest developments in science and mathematics—constitute a significant break with the program of German idealism, even as that program was in the process of formation. To a remarkable degree, Novalis used science and mathematics—disciplines in which he was well versed—as philosophical transports, carrying him far beyond the confines of the idealist I.

The earliest published fragment of Novalis, cited above, exemplifies his critique of idealism: the Un-thinged is not discoverable among things. In his notes on Fichte, Novalis elaborated on the consequences of this observation. The absolute I—which Fichte had defined as the very identity of being, the I/Eye that perceives itself in order to conceive itself—cannot unconditionally represent itself, that is, cannot "see" itself without at the same time delimiting and losing itself in the mirror-world of conditionality. By mirroring itself, the I also divides itself, and so becomes less than absolute. It is therefore impossible for the absolute I to become conscious of itself as such.[3] Arriving at this result, Novalis believed he had effectively crashed the idealist program that founded philosophy on the primacy of self-consciousness. "I am *not*," he wrote, "insofar as I posit myself but insofar as I suspend myself" (*NS* 2:196). Here, the absolute I presents itself as neither a starting point (as Fichte maintained) nor an endpoint (as Hegel would later argue), but a *breaking point*—a rupturous reversal, a state of flowing in two directions at once.

N: "Elastic mode of thought—to philosophize, from the appearances to the principles, and to go conversely back and forth—or better, to go simultaneously this way and that way—to ceaselessly push oneself in two directions. (*Vide* the magnetic flux. A *Fluidum* that, polarized, tears itself apart, moving immanently in opposing directions.)" (*NS* 3:58)

Novalis's "elastic mode of thought" differs markedly from that of the post-Kantian idealists, who were still utilizing the modalities of Aristotelian logic—analytic and synthetic operations—to reconstruct the world from the fact/act of self-consciousness—rebuilding the world brick by brick, as it were, upon the foundation of this first principle. Novalis, on the other hand, was proposing a new, antifoundational logic in which the act of self-positing brings about a state of suspension: "consciousness," he wrote, "is a being beyond being within being" (*NS* 2:106). This oscillatory force field is generated by the finite I's encounter with the infinite—which produces a feeling of *ek-stasis* (literally, of "standing outside") in the subject. And while the Absolute as such escapes reflection, it is at least possible, according to Novalis, to capture the flash of ekstasis in the mirror of thought. This ecstatic feeling constitutes an *un*knowing that, when reflected, becomes the object (the primal "stuff") of knowing.

N: "The I of feeling is the stuff—the I of reflection the form. . . . Thus, two mediated versions of the I are present—the I of feeling and the I of thought. The absolute I passes from the infinite to the finite, [but] the mediated I(s) [go] from the finite to the infinite" (*NS* 2:126). The passages of the mediated Is[4] are only "apparent," as Novalis emphasizes (2:117), possessing only the reality of reflections in a mirror. Yet the "wrong-way" reflection of the mediated Is (which vainly attempt a stepwise approach to the infinite) can be reversed by a second-order reflection (once more allowing the infinite its free play over finitude). This second reflection was motivated, no doubt, by Novalis's turn against Fichtean idealism, and his Romantic understanding of *arrival* as *reversal*. By means of this double reflection, the mind's attempt to engage the Absolute becomes an unknowing that *knows itself as such*, a "representation of the unrepresentable" that finally finds its expression not in philosophical, but in poetic, language (*NS* 3:685).[5]

And yet this concept of an *ordo inversus* (as Novalis termed it [*NS* 2:127]) must not be understood as the "starting point" of Novalis's "systemless system." Care must be taken not to apply the error of foundationalism—with its belief in a generative first principle—to Novalis's antifoundationalist thought. Within the infinite, there is no privileged point of arrival or departure. The strange relations between the Is of feeling and of reflection are no more than a local instance of the way that everything in the Universe flows in two directions at once: even infinity is subject to reversal, infinitesimally approaching zero.

Moreover, while treating of the reciprocal "potentialization" of opposites, the logic of Novalis is yet not "dialectical," inasmuch as the opposing terms are never reconciled in, or stabilized by, a higher synthesis. The main postulate of "Romantic philosophy," as stated earlier, is one of "alternating elevation and abasement."

N: "Philosophy lets everything *go*—relativizes the Universe—abrogates, like the Copernican system, every *fixed* point—and turns what lies at rest into something suspended. It teaches the relativity of all foundations and all attributes—the unending multiplicity and unity of the construction of a single thing, etc." (*NS* 3:378).

Romantic activity is relativizing because there is no starting point or endpoint whose position is not *accidental* in relation to infinity (or its inverted mirror-twin, zero). N: "Activity is primal power of accident—it is the infinitely accidental" (*NS* 2:215). Here, the Aristotelian distinction between substance and accident breaks down. Novalis writes (in a note where syntactic relation itself seems to break down): "In absolute stuff is stuff substance—determined and determining—accident. In absolute form is form—substance determined and determining—accident" (*NS* 2:128). More clearly, Novalis writes, "Thus it becomes clear that subject and object are precarious/apparent/accidents" (*NS* 2:119).

To romanticize—that is, to magic or to mimic the insurgencies of the Absolute—start anywhere. Then, to realize the necessity of this freedom, *exponentialize* that arbitrary thought or thing toward its opposite, its other. Romantic logic is a pandemonium of paradoxical symmetries.[6] N: "All determinations are accidents" (*NS* 2:286) and "Accidents always are polarized" (*NS* 3:258).

For Novalis, only a *science of accidents* could model these lines of flight. After his studies of Kant and Fichte—which concluded with his relativization of idealism's absolute self-positing—Novalis (pushing himself, along with the Universe, in two directions at once) turned to the study of *mathematics*, on the one hand, and *geology*, on the other: finding, in the opposing spheres of the most abstract and the most concrete, the most orderly and the most disordered, further configurations of the universal self-rend(er)ing he had first witnessed in the absolute I.

Hymns to Mathematics

Novalis's turn toward science and mathematics occurred in the context of the death of Sophie von Kühn, to whom he had been engaged. During Sophie's illness, Novalis wrote to his brother that "the sciences have wonderful healing powers—at least they, like opiates, stop pain and lift us into spheres suffused with eternal sunlight."[7] The "Hymns to Mathematics" in Novalis's notebooks may be regarded as the *ordo inversus* of his more famous "Hymns to the Night." In the aftermath of Sophie's death, Novalis wanted nothing more than to lose his mind among abstract relations: "Numbers are drugs," he wrote, and on the same page, "Pure mathematics is religion" (*NS* 3:594). His friend August Wilhelm Schlegel reported to Goethe that Novalis's "melancholy has thrown him with redoubled effort into the most abstract sciences."[8]

Yet even this realm of abstract relations was inevitably fractured by accident. Novalis had already stated his belief that "Philosophy is, as all synthetic knowledge like mathematics, *arbitrary*" (*NS* 3:690); in his view, neither philosophy nor mathematics possessed a foundational "first principle." The apparently self-evident truths of mathematical axioms rested not on reason, but on *sensation*: "What proceeds from an axiom is an artificial, pretended conviction" (*NS* 2:371). Though an axiom defined a starting point, any "true definition is a magic word" (*NS* 2:592), a conjuration out of nowhere.

What he was seeking here, as elsewhere, was evidence of the (n)ever-arriving wave of the Absolute. Three areas of mathematics appealed to the imagination of Novalis: calculus, in which motion was analyzed using a method of infinitely approximating zero; algebra, in which unknown quantities, symbolized by letters, transacted with the known; and combinatorial analysis, a now forgotten art in which all possible permutations between the elements of a system were to be integrated by a kind of conceptual kaleidoscope, or "difference engine."

In the calculus, Novalis discovered a mathematical analogue to his philosophical insight that the longing for the Absolute, the motion of the conditioned toward the Unconditioned, must consist of an "infinite approximation."[9] The calculus developed by Newton and Leibniz likewise involves an "infinite approximation": to account for varying rates of change, it divides time intervals into ever-smaller units, infinitesimally approaching zero. Now, mathematicians are wary of any operation involving infinity or zero because it often leads to paradoxical or meaningless results. And indeed, the practice of calculus was beset, during the first hundred years following its invention, with accusations that its operation involved *division by zero*, a mathematically meaningless concept. Although calculus had accurately predicted rates of change, its mathematical basis was still very much open to question in Novalis's time.

Such questioning, of course, only heightened Novalis's interest in calculus as a mode of expressing the inexpressible: "Infinitesimal calculus," he wrote, "really means *reckoning*, division or measurement of the undivided—the incomparable—*the immeasurable*" (*NS* 3:386). Where "reckoning" yielded a solution that the system of reckoning itself could not accommodate, there was an opening to the Absolute. Novalis considered the fusion of zero and infinity in the method of calculus to be one such opening and even asserted that "The basic formula of infinitesimal calculus [is] $a/\infty \bullet \infty = a$" (*NS* 3:66). This formula is a paradox: any quantity divided by infinity is zero; thus, Novalis is here multiplying zero (that is, a/∞) by infinity to yield "a." As Novalis himself admits, "This is a seeming operation—determination of the ideal—an *indirect*—polarized calculation. *Application of error*. (Truth is a *fully completed* error. As health (is) a *fully completed* illness)" (*NS* 3:66).

Algebraic equations in general attracted Novalis: here was a form of notation in which letters mingled with numbers, and in which letters served the special function of standing for the unknown. Might the *paradoxon* of the Universe be summed up in a single letter, a single magical symbol? N: "Universe—Multiverse—Omniverse. For the *highest* All-encompassing a *nameless* expression" (*NS* 3:290). The absolute symbol, toward which both science and art converge, must take the shape of an algebraic letter: "The basis of all sciences and arts must be a science and an art—that could be compared to algebra." In a crucial passage on the same page, Novalis wrote: "The highest elementary science is one that treats no *determinate* object at all—only a pure *N*. The same goes for art. The making that is done with hands is already a special, applied making. The *making* of N with the N organ is the object of this general aesthetics and art" (*NS* 3:257).

Here, then, is the poem of the Universe: *N*.

Unnameable N, which, in order to be unconditioned, cannot be the same as itself; which at once "tears itself apart" and flows back into itself. If the Absolute has a *structure* or a *function*, it has no other structure or function than this.

The site of such an exchange—and for Novalis, "Ideals are also products of transitional moments" (*NS* 3:414)—can be represented mathematically as a function, a relation between variables. Long ago, Käte Hamburger, in her study of Novalis's engagement with mathematics, pointed out that "he strives straightaway for the concept of function; he discerns that true 'being' must be characterized not by means of a dogmatic ontology's concept of substance, but much more by the relational character of function."[10] In a

"Universe—Multiverse—Omniverse" characterized by paradoxically polarized flows of the One into its Other, functions serve *as nodes within a network*, sites of transition at which opposing pairs briefly embrace before reversing their positions once again.

Novalis envisioned an absolute mathematics, an infinite self-relation of zero, a function in which the relata would vanish into their relations. On the one hand, Novalis demanded that "Our letters should become numbers, our speech arithmetic" (*NS* 3:50), and on the other, that "In pure algebra, no numbers are presented" (*NS* 3:128). Letters and numbers, then, are merely the vanishing variables of an absolute Function. Like the Absolute itself, however, this absolute Function was inexpressible, or expressible only within an endless combination of letters and numbers.

Novalis referred to this nexus as a "*TotalFunction*"—a fused term emblematic of the combinatorial operation itself. "Science as a whole," he wrote, "is thus above all the *TotalFunction* of *data* and *facts*—the N power of the *binomial series of data and facts*. Here *combinatorial analysis* becomes necessary" (*NS* 3:275). In the spirit of Leibniz, who had proposed an *ars combinatoria* (a kind of protocomputer in which the basic elements of knowledge would be reduced to symbols and endlessly recombined to yield new truths), Novalis argued that "In the combinatorial theory lies the principle of completeness— as in analysis—or the art of finding the unknown terms from given data" (*NS* 3:364).

Thus, the *ars combinatoria*, for Novalis as well as Leibniz, was also an *ars inveniendi*, mirroring the world's own self-making. Through this art, the knowledge that lay frozen in such static tabulations as the French *Encyclopédie* would turn fluid: the Romantic encyclopedia must resemble a magnetic or electric *Fluidum*, a force field of dynamically interacting elements.

One portion of Novalis's philosophical notebooks is in fact devoted to the construction of just such an encyclopedia: the pages of his *Allgemeine Brouillon* (literally, "general mishmash") consist of swarms of interdisciplinary data and ideas, awaiting their moment of integration by the *TotalFunction*. While this messianic moment never arrives, Novalis believed he was composing the rough draft of an absolute Book—the first adumbration of a "scientific Bible" that would eventually take its place beside the traditional Bible. "My book must become a scientific Bible—a real, and ideal archetype—and germinal nucleus of all books" (*NS* 3:363). And he confessed, in a letter to his friend Friedrich Schlegel, his desire to write a "new Bible" (*NS* 4:263).

In this new, scientific Bible, all the manifold aspects of Being, both real and ideal, would be integrated through a mathematical function. Even miracles would be accommodated, as unprecedentedly rare events resulting from the combinatorial play of possibilities. N: "Linkage between the sphere of miracles and of nature. Miracles *must* result from rules—natural effects from the *lack* of them. The sphere of miracles and of nature must become One. (The *regular* and *irregular*.) The irregular is the fantastic-regular—*the rule of the arbitrary*—the rule of accident—the rule of miracles." And on the same page, Novalis jotted: "The *regular*—direct law—indirect, (crooked) law = irregularity" (*NS* 3:409).

The *ars combinatoria*, which was no less an art of invention,[11] is recognized to be a precursor of modern probability theory and computer science; Novalis applied it liberally.[12] Here, then, was a *science of accidents* that could explain, at least in theory, even the most irregular aspects of nature, such as geological formations (whose chaotic appearance had, in part, given rise to the Kantian aesthetics of the sublime).[13] And, following Sophie's death, Novalis was enthused as much with mineralogy as with mathematics.[14] At Freiburg, he had taken courses in both disciplines in preparation for employment as an inspector of mines. Just as he had, in Jena, criticized the teachings of Fichte for being insufficiently grounded in the groundlessness of Being, Novalis immediately launched—again, in the name of the Infinite—a critique of the lessons of his new teacher, the geologist Abraham Gottlob Werner.

How to Write (Chaosophy Remix)

Like Fichte, Werner wished to ground his science in the self-evident simplicity of a first principle: for Werner, the literal ground was granite, which he defined as the simplest, earliest, most basic layer of the earth. All subsequent complications of the earth's surface were caused by a series of worldwide floods (Werner was a Neptunian) acting upon this layer. For Novalis, of course, reality (as well as ideality) was *always already* complex; all that appeared to be fixed in relation to its own identity was, in relation to infinity, unfixable.

Novalis conceived of nature, at least in one of its aspects, as an "infinite stone" (*NS* 3:89), but he also prized his friend Friedrich Schlegel's comment that "Nature *is* not infinite but *becomes* infinite" (*NS* 3:90): for both of these Romantic thinkers, the ultimate nature of things was processual. "Nature adds, subtracts, multiplies, potentializes etc. unceasingly," Novalis wrote (*NS* 3:52); the young poet—even while learning the technical trade of mine inspection—was looking for the "exponentials of stones" (*NS* 3:258).

His teacher Werner, however, wanted not to exponentialize but to stabilize geological science—to bring order to the apparent disorder of rock formations by imposing a taxonomic scheme rather like the Linnaean system of plant classification, based on the external characteristics of specimens. Novalis, unsurprisingly, soon grew impatient with this reductive schema: geological science, he believed, ought to look beyond the surface of things. Only combinatorial analysis could uncover the play of forces at work within each rock: "each body is a Chaos of numbers—figures—forces" (*NS* 3:90). A rock, then, existed as a kind of material N-function.

Moreover, the Infinite left its signature most indelibly in rock. Unlike the elements of fire, water, and air—each of which had been nominated in Greek antiquity as a world-creating power, but none of which could bear any trace upon themselves—earth had the power to preserve the inscriptions of forces acting upon it. These forces were chemical as well as mechanical.[15] The earth was itself an infinite Book: the chaotic texture of its surface might be interpreted as an Ur-text, as fossilized writing (mineralogical specimens in Novalis's time were commonly deemed "fossils," whether or not they contained organic remnants). Novalis faulted Werner for compiling a "vulgarly empirical" table of fossil-signs without knowing the abstract, combinatorial grammar that could make them speak.[16]

In the end, Novalis's "infinite" critique of the geologist Werner was never as fully developed as his antifoundational critique of the philosopher Fichte. For one thing, the limits of his technical training did not allow it; for another, his restless imagination was already taking him elsewhere. After a four-year period in which he had thrown himself, with almost mystical fervor, into the study of philosophy, science, and mathematics—as documented in the grand *combinatoire* of his notebook entries—Novalis felt that he was finally coming into his true vocation as a poet.

Shortly after leaving the mining academy, Novalis composed a brief text on language, which was later given the title "Monologue" by the editors of his writings. In this text (as well as in his story "The Apprentices at Saïs," also written around this period), Novalis, far from abandoning his views on the infinite *mathesis* of being, treats language as yet another force field of combinatorial possibilities, a system of signs designing itself beyond communication. The text is worth quoting in full:

> N: The case of speech and writing is actually maddening; right discourse is mere wordplay. It's a laughable error to think highly of the fact that people make meaning—they speak for the sake of things. No one knows that what is actually peculiar about language is that it concerns itself only with itself. That's why language is such a marvelous

and fruitful enigma—for when one speaks only in order to speak, one expresses just the most splendid and original truths. But if one wants to speak about something specific, then one is led by the playfulness of speech to say the most ridiculous and distorted things. From this arises the hatred for speech so many earnest people hold. They observe its mischievous qualities, but fail to notice that the chatter so despised by them is the infinitely earnest side of speech. If one could only make people realize that it's the same with language as it is with mathematical formulas, which constitute a world in themselves, engage in play only with themselves, and express nothing but their own marvelous nature. Which is exactly why they are so rich in expression, and why the strange relational play of things can be reflected in them. For they become parts of nature only through their freedom; only in their free movements does the world-soul express itself, and make of them a sensitive measure and ground-plan of things. It's the same with language—whoever has a fine feeling for its fingering, its beat, its musical spirit, whoever perceives within himself the delicate workings of its inner nature, and moves his tongue or his (writing) hand accordingly, will become a prophet. Oppositely, whoever knows well enough to write truths like these, but whose ear and sense for them is insufficient, will let language get the better of him, and will be mocked by people as Cassandra was by the Trojans. If I believe thereby to have stated most clearly the essence and office of poetry, then I know that, all the same, no one will understand it, and that I have said something foolish, because I intended to say it, and in this way no poetry can come to pass. How is this so, if I am yet driven to speak? And if this drive to speak is the characteristic of verbal inspiration, of the efficacy of language in me? And if my will also wills no more than that which I must do, then could this be, in the end, without my knowledge and belief, indeed poetry, and could this have made a secret of language understandable? And then would I be a professionally qualified writer, inasmuch as a writer really is just someone inspired by speech? (*NS* 2:672–73)

In a few quick steps, this statement moves beyond the Kantian position on autonomous art—as a form of "purposefulness without purpose"—toward something like the surrealist concept of automatic writing. Here, language is understood as a complex, self-organizing system whose "strange relational play" rhythmizes the cosmomathematical N-function. Using words to refer to things—to communicate a "specific" meaning—amounts to a falsification of language. Words, in their "free movements," are "parts of nature," exceeding the limits of human intentionality. The imperative for the poet must be to *let language speak itself.*

If poetic practice takes place beyond intentionality, then it must also be the art of *accident* and of the unknown. Novalis had already defined art algebraically as "making N with the N organ." The *TotalFunction* of poetry, then, is to arrive at N, symbol of the unknown, through a series of word-accidents: for "everything arbitrary, accidental, indivisible can become our cosmic organ" (*NS* 3:684); "the sense for poetry" is "the sense for the singular, the individual, the unknown, the mysterious, unto *revelation*, the necessary-accidental" (*NS* 3:85). "The poet," wrote Novalis, "prays to chance" (*NS* 3:449). Anticipating the surrealist practice of free association, Novalis asserted that "All of poetry depends on the active association of ideas—on self-activating, intentional *chance-production*" (*NS* 3:451).

If the highest function of language is both nonintentional and nonreferential, then it must become a kind of wind-harp, sensitive to—its tones participating in—the "strange relational play" of the elements.[17] Verbal language was for Novalis merely a subset of the "general N-language of music" (*NS* 3:283).[18] The very letters of the alphabet, in his eyes, dissolved into vibrational patterns: "Figurations of sound waves like *letters.* (The letters originally must have been *acoustical figures.* A priori letters?)" (*NS* 3:305). It must be remembered that Novalis viewed letters as having both alphabetic and algebraic value: the common ancestor of language and mathematics was therefore the musical force field of the N-function.

Novalis had been provoked into thinking about "sound writing itself" by the German physicist Ernst Chladni's book *Discoveries in the Theory of Sound,* published in 1787. The book described how Chladni first scattered flour or sand on glass or metal plates and then stroked the plates with a violin bow: as the plates resonated, force field–like patterns appeared in the material covering their surfaces. For Novalis, these "figurations of sound waves" were the "a priori letters" of a universal script.[19]

The world, in fact, was littered with the letters of the Absolute: anything, real or ideal, that underwent a self-complicating (ultimately musical) pattern of interaction was a sign of the processual emergence of the Infinite within the finite.

> N: People follow many different paths. Whoever traces these paths and compares them will see marvelous patterns arise; patterns that appear to belong to that great cipher-writing that one glimpses everywhere, on

wings, eggshells, in clouds, in snow, in crystals and in rock formations, on frozen water, in the interior and exterior of mountains, of plants, of animals, of people, in the lights of the sky, when tapping and stroking plates of resin and glass, in the filings around a magnet, and the singular conjunctures of chance. In them one feels a presentiment of the deciphering of this miraculous script, as of its very grammar; yet this presentiment will not submit itself to any fixed form, and appears unwilling to become a higher deciphering. An *alcahest* (universal solvent) appears to have been poured over the human organs of perception. Only in the flash of an instant do our wishes, our thoughts appear to solidify. Thus arise our presentiments, but after a short while everything swims away from our sight, as before. . . . One fails to comprehend language, because language doesn't comprehend itself, and doesn't want to comprehend itself. The true Sanskrit (i.e., the root language) speaks for the sake of speaking, because speaking is its passion and its essence. (*NS* 1:79)

This well-known paragraph, which opens Novalis's story "The Apprentices at Saïs," marks the end of his practice of keeping "philosophical notebooks" and the beginning of his literary production proper. (Though this story counts as his first mature literary work, the influence of his scientific studies remains strong; and the story's compositional style still resembles that of the notebooks.) And yet Novalis's work in fiction and poetry never achieved the radicality of his own poetics, according to which language must "speak itself" by chance associations, producing the force field of the N-function as a saying of the Unsayable. It would require the poetic innovations of symbolism and surrealism to come close to fulfilling the promise of—the *prevision* of—the poetics of Novalis.[20]

However, the relevance of Novalis's poetics does not end with the innovations of High Modernism but extends into the present moment—a moment in which the twentieth century's "linguistic turn," and the poetics associated with it, is becoming superseded by an "ontological turn" whose poetics are not yet clearly defined.

Adding impetus to the ontological turn in philosophy has been the growing recognition in the sciences that most natural systems are characterized by self-organized, emergent orders of complexity.[21] Or, as Novalis put it, "each body is a Chaos of numbers—figures—forces." Recent developments in chaos and complexity theory have brought the scientific model of the universe ever closer to Novalis's vision of the Absolute as a combinatorial force field; in

this new model, complex random interactions are seen to give rise sponta-
neously to (in Novalis's words) "marvelous patterns" driven by "the singular
conjunctures of chance." Even inorganic systems of sufficient complexity
(some examples are listed above by Novalis) exhibit this self-organizing, innovative behavior. Such nomadic multiplicities are prioritized in the work
of neomaterialist philosophers Deleuze and Badiou; their work is considered to have enacted a "speculative turn," decisively moving the philosophical debate beyond the categories of Derridean poststructuralism into an ontological zone prepared by the concepts of chaos and complexity theory.[22]

To register this ontological turn in poetic practice would require moving
beyond social constructivism, still the dominant paradigm of avant-garde
writing in the United States and heavily indebted to the theories of the twentieth century's "linguistic turn." The Romantic poetics of Novalis, which finds
the source of *poiesis* neither in the self nor in society, may yet show us the
way out of the prison-house of language—for the Word makes itself in the
same way that the World does, as a form of Accident over N.

Notes

1. This is the famous opening line of *Blütenstaub* (Pollen), a collection of
Novalis's fragments compiled by his friend Friedrich Schlegel and published in
the first issue of *Athenaeum* (1798), the journal that inaugurated German Romanticism.

2. Novalis 2:257. Citations to this edition of Novalis's collected works will
be given as *NS*, followed by volume and page number. All translations are mine.

3. Hölderlin had, in his brief statement "Judgment and Being," mounted a
similar critique of Fichte's idealism; that two poets could participate so decisively in the discourse of philosophy is indicative of the cultural ferment during this period. The case for granting priority to Hölderlin's critique has been
made most fully by Dieter Henrich; while Manfred Frank has insisted on the
"technical-argumenative superiority" of Novalis's critique "as compared with
Hölderlin's rather rudimentary notes" (Frank, *Philosophical Foundations* 152).

4. How marvelous that, in English, and in this context, the plural of "I" is
"Is"—and that "Is" carry the sound of "eyes"!

5. Novalis's concept of an *ordo inversus* is most fully investigated in Manfred
Frank's *Das Problem "Zeit"* (141–57). See also Frank, *Einführung* 248–61.

6. This phrase is borrowed from E. M. Cioran's *On the Heights of Despair*
(90), where it is used to describe the "original chaos."

7. Cited in German in Dyck 32; my translation.

8. Ibid. 33; my translation.

9. See Manfred Frank's massive survey *"Unendliche Annäherung": Die Anfänge der philosophischen Frühromantik*, in which he traces the trope of the "infinite approximation" of the Absolute throughout the history of early German Romanticism. For Novalis, such approximation was the "only possible Absolute that can be given to us and that we discover only through our inability to attain and to know an Absolute" (*NS* 2:270).

10. Hamburger's paper was published in 1929. The passage is quoted in German in Dyck 32; my translation.

11. "The combinatorial analysis of physics would be the indirect art of invention that Bacon had sought" (*NS* 3:128).

12. "The true mathematician is an enthusiast per se. Without enthusiasm no mathematics" (*NS* 3:593).

13. See Nicolson.

14. Two recent studies of Novalis's engagement with mineralogy are Laurent Margantin's *Système minéralogique et cosmologie chez Novalis*, which offers a decidedly Deleuzean reading; and Irene Bark's *Steine in Pontenzen: konstruktive Rezeption der Minerologie bei Novalis*.

15. Novalis, while at Freiburg, followed the latest advances in chemistry and was drawn especially to Lavoisier's combinatorial algebra of elements. See Neubauer 63–64. Neubauer's book is an interesting study of the elective affinities between combinatorial analysis and Romantic and Symbolist poetics.

16. Margantin 154.

17. N: "Immeasurable multiplicity of wind-harp tones and *simplicity* of the moving power" (*NS* 3:434). Novalis got the idea of a simple system producing complex results from Leibnizian analysis; the notion has become relevant again in the chaos and complexity theory of the present era. See Mahoney 107–20.

18. On the same page of his notebooks, Novalis freely associates the systems of music, mathematics, and language: "Doesn't music partake of combinatorial analysis and vice versa? . . . Numbers are mathematical vowels. . . . Combinatorial analysis induces numeric fantasizing. . . . Language is a musical idea-instrument" (*NS* 3:360).

19. See the editor's note in *NS* 3:928.

20. Of course, it is tempting to read the notebooks themselves as an absolute Book—comparable to, but much vaster than, Mallarmé's unfinished *Livre*—embodying the poetics of an infinitely playful combinatorial *hasard*.

21. Ilya Prigogine, the Nobel Prize–winning chemist and leading theorist of complex systems, has stated that "we are living in a nature in which the rule is non-integrability. . . . Nonintegrable fields are systems of an infinite number of

degrees of freedom with persistent interactions. . . . The physical universe comes closer now to the biological universe. The emergence and evolution of stars and galaxies are non-equilibrium processes like self-organization in biology. In both cases you have billions of particles, which follow each other to form complex non-equilibrium structures" (see Prigogine and Stengers 16, 38, 59).

22. For the scientific aspects of the new model, see Prigogine and Stengers; for the philosophical aspects, see Bryant, Srnicek, and Harman.

Bibliography

Adorno, Theodor. *Minima Moralia: Reflections from Damaged Life*. Trans. E. F. N. Jephcott. London: Verso, 1978.

——. *Negative Dialektik*. Frankfurt am Main: Suhrkamp, 1973.

——. *Notes to Literature*. Vol 1. Trans. Shierry Weber Nicholson. New York: Columbia UP, 1991.

Agamben, Giorgio. *The End of the Poem: Studies in Poetics*. Trans. Daniel Helle-Roazen. Stanford: Stanford UP, 1999.

——. "Time and History: Critique of the Instant and the Continuum." *Infancy and History: Essays on the Destruction of Experience*. Trans. Liz Heron. London: Verso, 1993. 89–105.

——. *The Time That Remains: A Commentary on the Letter to the Romans*. Trans. Patricia Dailey. Stanford: Stanford UP, 2005.

Allen, Donald. *The Poetics of the New American Poetry*. New York: Grove Press, 1973.

Allen Ginsberg Library, Naropa University. http://www.naropa.edu/allen-ginsberg -library/ (for lectures/readings on Shelley by Diane di Prima, Gregory Corso, Allen Ginsberg, and others).

Allison, Alexander W. et al., eds. *The Norton Anthology of Poetry*. 3rd ed. 1970. New York: W. W. Norton, 1983.

Arberry, A. J. Introduction. *Muslim Saints and Mystics: Episodes from the Tadhkirat al-Auliya' (Memorial of the Saints)*. By Farid al-Din Attar. Ames, IA: Omphaloskepsis, 2000. vii–xxv.

Armstrong, Isobel. "The Gush of the Feminine: How Can We Read Women's Poetry of the Romantic Period?" *Romantic Women Writers: Voices and Countervoices*. Eds. Paula R. Feldman and Theresa M. Kelley. Hanover: UP of New England, 1995. 13–32.

——. *Victorian Poetry: Poetry, Poetics and Politics*. London: Routledge, 1993.

Attar, Farid ud-Din. *The Conference of the Birds* [Manteq at-Tair]. Trans. and introduction Afkham Darbandi and Dick Davis. New York: Penguin, 1984.

Attridge, Derek. *The Rhythms of English Poetry*. London: Longman, 1982.

Bakhtin, M. M., and P. N. Medvedev. *The Formal Method in Literary Scholarship: A Critical Introduction to Sociological Poetics*. 1928. Trans. Albert J. Wehrle. Baltimore: Johns Hopkins UP, 1978.

Balibar, Etienne. *Politics and the Other Scene*. London: Verson, 2012.

Ball, Patricia M. *The Science of Aspects: The Changing Role of Fact in the Work of Coleridge, Ruskin, and Hopkins*. London: Athlone Press, 1971.

Barbauld, Anna Laetitia. *Eighteen Hundred and Eleven*. *The Works of Anna Laetitia Barbauld*. Vol. 1. London: Longman, 1825. 232–50.

Bark, Irene. *Steine in Pontenzen: konstruktive Rezeption der Minerologie bei Novalis*. Tübingen, Germany: M. Niemeyer, 1999.

Basker, James G. "Scotticisms and the Problem of Cultural Identity in Eighteenth-Century Britain." *Eighteenth-Century Life* 15 (1991), 81–95.

Bate, Jonathan. *John Clare: A Biography*. New York: Farrar, Straus and Giroux, 2003.

Beachy-Quick, Dan. *This Nest, Swift Passerine*. North Adams, MA: Tupelo Press, 2009.

Benjamin, Walter. *Begriff der Kunstkritik in der Deutschen Romantik*. French trans. Philippe Lacoue-Labarthe. *Le Concept de critique esthétique dans le Romantisme allemand*. Paris: Flammarion, 1986.

———. *Illuminations: Essays and Reflections*. Ed. Hannah Arendt. Trans. Harry Zohn. New York: Schocken Books. 1969.

———. "Theses on the Philosophy of History." Benjamin, *Illuminations* 253–64.

Bentman, Raymond. "Robert Burns's Use of Scottish Diction." *From Sensibility to Romanticism*. Eds. Frederick Hilles and Harold Bloom. Oxford: Oxford UP, 1965. 239–50.

Bergvall, Caroline, Laynie Browne, Teresa Carmody, and Vanessa Place, eds. *I'll Drown My Book: Conceptual Writing by Women*. Los Angeles: Les Figues Press, 2012.

Bernstein, Charles. "Artifice of Absorption," from *A Poetics*. Cambridge, MA: Harvard UP, 1992.

Blackstone, Bernard. "Byron and Islam: The Triple Eros." *Journal of European Studies* 4 (1974): 325–63.

Blake, William. *Blake's Poetry and Designs*. Eds. Mary Lynn Johnson and John E. Grant. New York: W. W. Norton, 1979.

Bonney, Sean. *Happiness*. London: Unkant Publishing, 2011.

Brooks, Harold F. Introduction. *The Poems of John Oldham*. Eds. Harold F. Brooks and Raman Selden. Oxford: Clarendon Press, 1987. xxxvii–xxxviii.

Bryant, Levi, Nick Srnicek, and Graham Harman, eds. *The Speculative Turn: Continental Materialism and Realism*. Melbourne: re.press, 2011.

Buckley, Jerome Hamilton. *The Triumph of Time: A Study of the Victorian Concepts of Time, History, Progress, and Decadence*. Cambridge, MA: Belknap Press, 1966.

Bump, Jerome. "The Victorian Radicals: Time, Typology, and Ontology in Hopkins, Pusey, and Muller." *Victorian Religious Discourse: New Directions in Criticism.* Ed. Jude V. Nixon. New York: Palgrave, 2004. 27–49.

Burns, Robert. *Poems and Songs.* Ed. James Kinsley. 3 vols. Oxford: Oxford UP, 1968.

———. *Poems Chiefly in the Scottish Dialect.* Kilmarnock, UK: John Wilson, 1786.

Byron, George Gordon. *Beppo: A Venetian Story.* 6th ed. London: John Murray, 1818.

———. *Childe Harold's Pilgrimage: A Romaunt.* 2nd ed. London: John Murray, 1812.

———. *The Corsair: A Tale.* 9th ed. London: John Murray, 1815.

Caldwell, Deborah. "Mohammad Ali's New Spiritual Quest." n.d. [March 2005]. *Beliefnet.* 29 July 2012. http://www.beliefnet.com/Faiths/Islam/2005/02/Muhammad-Alis-New-Spiritual-Quest.aspx

Carlyle, Thomas. *The French Revolution: A History.* New York: American Book Exchange, 1881.

Carr, Julie. Interview with Lisa Robertson. *The Volta.* 8 Oct. 2013. http://www.thevolta.org/ewc-mainpage.html.

———. *Surface Tension: Ruptural Time and the Poetics of Desire in Late Victorian Poetry.* Champaigne, IL: Dalkey Archive Press, 2013.

Carruthers, Gerard. *Scottish Literature.* Edinburgh: Edinburgh UP, 2009.

Catullus. "A New Translation." Trans. James Brophy. Honors thesis, University of Maine, 2009.

Chadwick, Owen. *The Secularization of the European Mind in the Nineteenth Century.* Cambridge: Cambridge UP, 1975.

Chandler, James. *England in 1819: The Politics of Literary Culture and the Case of Romantic Historicism.* Chicago: U of Chicago P, 1998.

Chittick, William C. *The Self-Disclosure of God: Principles of Ibn al-'Arabi's Cosmology.* Albany: SUNY Press, 1998.

———. *Ibn 'Arabi: Heir to the Prophets.* Oxford: Oneworld Publications, 2005.

Cioran, E. M. *On the Heights of Despair.* Trans. Ilinca Zarifopol-Johnston. Chicago: U of Chicago P, 1992.

Clare, John. *John Clare by Himself.* Eds. Eric Robinson and David Powell. New York: Routledge, 2002.

Coleridge, Samuel Taylor. *Biographia Literaria.* Ed. Nigel Leask. London: Everyman, 1996.

———. *The Poems of Samuel Taylor Coleridge.* Ed. Ernest Hartley Coleridge. London: Oxford UP, 1961.

———. *Selected Poetry and Prose.* Ed. Donald Stauffer. New York: Modern Library, 1951.

———. *Sibylline Leaves: A Collection of Poems.* London: Rest Fenner, 1817.

Collingwood, David, and Jacques Khalip. "The Present Time of 'Live Ashes.'" Introduction, *Romanticism and Disaster.* Eds. Jacques Khalip and David Colling.

Romantic Circles (Jan. 2012). 11 July 2012. http://www.rc.umd.edu/blog_rc
/archive/201207

Collins, William. "The Passions. An Ode for Music," *Odes on Several Descriptive and Allegorical Subjects.* London, 1747.

Congreve, William. *A Pindarique Ode, Offer'd to the Queen, on the Victorious Progress of Her Majesty's Arms, under the Conduct of the Duke of Marlborough.* London, 1706.

Cooke, Jennifer. "The Laughter of Narcissism: Loving *Hot White Andy* and the Troubling Chain of Equivalence." Ladkin and Purves 323–40.

Corless-Smith, Martin. *Nota.* New York: Fence Books, 2003.

Corso, Gregory. *An Accidental Autobiography: The Selected Letters of Gregory Corso.* Ed. Bill Morgan. New York: New Directions Books, 2003.

——. *The Happy Birthday of Death.* New York: New Directions, 1960.

Cowley, Abraham. *The English Writings of Abraham Cowley. Poems: Miscellanies, The Mistress, Pindarique Odes, etc..* Ed. A. R. Waller. Cambridge: Cambridge UP, 1905.

Craciun, Adriana. "Romantic Poetry, Sexuality, Gender." *The Cambridge Companion to British Romantic Poetry.* Eds. James Chandler and Maureen N. McLane. Cambridge: Cambridge UP, 2008. 155–77.

Craig, Cairns. *Out of History: Narrative Paradigms in Scottish and British Culture.* Edinburgh: Polygon, 1996.

Craig, David. *Scottish Literature and the Scottish People, 1680–1830.* London: Chatto and Windus, 1961.

Crane, Hart. *The Complete Poems of Hart Crane.* Ed. Marc Simon. New York: Liveright, 1993.

Crawford, Robert, ed. *Apollos of the North: Selected Poems of George Buchanan and Arthur Johnston.* Edinburgh: Polygon, 2006.

——. *Devolving English Literature.* 2nd ed. Edinburgh: Edinburgh UP, 2000.

——, ed. *Robert Burns and Cultural Authority.* Edinburgh: Polygon, 1999.

——, ed. *The Scottish Invention of English Literature.* Cambridge: Cambridge UP, 1998.

Crawford, Thomas. *Society and the Lyric: A Study of the Song Culture of Eighteenth-Century Scotland.* Edinburgh: Scottish Academic Press, 1979.

Cross, Ashley. "Coleridge and Robinson: Harping on Lyrical Exchange." *Fellow Romantics: Male and Female British Writers, 1790–1835.* Ed. Beth Lau. Farnham, UK: Ashgate Publishing, 2009. 39–70.

Culler, Jonathan. "Why Lyric?" *Publications of the Modern Language Association of America* 123.1 (Jan. 2008): 201–6.

——. *The Pursuit of Signs.* Ithaca: Cornell UP, 1981.

Cuojati, Francesca. "John Clare: The Poetics and Politics of Taxonomy." *The Exhibit in the Text: The Museological Practices of Literature.* Eds. Caroline Patey and Laura Scuriatti. Bern: Peter Lang, 2009. 29–38.

Curran, Stuart. *Poetic Form in British Romanticism.* New York: Oxford UP, 1986.

Darras, Jacques. *Van Eyck et les rivières (dont la Maye)*. Le Cri, Brussels: 1996.

Darwin, Erasmus. *The Botanic Garden: A Poem, in Two Parts*. London: J. Johnson, 1791.

———. *Plan for the Conduct of Female Education in Boarding Schools*. London: J. Johnson, 1797.

Davis, Herbert, ed. *Pope: Poetical Works*, with introduction by Pat Rogers. Oxford: Oxford UP, 1978.

D'Emilio, John. *Sexual Politics, Sexual Communities. The Making of a Homosexual Minority in the United States, 1940–1970*. 1983. Chicago: U of Chicago P, 1998.

Derksen, Jeff. *Annihilated Time: Poetry and Other Politics*. Vancouver: Talonbooks, 2009.

de Silentio, Johannes. "Fear and Trembling: Dialectical Lyric." *Fear and Trembling and Repetition: Søren Kierkegaard*. Eds. and trans. Howard V. Hong and Edna H. Hong. Princeton, NJ: Princeton UP, 1983. 1–123.

de Staël, Germaine. *Corinne, or Italy*. trans. Isabel Hill, 1833

Donne, John. *The Complete Poetry and Selected Prose of John Donne*. Ed. Charles M. Coffin. New York: Modern Library, 1994.

———. "A Sermon Preached at the Earl of Bridge-waters house in London at the marriage of his daughter, the Lady Mary, to the Eldest sonne of the Lord Herbert of Castle-iland, Novemb. 19. 1627." *The Sermons*. Eds. Evelyn M. Simpson and George R. Potter. 10 vols. Berkeley: U of California P, 1956. 94–109.

Doris, Stacy. *Conference*. Bedford, MA: Potes and Poets Press, 2001.

———. *Paramour*. San Francisco: Krupskaya, 2000.

———. Reading of *Conference*. Poetics Program, SUNY Buffalo. 30 Oct. 2011. PennSound. 23 July 2012.

Drew, Philip. "Matthew Arnold and the Passage of Time: A Study of *The Scholar-Gypsy* and *Thyrsis*." *The Major Victorian Poets: Reconsiderations*. Ed. Isobel Armstrong. New York: Routledge, 2012. 199–224.

Duncan, Ian. *Scott's Shadow*. Princeton, NJ: Princeton UP, 2007.

Duncan, Robert. *Bending the Bow*. New York: New Directions, 1963.

———. *Fictive Certainties*. New York: New Directions, 1985.

———. *The Opening of the Field*. New York: Grove Press, 1960.

———. *Roots and Branches*. New York: New Directions, 1964.

———. *A Selected Prose*. Ed. Robert J. Bertholf. New York: New Directions, 1995.

Duncan, Robert, and Denise Levertov. *Letters of Robert Duncan and Denise Levertov*. Eds. Robert J. Bertholf and Albert Gelpi. Palo Alto: Stanford UP, 2003.

Dunn, Douglas. "'A Very Scottish Kind of Dash': Burns' Native Metric." *Robert Burns and Cultural Authority*. Ed. Robert Crawford. Iowa City: U of Iowa P. 1997. 58–85.

DuPlessis, Rachel Blau. *Blue Studios: Poetry and Its Cultural Work*. Tuscaloosa: U of Alabama P, 2006.

——. *Purple Passages: Pound, Eliot, Zukofsky, Olson, Creeley, and the Ends of Patriarchal Poetry*. Iowa City: U of Iowa P, 2012.

——. *Surge: Drafts 96–114*. Norfolk, UK: Salt Publishing, 2013.

Dyck, Martin. *Novalis and Mathematics*. New York: AMS Press, 1960.

Eliot, T. S. *Selected Essays*. 3rd ed. London: Faber and Faber, 1951.

Emerson, Ralph Waldo. *Selected Essays, Lectures, Poems*. Ed. Robert D. Richardson. New York: Bantam Classics, 1990.

Empson, William. *Some Versions of Pastoral*. New York: New Directions, 1974.

Favret, Mary. *War at a Distance: Romanticism and the Making of Modern Warfare*. Princeton, NJ: Princeton UP, 2010.

Fierle-Hedrick, Kai. "Lifted: An Interview with Lisa Robertson." *Chicago Review* 51.4, 52.1 (Spring 2006): 38–54.

Finburgh, Clare. "Unveiling the Void: The Presence of Absence in the Scenography of Jean Genet's *The Screens*." *Theatre Journal* 56 (2004): 205–24.

Finlay, Alec, ed. *Ian Hamilton Finlay: Selections*. Berkeley: U of California P, 2012.

Fishman, Lisa. "Shelley's 'Secret Alchemy': Mercury Unbound." Diss. University of Utah.

Fitterman, Robert, and Vanessa Place. *Notes on Conceptualisms*. Brooklyn: Ugly Duckling Press, 2009.

Ford, George H. *Keats and the Victorians: A Study of His Influence and Rise to Fame, 1821–1895*. North Haven, CT: Archon Books, 1962.

Fowler, Roger. "Three Blank Verse Textures." *The Languages of Literature: Some Linguistic Contributions to Criticism*. London: Routledge and Kegan Paul, 1971. 184–99.

Francis, Mark, and John Morrow. *A History of English Political Thought in the 19th Century*. New York: St. Martin's Press, 1994.

Frank, Manfred. *Das Problem "Zeit" in der deutschen Romantik*. Munich: Winkler Verlag, 1972.

——. *Einführung in die frühromantische Ästhetik*. Frankfurt: Suhrkamp Verlag, 1989.

——. *The Philosophical Foundations of Early German Romanticism*. Albany, NY: SUNY Press, 2004.

——. *"Unendliche Annäherung": Die Anfänge der philosophischen Frühromantik*. Frankfurt: Suhrkamp Verlag, 1997.

Freud, Sigmund. *General Psychological Theory*. New York: Macmillan, 1963.

——. *Three Essays on the Theory of Sexuality*. Trans. James Strachey. New York: Basic Books, 2000.

Furniss, Tom. "Mary Wollstonecraft's French Revolution." *The Cambridge Companion to Mary Wollstonecraft*. Ed. Claudia Johnson. Cambridge: Cambridge UP, 2002. 59–81.

Gallagher, Catherine. "Formalism in Time." *MLQ* 61.1 (March 2000): 230–51.

Gamer, Michael, and Terry F. Robinson. "Mary Robinson and the Dramatic Art of the Comeback." *Studies in Romanticism* 48.2 (Summer 2009): 219–56.

Geddes, Alexander. "Three Scottish Poems, with a Previous Dissertation on the Scoto-Saxon Dialect." *Transactions of the Society of the Antiquaries of Scotland*. Vol. 1. Edinburgh: 1792.

Genet, Jean. *The Screens*. Trans. Bernard Frechtman. New York: Grove Press, 1962.

Gittings, Robert. *The Mask of Keats*. Cambridge, MA: Harvard UP, 1956.

Goodridge, John, ed. *Eighteenth-Century Labouring Class Poets*. 3 vols. London: Pickering and Chatto, 2003.

Goya y Lucientes, Francisco. *Los Caprichos*. New York: Dover Publications, 1969.

Grieve, Dorian. "MacDiarmid's Language." *The Edinburgh Companion to Hugh MacDiarmid*. Eds. Scott Lyell and Margery Palmer McCulloch. Edinburgh: Edinburgh UP, 2011. 23–35.

Griggs, Earl Leslie. "Coleridge and Mrs. Mary Robinson." *Modern Language Notes* 45.2 (Feb. 1930): 90–95.

Guest, Barbara. *The Barbara Guest Memory Bank*. 8 Oct. 2013. http://www.asu .edu/pipercwcenter/how2journal/bg_memorybank/bg_memory.html

Guillory, John. *Cultural Capital: The Problem of Literary Canon Formation*. Chicago: U of Chicago P, 1993.

Guthrie, W. K. C. *Orpheus and Greek Religion*. Princeton, NJ: Princeton UP, 1993.

Hall, Spencer T. *Biographical Sketches of Remarkable People, Chiefly from Personal Recollection*. London: Simpkin, Marshall, 1873.

Halsey, Alan. *The Text of Shelley's Death*. Sheffield: West House Books, 2001.

Hameen-Anttila, Jaakko. "The Immutable Entities and Time." *Journal of the Muhyiddin Ibn 'Arabi Society* 39 (2006). n. pag. 23 July 2012.

Hannoum, Abdelmajid. "What Is an Order of Time?" *History and Theory* 47.3 (Oct. 2008): 458–71. http://www.ibnarabisociety.org/search/search.php?zoom _sort=0&zoom_query=Hameen-Anttila%2C+Jaakko.+%22The+Immutable +Entities+and+Time.%22+&zoom_per_page=10&zoom_and=0.

Hartog, François. "Time and Heritage." *Museum International* 57.3 (2005): 7–18.

Hawley, Judith. "Romantic Patronage: Mary Robinson and Coleridge Revisited." *British Women's Writing in the Long Eighteenth Century*. Eds. Jennie Batchelor and Cora Kaplan. Hampshire, UK: Palgrave Macmillan, 2005. 62–75.

H. D. *Notes on Thought and Vision*. San Francisco: City Lights Books, 1982.

Heine, Heinrich. *The Romantic School and Other Essays*. New York: Continuum, 2002.

Hejinian, Lyn. *The Beginner*. Berkeley: Tuumba Press, 2002.

Henrich, Dieter. *Der Grund im Bewußtsein*. Stuttgart: Klett-Cotta, 1992.

Hirtenstein, Stephen. *The Unlimited Mercifier: The Spiritual Life and Thought of Ibn 'Arabi*. Oxford: Anqa Publishing, 1999.

Hoffman, Eric. "Legislator of the Unacknowledged World: George Oppen and Shelley." *All This Strangeness: A Garland for George Oppen*. Ed. Eric Hoffman. 8 Oct. 2013. http://www.bigbridge.org/BB14/OPPEN.HTM

Hogg, James. *The Three Perils of Woman*. Eds. David Groves, Antony Haslar, and Douglas S. Mack. Edinburgh: Edinburgh UP, 1995.

Hölderlin, Friedrich. *Essays and Letters on Theory*. Trans. Thomas Pfau. Albany: SUNY Press, 1988.

——. *Selected Poems*. Trans. Maxine Chernoff and Paul Hoover. Richmond, CA: Omnidawn Publishing, 2008.

Hopkins, Gerard Manley. *The Poetical Works of Gerard Manley Hopkins*. Ed. Norman H. Mackenzie. Oxford: Clarendon Press, 1990.

Howe, Susan. *The Birthmark: Unsettling the Wilderness in American Literary History*. Middletown, CT: Wesleyan UP, 1993.

Huizinga, Johan. *The Waning of the Middle Ages*. New York: Penguin, 1982.

"Iranian Satellites Fajr, Nahid and Zafar to Be Launched on Schedule." *Islamic Republic News Agency*. 23 June 2012. 23 July 2012. http://article.wn.com/view /2012/06/23/Iranian_satellites_Fajr_Nahid_and_Zafar_to_be_launched_on_sc/

Jakobson, Roman. "What Is Poetry?" *Language in Literature*. Eds. Krystyna Pomorska and Stephen Rudy. Cambridge, MA: Harvard UP, 1987. 368–78.

Jameson, Frederic. "Marx's Purloined Letter." *Ghostly Demarcations: A Symposium on Jacques Derrida's Specters of Marx*. Ed. Michael Sprinker. London: Verso, 1999. 26–67.

Johnson, Barbara. *A World of Difference*. Baltimore: Johns Hopkins UP, 1987.

Johnston, Devin. *Precipitations*. Middletown, CT: Wesleyan UP, 2002.

Jones, Charles. *A Language Suppressed: The Pronunciation of Scots in the 18th Century*. Edinburgh: John Donald, 1995.

Joris, Pierre. *Justifying the Margins*. Cambridge, UK: Salt Publishing, 2009.

Juengel, Scott J. "Mary Wollstonecraft's Perpetual Disaster." *Romanticism and Disaster*. Eds. Jacques Khalip and David Colling. *Romantic Circles* (Jan. 2012). 11 July 2012. www.rc.umd.edu/praxis/disaster/HTML/praxis.2012.juengel.html

Kaufman, Robert. "Legislators of the Post-Everything World: Shelley's *Defence* of Adorno." *ELH* 63 (1996): 707–33.

——. "Red Kant, or the Persistence of the Third *Critique* in Adorno and Jameson." *Critical Inquiry* 26 (Summer 2000): 682–724.

Keach, William. *Arbitrary Power: Romanticism, Language, Politics*. Princeton: Princeton University Press, 2004.

——. "The Ruins of Empire and the Contradictions of Restoration: Barbauld, Byron, Hemans." *Romanticism and Disaster*. Eds. Jacques Khalip and David Colling. *Romantic Circles* (Jan. 2012). 11 July 2012. http://www.rc.umd.edu /praxis/disaster/HTML/praxis.2012.keach.html

Keats, John. *Complete Poems*. Ed. Jack Stillinger. Cambridge, MA: Harvard UP, 1982.

——. *The Selected Letters of John Keats*. Ed. Grant F. Scott. Cambridge, MA: Harvard UP, 2005.

Kelly, Robert. *Mont Blanc*. Ann Arbor: OtherWind Press, 1994.

Kerrigan, John. *Archipelagic English*. Oxford: Oxford UP, 2008.

Koselleck, Reinhart. *Futures Past: On the Semantics of Historical Time.* Trans. Keith Tribe. Cambridge, MA: MIT Press, 1985.

Lacoue-Labarthe, Philippe. *Nancy, Jean-Luc. L'absolu littéraire.* Collection Poétique. Paris: Le Seuil, 1978.

Ladkin, Sam. "Problems for Lyric Poetry." Ladkin and Purves 271–322.

Ladkin, Sam, and Robin Purves, eds. *Complicities: British Poetry 1945–2007.* Prague: Litteraria Pragensia, 2007.

Leask, Nigel. "Burns, Wordsworth, and the Politics of Vernacular Poetry." *Land, Nation, Culture, 740–1840: Thinking the Republic of Taste.* Eds. Peter de Bolla, Nigel Leask, and David Simpson. Basingstoke, UK: Palgrave Macmillan, 2005.

———. *The Politics of Imagination in Coleridge's Critical Thought.* London: Macmillan, 1988.

———. *Robert Burns and Pastoral: Poetry and Improvement in Late Eighteenth-Century Scotland.* Oxford: Oxford UP, 2010.

Lefebvre, Henri. *Introduction to Modernity.* London: Verso, 2011.

Leonard, Tom, ed. *Radical Renfrew: Poetry from the French Revolution to the First World War.* Edinburgh: Polygon, 1990.

Lezama Lima, José. *La expresión americana.* Ed. Irlemar Chiampi. Mexico City: Fondo de Cultura Económica, 1993.

Lockhart, John Gibson. *Peter's Letters to His Kinsfolk.* 3rd ed. 3 vols. Edinburgh, 1819.

Lokke, Kari E. "The Last Man." *The Cambridge Companion to Mary Shelley.* Ed. Esther Schor. Cambridge: Cambridge UP, 2004. 116–34.

The Longman Anthology of British Literature. 2nd ed. Vol. 2A. "The Romantics and Their Contemporaries." Eds. Susan Wolfson and Peter Manning. New York: Longman, 2003.

Lorca, Federico García. *Deep Song and Other Prose.* New York: New Directions, 1980.

Low, Donald A., ed. *Robert Burns: The Critical Heritage.* London: Routledge and Kegan Paul, 1974.

Lyotard, Jean-François. *The Differend: Phrases in Dispute.* Trans. Georges Van Den Abbeele. Minneapolis: U of Minnesota P, 1988.

———. *The Inhuman: Reflections on Time.* Palo Alto: Stanford UP, 1991.

MacDiarmid, Hugh. *Selected Prose.* Ed. Alan Riach. Manchester, UK: Carcanet, 1992.

Mahoney, Dennis F. "Hardenbergs Naturbegriff und—darstellung im Lichte moderner Chaostheorien." *Novalis und die Wissenschaften.* Ed. Herbert Uerlings. Tübingen, Germany: Max Niemeyer Verlag, 1997.

Makdisi, Saree. "Literature, National Identity, and Empire." *The Cambridge Companion to English Literature, 1740–1830.* Eds. Thomas Keymer and Jon Mee. Cambridge: Cambridge UP, 2004. 61–79.

———. *Romantic Imperialism: University Empire and the Culture of Modernity.* Cambridge: Cambridge UP, 1998.

Malthus, Thomas. *An Essay on the Principle of Population, as it affects the Future Improvement of Society. With remarks on the Speculations of Mr. Godwin, M. Condorcet, and Other Writers.* London: J. Johnson, 1798.

Marcuse, Herbert. "The Affirmative Character of Culture." *Negations.* Boston: Beacon Press, 1969.

Margantin, Laurent. *Système minéralogique et cosmologie chez Novalis.* Paris: L'Harmattan, 1998.

Mariani, Paul. *The Broken Tower: The Life of Hart Crane.* New York: W. W. Norton, 1999.

~~Martínez, Juan Luis,~~[sic] and ~~Juan de Dios Martínez~~[sic]. *La nueva novela.* 1977. Santiago, Chile: Ediciones Archivo: 1985.

McGann, Jerome, ed. *The New Oxford Book of Romantic Period Verse.* Oxford: Oxford UP, 1993.

———. *The Poetics of Sensibility: A Revolution in Literary Style.* Oxford: Oxford UP, 1996.

———. and Lisa Samuels, "Deformance and Interpretation," ed. Jerome McGann, *Radiant Textuality.* New York: Palgrave, 2001.

McGonigal, James. *Beyond the Last Dragon: A Life of Edwin Morgan.* Dingwall, UK: Sandstone Press, 2010.

McGuirk, Carol. *Robert Burns and the Sentimental Era.* Athens: U of Georgia P, 1985.

McIlvanney, William. "Afterword to *Burdalane.*" *Headshook: Contemporary Novelists and Poets Writing on Scotland's Future.* Ed. Stuart Kelly. Hachette Scotland: *Scotland on Sunday,* 2009.

McKusick, James. "Beyond the Visionary Company: John Clare's Resistance to Romanticism." *John Clare in Context.* Eds. Hugh Haughton et al. Cambridge: Cambridge UP, 1994. 221–37.

McLane, Maureen. *Romanticism and the Human Sciences: Poetry, Population, and the Discourse of the Species.* Cambridge: Cambridge UP, 2000.

Meier, Paul. *William Morris: The Marxist Dreamer.* Trans. Frank Grubb. Sussex, UK: Harvester Press, 1978.

Milton, John. *Paradise Lost. A Poem Written in Ten Books.* London: Peter Parker, 1667.

Morgan, Edwin. "The Young Writer in Scotland." *Edinburgh International Festival, 1962, "The Novel Today," International Writers' Conference.* Kilkerran, UK: Zeticula, 2012. 35–38.

Mosès, Stéphane. *The Angel of History: Rosenzweig, Benjamin, Scholem.* Trans. Barbara Harshav. Stanford: Stanford UP, 2009.

Mossin, Andrew. *Drafts for Shelley.* Cedar Ridge, CA: Facture Books, 2001.

Mouffe, Chantel. *The Democratic Paradox.* London: Verso, 2005.

Mount, Kevin. "Long lost reply." Message to Judith Goldman. 23 July 2013. E-mail.

———. "Stacy Doris." Message to Judith Goldman. 8 Aug. 2012. E-mail.

Moxley, Jennifer. "Rimbaud's Foolish Virgin, Wieners's 'Feminine Soliloquy,' and the

Metaphorical Resistance of the Lyric Body." *Talisman* 34 (2007). Reprinted online, *Jacket* 34 (2007). http://jacketmagazine.com/34/moxley-rimbaud-wieners .shtml.

Muir, Edwin. *Scott and Scotland: The Predicament of the Scottish Writer*. Edinburgh: Polygon, 1982.

Mullen, Laura. "Late Spring (1973)." *Court Green* 7 (2010).

Murison, David. "The Language of Burns." *Critical Essays on Robert Burns*. Ed. Donald Low. London: RKP, 1975. 54–69.

———. "The Speech of Ayrshire in the Time of Burns." *Ayrshire at the Time of Burns*. Ed. John Strawhorn. Kilmarnock, UK: Ayrshire Archaeological and Natural History Society, 1959. 222–31.

Myles, Eileen. *The Inferno*. New York: OR Books, 2010.

Neruda, Pablo. *Obras completas*. Vol. 2. Buenos Aires: Losada, 1968.

———. "Walking Around." Trans. Jerome Rothenberg. *The Oxford Book of Latin American Poetry*. Eds. Cecilia Vicuña and Ernesto Livon-Grosman. Oxford: Oxford UP, 2009.

Neubauer, John. *Symbolismus und symbolische Logik*. Munich: Wilhelm Fink Verlag, 1978.

The New Penguin Book of Romantic Poetry. Eds. Jonathan Wordsworth and Jessica Wordsworth. London: Penguin Books, 2001.

The New Princeton Encyclopedia of Poetry and Poetics. Eds. Alex Preminger and T. V. F. Brogan. Princeton, NJ: Princeton UP, 1993.

Ni, Siobhan. "'Why May Not Man One Day Be Immortal?' Population, Perfectibility, and the Immortal Question in Godwin's Political Justice." *History of European Ideas* 33 (2007): 25–39.

Nicolson, Marjorie Hope. *Mountain Gloom and Mountain Glory: The Development of the Aesthetics of the Infinite*. Ithaca: Cornell UP, 1959.

Niecks, Frederick. "The Flat, Sharp, and Natural: A Historical Sketch." *Proceedings of the Musical Association* 16th Session (1889–90). 79–100.

The Norton Anthology of English Literature. Ed. Deidre Shauna Lynch and Jack Stillinger. Vol. 2. New York: W. W. Norton, 2012.

Novalis. *Schriften*. Ed. Paul Kluckhohn and Richard Samuel. 4 vols. Stuttgart: Verlag W. Kohlhammer, 1977–83.

O'Hara, Frank. *Meditations in an Emergency*. New York: Grove Press, 1957.

O'Neill, Michael. *The All-Sustaining Air: Romantic Legacies and Renewals in British, American, and Irish Poetry since 1900*. Oxford: Oxford UP, 2007.

———. *Romanticism and the Self-Conscious Poem*. Oxford: Clarendon Press, 1997.

Oppen, George. *New Collected Poems*. Ed. Michael Davidson. New York: New Directions Books, 2002.

Ovid. *The Metamorphoses*. Trans. Rolfe Humphries. Bloomington: Indiana UP, 1955.

Paley, Morton D. "Mary Shelley's *The Last Man*: Apocalypse without Millennium." *Keats-Shelley Review* 4 (Autumn 1989): 1–25.

Palmer, Michael. "Some Notes on Shelley, Poetics and the Present." *Active Boundaries*. New York: New Directions Books, 2008. 195–206.

Parra, Nicanor. *Obras completas & Algo † (1935–1972)*. Barcelona: Galaxia Gutenberg, 2006.

Pascoe, Judith. "Mary Robinson and the Literary Marketplace." *Romantic Women Writers: Voices and Countervoices*. Eds. Paula R. Feldman and Theresa M. Kelley. Hanover: UP of New England, 1995. 252–68.

Pater, Walter. *Appreciations with an Essay on Style*. London: Macmillan, 1889.

Patterson, Annabel. *Pastoral and Ideology: Virgil to Valery*. Oxford: Clarendon Press, 1988.

Pattison, Neil. "Lyric Purity in Keston Sutherland's *Hot White Andy*." *Hot Gun!* 1 (Summer 2008): 84–94.

Paulin, Tom, ed. *The Faber Book of Vernacular Verse*. London: Faber and Faber, 1990.

Pinson, Jean-Claude. *Habiter en Poète*. Paris: Verdier, 1995.

Pittock, Murray. *Scottish and Irish Romanticism*. Oxford: Oxford UP, 2008.

Poggioli, Renato. *The Oaten Flute*. Cambridge: Harvard UP, 1975.

Pope, Alexander. *Ode for Musick*. London, 1713.

Pound, Ezra. *Active Anthology*. London: Faber and Faber, 1933.

———. *Literary Essays of Ezra Pound*. New York: New Directions, 1968.

Prickett, Stephen. *European Romanticism: A Reader*. London: Continuum, 2012.

Prigogine, Ilya. *Is Future Given?* Singapore: World Scientific, 2003.

Prigogine, Ilya, and Isabelle Stengers. *Order Out of Chaos*. New York: Bantam Books, 1984.

Prynne, J. H. *Field Notes: 'The Solitary Reaper' and Others*. Cambridge: Cambridge Printers Limited, 2007.

———. "Keston Sutherland: *Hot White Andy* reviewed by J. H. Prynne, 26th November 2007." *Hot Gun!* 1 (Summer 2008): 78–83.

Queyras, Sina. "All Sides Now: A Correspondence with Lisa Robertson." Mar. 2014. http://www.poetryfoundation.org/harriet/2010/03/on-rs-boat-correspondence -with-lisa-robertson/. Accessed March 2014.

Ramke, Bin. "Articulation." *Fence* (Fall 2011): 157–60.

Ramsay, Allen, *Works*. Eds. Alexander Kinghorn and Alexander Law, Scottish Text Society. 6 vols. Edinburgh: Blackwood, 1953–74.

Rancière, Jacques. *Aesthetics and Its Discontents*. Cambridge, UK: Polity Press, 2009.

Rasula, Jed. *Modernism and Poetic Inspiration: The Shadow Mouth*. New York: Palgrave Macmillan, 2009.

Reitan, Albert G. "Specialist's Factual Report of Investigation DCA00MA006." Washington, DC: National Transportation Safety Board, 2000. 23 July 2012. http://books.google.co.uk/books

Riach, Alan. "MacDiarmid's Burns." *Robert Burns and Cultural Authority*. Ed. Robert Crawford. Edinburgh: Polygon, 1999.

Ricks, Christopher. *Allusion to the Poets*. Oxford: Oxford UP, 2002.

Riding, Laura. *Anarchism Is Not Enough*. Ed. Lisa Samuels. 1928. Berkeley: U of California P, 2001.

Rilke, Rainer Maria. *Ahead of All Parting: The Selected Poetry and Prose of Rainer Maria Rilke*. Ed. and trans. Stephen Mitchell. New York: Random House, Modern Library Edition, 1995.

———. *Letters of Rainer Maria Rilke 1892–1910*. Trans. Jane Bannard Greene and M. D. Herter Norton. New York: W. W. Norton, 1969.

———. *Letters of Rainer Maria Rilke 1910–1926*. Trans. Jane Bannard Greene and M. D. Herter Norton. New York: W. W. Norton, 1969.

Rimbaud, Arthur. "The 'Voyant' Letter to Paul Demy." *Toward the Open Field: Poets on the Art of Poetry 1800–1950*. Ed. Melissa Kwasny. Middletown, CT: Wesleyan UP, 2004.

Robertson, Lisa. *Lisa Robertson's Magenta Soul Whip*. Toronto: Coach House Books, 2009.

———. *Occasional Work and 7 Walks from the Office for Soft Architecture*. 2003. Toronto: Coach House Books, 2006.

———. *R's Boat*. Berkeley: U of California P, 2010.

Robinson, Daniel. "From 'Mingled Measure' to 'Ecstatic Measures': Mary Robinson's Poetic Reading of 'Kubla Khan.'" *The Wordsworth Circle* 26.1 (1995): 4–7.

Robinson, Jeffrey C. *Spliced Romanticism*. Lampeter, UK: Edwin Mellen Press, 1997.

———. *Unfettering Poetry: The Fancy in British Romanticism*. New York: Palgrave Macmillan, 2006.

Robinson, Mary. "A Letter to the Women of England on the Injustice of Mental Subordination" [w. 1798, pub. 1799, under the pseudonym Anne Frances Randall]. London: Printed for T. N. Longman and O. Rees, No. 39, Paternoster Row, 1799. Eds. Adriana Craciun, Anne Irmen Close, Megan Musgrave, and Orianne Smith. Hypertext ed. from the *Romantic Circles*, University of Maryland. 21 Apr. 2012. www.rc.umd.edu/editions/robinson/cover.htm.

———. *Selected Poems*. Ed. Judith Pascoe. Peterborough, ON: Broadview Press, 2000.

Rohrbach, Emily. "Anna Barbauld's History of the Future." *European Romantic Review* 17.2 (2006): 179–84.

Ross, Christine. "The Suspension of History in Contemporary Media Arts." *Intermediality: History and Theory of the Arts, Literature and Technologies* 11 (2008): 125–48.

Ross, Kristin. *The Emergence of Social Space: Rimbaud and the Paris Commune*. London: Verso, 2008.

Rossetti, Dante Gabriel. *Collected Poetry and Prose*. Ed. Jerome McGann. New Haven, CT: Yale UP, 2003.

Rothenberg, Jerome. *A Book of Witness*. New York: New Directions, 2003.

———. *Concealments and Caprichos*. Boston: Black Widow Press, 2010.

Rothenberg, Jerome, and Jeffrey C. Robinson, eds. *Poems for the Millennium, Volume Three: The University of California Book of Romantic and Postromantic Poetry*. Berkeley: U of California P, 2009.

Rothenberg, Jerome, and Diane Rothenberg, eds. *Symposium of the Whole: A Range of Discourse toward an Ethnopoetics*. Berkeley: U of California P, 1983.

Said, Edward. *Orientalism*. New York: Vintage Books, 1979.

Schlegel, Friedrich. *Lucinde and the Fragments*. Trans. Peter Firchow. Minneapolis: U of Minnesota P, 1971.

———. *The Philosophical Foundations of Early German Romanticism*. Trans. Elizabeth Millán-Zeibert. Albany: SUNY Press, 2004.

———. *Philosophical Fragments*. Trans. Peter Firchow, foreword by Rodolphe Gasché. Minneapolis: U of Minnesota P, 1971.

Schwab, Raymond. "The Asiatic Society of Calcutta." *Orientalism: A Reader*. Ed. A. L. Macfie. New York: New York UP, 2001. 31–35.

Scodel, Joshua. "The Cowleyan Pindaric Ode and Sublime Diversions." *A Nation Transformed*. Eds. Alan Houston and Steve Pincus. Cambridge: Cambridge UP, 2001. 180–210.

Sharafuddin, Mohammed. *Islam and Romantic Orientalism: Literary Encounters with the Orient*. New York: St. Martin's Press, 1996.

Shelley, Mary. *The Last Man*. Ed. Morton D. Paley. Oxford: Oxford UP, 1994.

Shelley, Percy Bysshe. *The Complete Poetical Works of Percy Bysshe Shelley*. Ed. Thomas Hutchinson. London: Oxford UP, 1934.

———. "A Defence of Poetry." *Shelley's Poetry and Prose*. Eds. Donald H. Reiman and Sharon B. Powers. New York: W. W. Norton, 1977. 478–508.

———. "The Revolt of Islam" (1818). *The Complete Poetical Works of Percy Bysshe Shelley*. Ed. George Edward Woodberry. New York: Houghton Mifflin, 1901. 43–136.

———. *Shelley, Percy Bysshe*. Vol. 20. Ed. Michael O'Neill. New York: Garland Publishing. 1994.

Silverman, Kaja. *Flesh of My Flesh*. Stanford, CA: Stanford UP, 2009.

Simay, Philippe. "Tradition as Injunction: Benjamin and the Critique of Historicisms." *Walter Benjamin and History*. Trans. Carlo Salzani. Ed. Andrew Benjamin. London: Continuum, 2005. 137–55.

Simpson, David. *9/11: The Culture of Commemoration*. Chicago: U of Chicago P, 2006.

Skau, Michael. *"A Clown in a Grave": Complexities and Tensions in the Work of Gregory Corso*. Carbondale: Southern Illinois UP, 1999.

Skoblow, Jeffrey. *Dooble Tongue: Scots, Burns, Contradiction*. Newark: U of Delaware P, 2001.

Smith, Adam. *Lectures on Rhetoric and Belles Lettres*. Ed. J. C. Bryce. Glasgow Edition of the Works and Correspondence of Adam Smith. Indianapolis: Liberty Fund, 1985.

Smith, G. Gregory. *Scottish Literature: Character and Influence*. London: Macmillan, 1919.

Smith, Jeremy. "*Copia Verborum*: Linguistic Choices in Robert Burns." *Review of English Studies* 58.233 (2007): 73–88.

Sorensen, Janet. *The Grammar of Empire in Eighteenth-Century British Writing*. Cambridge: Cambridge UP, 2000.

Spicer, Jack. *The House That Jack Built: The Collected Lectures of Jack Spicer*. Ed. Peter Gizzi. Hanover: UP of New England, 1998.

Stelzig, Eugene. "'Spirit divine! With thee I'll wander': Mary Robinson and Coleridge in Poetic Dialogue." *Wordsworth Circle* 35.3 (Summer 2004): 118–22.

Stoler, Ann Laura. "Imperial Debris: Reflections on Ruins and Ruination." *Cultural Anthropology* 23.2 (May 2008): 191–219.

Storey, Mark. *The Problem of Poetry in the Romantic Period*. Basingstoke, UK: Macmillan, 2000.

Strachan, John. "Poets and Pugilists." *History Today* 59.1 (Jan. 2009).

Sulloway, Alison. *Gerard Manley Hopkins and the Victorian Temper*. London: Routledge, 1972.

Sutherland, Keston. *Stupefaction: A Radical Anatomy of Phantoms*. London: Seagull Books, 2011.

Thompson, E. P. *William Morris: Romantic to Revolutionary*. New York: Pantheon Books, 1976.

Thoreau, Henry David. *The Heart of Thoreau's Journals*. Ed. Odell Shepard. New York: Dover, 1961.

———. *Walden and Other Writings*. Ed. Joseph Wood Krutch. New York: Bantam Classics, 1981.

Toufic, Jalal. *Distracted*. 2nd ed. Berkeley: Tuumba Press, 2003.

———. *Over-Sensitivity*. Los Angeles: Sun and Moon Press, 1996.

———. *(Vampires): An Uneasy Essay on the Undead in Film*. Rev. ed. Sausalito: Post-Apollo Press, 2003.

Vendler, Helen. *The Odes of John Keats*. Cambridge, MA: Harvard UP, 1983.

Wagner, Catherine. *My New Job*. Albany, NY: Fence Books, 2009.

Watson, Roderick, "Living with the Double Tongue: Modern Poetry in Scots." *Edinburgh History of Scottish Literature*. Ed. Ian Brown. 3 vols. Edinburgh: Edinburgh UP, 2007. 3: 163–75.

Weiner, Stephanie Kuduk. *Republican Politics and English Poetry, 1789–1874*. New York: Palgrave Macmillan, 2005.

Weisman, Alan. *The World without Us*. New York: Picador, 2007.

When We Were Kings. Dir. Leon Gast. Perf. Muhammad Ali, George Foreman, and Don King. Polygram Filmed Entertainment, 1996.

Whitman, Walt. *Walt Whitman: Poetry and Prose*. New York: Library of America, 1982.

Wieners, John. *Cultural Affairs in Boston*. Preface by Robert Creeley. Santa Rosa, CA: Black Sparrow, 1988.

———— *Selected Poems 1958–1984*. Santa Barbara, CA: Black Sparrow, 1986.

Wilkinson, John, 2008. "Mandarin Ducks and Chee-Chee Chokes." *Jacket* 35 (early 2008). 1 July 2009. http://jacketmagazine.com/35/r-sutherland-rb-wilkinson .shtml.

Williams, Raymond. *Culture and Society 1780–1950*. New York: Harper and Row, 1958.

Williams, William Carlos. *Pictures from Brueghel and Other Poems*. New York: New Directions, 1962.

Willis, Elizabeth. *Meteoric Flowers*. Middletown: Wesleyan UP, 2006.

Wolfson, Susan J. *Borderlines: The Shiftings of Gender in British Romanticism*. Stanford: Stanford UP, 2006.

Wollstonecraft, Mary. *Letters Written during a Short Residence in Sweden, Norway and Denmark*. London: J. Johnson, 1796.

————. *A Vindication of the Rights of Woman*. Ed. Carol H. Poston. 1792. New York: W. W. Norton, 1975.

Wordsworth, William. *Lyrical Ballads and Other Poems, 1797–1800*. Eds. James Butler and Karen Green. Ithaca: Cornell UP, 1992.

————. "Preface to the Second Edition of *Lyrical Ballads*." *Toward the Open Field: Poets on the Art of Poetry 1800–1950*. Ed. Melissa Kwasny. Middletown, CT: Wesleyan UP, 2004.

————. *The Prose Works of William Wordsworth*. Eds. W. J. B. Owen and Jane Worthington Smyser. Vol 1. Oxford: Clarendon Press, 1974.

————. *William Wordsworth: The Oxford Authors*. Ed. Stephen Gill. Oxford: Oxford UP, 1984.

————. *Wordsworth: The Poems*. Ed. John O. Hayden. 3 vols. Harmondsworth, UK: Penguin, 1977.

Wordsworth, William, and Samuel Taylor Coleridge. *Lyrical Ballads* (1800). Ed. R. L. Brett and A. R. Jones. 2nd ed. London: Routledge, 1991.

Wroe, Ann. *Being Shelley*. New York: Pantheon, 2007.

Yeats, William Butler. *Autobiography*. New York: Scribner, 1986.

————. *Essays and Introductions*. New York: Palgrave Macmillan, 1961.

————. *The Collected Poems of W. B. Yeats*, ed. Richard J. Finneran. New York: Simon & Schuster Inc, 1996.

Yingling, Thomas. *Hart Crane and the Homosexual Text*. Chicago: U of Chicago P, 1990.

Yohannan, John D. "The Persian Poetry Fad in England, 1770–1825." *Comparative Literature* 4.2 (Spring 1952): 137–60.

Young, Edward. "Epistle I. To Mr. Pope." *Two Epistles to Mr.Pope. Concerning the Authors of the Age*. London and Dublin, 1730.

Young, Robert. *Colonial Desire: Hybridity in Theory, Culture, and Race*. London: Routledge, 1995.

"Yucca Mountain Nuclear Waste Repository." *Wikipedia*. 23 July 2012. http:// en.wikipedia.org/wiki/Yucca_Mountain_nuclear_waste_repository

Contributors

Dan Beachy-Quick is the author of five books of poetry, *Circle's Apprentice*, *North True South Bright*, *Spell*, *Mulberry*, and *This Nest, Swift Passerine*; five chapbooks, *Apology for the Book of Creatures*, *Overtakelesness*, *Heroisms*, *Canto*, and *Mobius Crowns* (the latter two both written in collaboration with the poet Srikanth Reddy); and *A Whaler's Dictionary*, a book of interlinked essays on *Moby-Dick*. Reddy and Beachy-Quick's collaboration has recently been released as a full-length collection, *Conversities*, from 1913 Press. Milkweed Editions has also published a new collection of essays, meditations, and tales, *Wonderful Investigations*. He is a contributing editor for the journals *A Public Space*, *Dear Navigator*, and *West Branch*. He has taught at Grinnell College and the School of the Art Institute of Chicago and is currently teaching in the MFA Writing Program at Colorado State University. His work has been a winner of the Colorado Book Award and has been a finalist for the William Carlos Williams Prize and the PEN/USA Literary Award in Poetry. He is the recipient of a Lannan Foundation residency and taught as visiting faculty at the Iowa Writers' Workshop in spring 2010.

Julie Carr is the author of five books of poetry, *Mead: An Epithalamion*, *Equivocal*, *100 Notes on Violence* (winner of the Sawtooth Award), *Sarah—Of Fragments and Lines* (a National Poetry Series selection), and RAG. Her critical study of Victorian poetry, *Surface Tension: Ruptural Time and the Poetics of Desire in Late Victorian Poetry*, was published by Dalkey Archive in 2013. She is an associate professor of English and creative writing at the University of Colorado, Boulder. She was the recipient of a National Endowment for the Arts Fellowship for 2011–2012. *Think Tank*, a book of poetry, is forthcoming from Solid Objects Press in 2015.

Jacques Darras is a poet, essayist, and translator as well as professor emeritus in English and American poetry at the University of Picardy in Amiens.

He is currently completing a *Poem in 8 Cantos*, begun in 1988, about the little Northern River *La Maye*, which flows into the Somme at its channel mouth. Cantos 1, 2, 3, 4, and 7 were published by Le Cri in Brussels, while Cantos 5 and 6 were published by Gallimard/L'Arbalète in Paris. He has translated Walt Whitman, Samuel Taylor Coleridge, Ezra Pound, William Carlos Williams, Malcolm Lowry, Basil Bunting, Ted Hughes, Geoffrey Hill, and others. In 1989, he was the first French person and European to deliver the Reith Lectures on the BBC. He was awarded the Prix Apollinaire in 2004 and the Grand Prix de Poésie de l'Académie Française in 2006. In the previous year he published "Nous sommes tous des Romantiques allemands" (We are all German Romantics) at Calmann-Lévy, Paris.

Rachel Blau DuPlessis is the creator of recent poetry and visual works including *The Collage Poems of Drafts* (Salt Publishing, 2011) and *Pitch: Drafts 77–95* (Salt Publishing, 2010), both from the long poem *Drafts. Surge: Drafts 96–114* was published in 2013, bringing this work to a temporary fold. Her *Purple Passages: Pound, Eliot, Zukofsky, Olson, Creeley, and the Ends of Patriarchal Poetry* (U of Iowa P, 2012) is part of a trilogy of works about gender and poetics that includes *The Pink Guitar: Writing as Feminist Practice* and *Blue Studios: Poetry and Its Cultural Work*. She has published three other critical books and three coedited anthologies as well as editing *The Selected Letters of George Oppen*. French and Italian book-length translations of selections of *Drafts* appeared in 2013. A Jacket2 feature on *Drafts* appeared in December 2011 at jacket2.org/feature/drafting-beyond-ending. She is professor emerita at Temple University.

Judith Goldman is the author of *Vocoder* (Roof Books, 2001), *Deathstar/Ricochet* (O Books, 2006), and *l.b.; or, catenaries* (Krupskaya, 2011). She coedited the annual journal *War and Peace* with Leslie Scalapino from 2005 to 2009; she currently serves as the poetry features editor for the online academic journal *Postmodern Culture*. She taught in the creative writing program and the interarts humanities core at the University of Chicago from 2007 to 2011. In 2011–2012, she was the Roberta C. Holloway Lecturer in the Practice of Poetry at the University of California, Berkeley. She joined the core faculty of the Poetics Program at SUNY Buffalo in fall 2012.

Jen Hofer is a Los Angeles-based poet, translator, social justice interpreter, teacher, knitter, book-maker, public letter-writer, urban cyclist, and co-founder (with John Pluecker) of the language justice and language experimentation collaborative Antena (www.antenaantena.org). She publishes poems and translations with numerous small presses, including Action Books, Atelos, belladonna, Counterpath Press, Kenning Editions, Insert Press, Les

Figues Press, Litmus Press, LRL Textile Editions, newlights press, Palm Press, Subpress, Ugly Duckling Presse, and in various DIY/DIT incarnations. Her visual-textual work is currently on view at the Center for Land Use Interpretation's Wendover site. She teaches poetics, translation, and bookmaking at California Institute of the Arts and at Otis College of Art and Design.

Simon Jarvis is the Gorley Putt Professor of Poetry and Poetics at the University of Cambridge. Among his prose works are *Wordsworth's Philosophic Song* (Cambridge, 2007) and many essays on poetry and prosody; his compositions in verse include *Dionysus Crucified: Choral Lyric for Two Soloists and Messenger* (Grasp, 2011), *The Unconditional: A Lyric* (Barque, 2005), and *Eighteen Poems* (Eyewear, 2012).

Andrew Joron is the author of *Trance Archive: New and Selected Poems* (City Lights, 2010). Joron's previous poetry collections include *The Removes* (Hard Press, 1999), *Fathom* (Black Square Editions, 2003), and *The Sound Mirror* (Flood Editions, 2008). *The Cry at Zero*, a selection of his prose poems and critical essays, was published by Counterpath Press in 2007. From German, he has translated the *Literary Essays* of Marxist-Utopian philosopher Ernst Bloch (Stanford UP, 1998) and *The Perpetual Motion Machine* by the proto-Dada fantasist Paul Scheerbart (Wakefield Press, 2011). Joron lives in El Cerrito, California, where he theorizes using the theremin.

Nigel Leask was appointed to the University of Glasgow's Regius Chair of English Language and Literature in 2004 and is currently head of the School of Critical Studies. He was previously Reader in Romantic Literature on the English faculty at Cambridge University and has also taught at the University of Bologna, Italy, and the National Autonomous University of Mexico. He has published widely in the area of Romantic literature and culture, with a special emphasis on empire, Orientalism, and travel writing, as well as Scottish literature and thought from 1750 to 1850. His most recent book, *Robert Burns and Pastoral: Poetry and Improvement in Late Eighteenth-Century Scotland* (Oxford UP, 2010) won the Saltire Prize for the best Scottish research book of 2010. He is currently editing *Commonplace Books, Tour Journals, and Miscellaneous Prose Writings*, volume 1 of the AHRC-funded Oxford edition of the *Collected Works of Robert Burns* (general editor, Prof. Gerard Carruthers). He is a Fellow of the British Academy and the Royal Society of Edinburgh.

Jennifer Moxley's collections include: *Clampdown, The Line, Often Capital, The Sense Record*, and *Imagination Verses*. Her poem "Behind the Orbits" was chosen by Robert Creeley for inclusion in *The Best American Poetry 2002*. In addition to her books of poetry she has published a memoir, a volume of essays, and three books of translation from the French. Though a California native, she now lives in Maine with her husband, scholar Steve Evans, and her cat Odette. She teaches poetry and poetics at the University of Maine. For more information on Moxley visit: http://epc.buffalo.edu/authors/moxley/.

Bob Perelman has published numerous books of poems, including: *Iflife* (Roof Books, 2006); *Playing Bodies*, in collaboration with painter Francie Shaw (Granary Books, 2004); and *Ten to One: Selected Poems* (Wesleyan UP, 1999). His critical books are *The Marginalization of Poetry: Language Writing and Literary History*, and *The Trouble with Genius: Reading Pound, Joyce, Stein, and Zukofsky*. His work can be accessed on Penn Sound at http://www.writing.upenn.edu/pennsound; his website is http://writing.upenn.edu/pepc/authors/perelman/; a feature on his work appears in *Jacket* 39 (http://jacketmagazine.com/39/index.shtml). He teaches at the University of Pennsylvania.

Jeffrey C. Robinson attempts to rethink the fundamental principles of the poetics of Romanticism in most of his writing and teaching. Among his books are *Radical Literary Education: A Classroom Experiment with Wordsworth's Ode* (1987); *The Walk: Notes on a Romantic Image* (1989, repr. 2006); *The Current of Romantic Passion* (1991); *Romantic Presences: Living Images from the Age of Wordsworth and Shelley* (1995); *Reception and Poetics in Keats* (1998); *Wordsworth Day by Day: Reading His Work into Poetry Now* (2005); and *Unfettering Poetry: The Fancy in British Romanticism* (2006). He has coedited with Jerome Rothenberg *Poems for the Millennium, Volume Three: The University of California Book of Romantic and Postromantic Poetry* (2009, American Book Award 2010) and has also published books and chapbooks of his own poetry based on Romantic materials, most recently *Untam'd Wing: Riffs on Romantic Poetry* (2010). Professor emeritus at the University of Colorado, he is currently professor of Romantic poetry at the University of Glasgow.

Jerome Rothenberg is an internationally known poet with over eighty books of poetry and several assemblages of traditional and avant-garde poetry such as *Technicians of the Sacred* and, with Pierre Joris and Jeffrey Robinson, *Poems for the Millennium, Volumes 1–3*. Recent books of poems include *Triptych, Gematria Complete, Concealments & Caprichos*, and *Retrievals: Uncollected & New Poems 1955–2010*. He is now working on a global anthology of "outside and subterranean poetry" and has just published, with Heriberto Yépez, *Eye of Witness: A Jerome Rothenberg Reader* for Black Widow Press. He has until recently been a professor of visual arts and literature at the University of California, San Diego.

Elizabeth Willis's most recent book, *Address* (Wesleyan UP, 2011), won the PEN New England / L. L. Winship Award for Poetry. Her other books of poetry include *Meteoric Flowers* (Wesleyan UP, 2006); *Turneresque* (Burning Deck, 2003); and *The Human Abstract* (Penguin, 1995). She has also written widely on nineteenth- and twentieth-century poetry and has edited a volume of essays entitled *Radical Vernacular: Lorine Niedecker and the Poetics of Place* (U of Iowa P, 2008). She teaches at Wesleyan University, where she is Shapiro-Silverberg Professor of Creative Writing.

Heriberto Yépez is a writer from Mexico, where he studied philosophy and Gestalt psychotherapy. He has been a professor at the Facultad de Artes, Universidad Autónoma de Baja California (Tijuana) for the last decade and is now a student at the Department of Spanish and Portuguese at the University of California, Berkeley. His fiction, poetry, and criticism have been widely published in Mexico. He also edited and translated *Ojo del testimonio. Escritos selectos 1951–2010* (Aldus), a compilation of Jerome Rothenberg's prose into Spanish, and he edited and cotranslated *El l*en*g*u*a*je* contraataca! Poéticas selectas (1974–2011)* (Aldus), a collection of Charles Bernstein poetics in Spanish. In English he coedited with the author *Eye of Witness: A Jerome Rothenberg Reader* (Black Widow Press). His experimental fiction *Wars. Threesomes. Drafts. and Mothers* was published by Factory School, and the translation of his critical book around Charles Olson's Mexican experience, *The Empire of Neomemory*, by Chain Links. He now lives between Tijuana and the Bay Area. He defines himself as a postnational writer.

Index